Jesus as Means and Locus of Worship
in the Fourth Gospel

Jesus as Means and Locus of Worship in the Fourth Gospel

Sacrifice and Worship Space in John

Kathleen Troost-Cramer

☙PICKWICK Publications · Eugene, Oregon

JESUS AS MEANS AND LOCUS OF WORSHIP IN THE FOURTH GOSPEL
Sacrifice and Worship Space in John

Copyright © 2017 Kathleen Troost-Cramer. All rights reserved. Except for brief quotations in critical publications or reviews, no part of this book may be reproduced in any manner without prior written permission from the publisher. Write: Permissions, Wipf and Stock Publishers, 199 W. 8th Ave., Suite 3, Eugene, OR 97401.

Pickwick Publications
An Imprint of Wipf and Stock Publishers
199 W. 8th Ave., Suite 3
Eugene, OR 97401

www.wipfandstock.com

PAPERBACK ISBN: 978-1-5326-1285-5
HARDCOVER ISBN: 978-1-5326-1287-9
EBOOK ISBN: 978-1-5326-1286-2

Cataloguing-in-Publication data:

Names: Troost-Cramer, Kathleen

Title: Jesus as means and locus of worship in the fourth gospel : sacrifice and worship space in John / by Kathleen Troost-Cramer.

Description: Eugene, OR: Pickwick Publications, 2017 | Includes bibliographical references and index.

Identifiers: ISBN 978-1-5326-1285-5 (paperback) | ISBN 978-1-5326-1287-9 (hardcover) | ISBN 978-1-5326-1286-2 (ebook)

Subjects: LCSH: Bible. John—Criticism, interpretation, etc. | Worship—Biblical teaching. | Sacrifice—Biblical teaching. | Bible. John—Theology. | Jesus Christ—Person and office.

Classification: LCC BS2615.52 T71 2017 (print) | LCC BS2615.52 (ebook)

Unless otherwise noted, Scripture citations are from the New Revised Standard Version Bible, copyright © 1989 the Division of Christian Education of the National Council of the Churches of Christ in the United States of America. Used by permission. All rights reserved.

Manufactured in the U.S.A.   11/20/17

For my mother Donna
and the Sisters Faithful Companions of Jesus
who were the first to teach me the wonder of God's Word;
and for Mary, *Virgo Potens*.

Tuus totus ego sum,
et omnia mea tua sunt.

Contents

List of Figures | ix
Acknowledgments | xi
Abbreviations | xiii

1 **Introduction to This Study** | 1
   Corollaries in the Dead Sea Scrolls | 5
   References to Sacrificial Worship in John | 6
   The Jesus-Temple as Anti-Roman Polemic | 8
   An Essential Translation Problem: The Temple and the Ἰουδαῖοι in John | 9
   Methodology | 18

2 **The Johannine Jesus Fulfills the Functions of the Temple** | 23
   Worship is Sacrifice; Sacrifice is Worship | 24
   The *Tāmîd* Offering | 27
   The *Tôdāh* Offering | 38
   Models of Passover as a Thanksgiving Sacrifice in Philo and Josephus | 52
   Jesus/Isaac | 55
   Discursus: The Suffering Servant | 58
   Summary and Conclusions: Jesus as Sacrifice in John | 66

CONTENTS

3 **The Johannine Passion as Sacrifice Event Revealing the Place of Worship** | 69

Jesus' Arrest and Trial | 69

The Crucifixion | 74

Son of Man as Temple | 88

The Johannine Resurrection | 89

Temple as Eden | 92

Summary and Conclusions | 94

4 **Relocation of Worship Space: From Institution to Person** | 95

"Mobile Sanctity" | 96

John's Worship Shift as Anti-imperial Polemic | 99

Ancient Ritual Theory | 100

John's Jesus-Temple and Spatial Theory | 102

John 4:6–26: Worship Space in Jesus' Discourse with the Samaritan Woman | 109

Summary and Conclusions | 114

5 **The Translation of Ἰουδαιοι as "Judeans": Fundamental to John's Theme of Jesus as Temple and Sacrifice** | 115

Ἰουδαῖοι and Ἰσραήλ | 116

Individual Passages | 129

Jesus' Origins | 142

Summary and Conclusions | 143

6 **Conclusion: Summary of Findings and Contributions of This Study** | 146

Bibliography | 149

Subject Index | 165

Ancient Document Index | 169

List of Figures

Figure 1: Akedah Tradition Chronology | 20

Figure 2: Worship Spaces in Judea and in Samaria/Galilee | 103

Figure 3: Re-orientation of worship space in John | 108

Acknowledgments

To say that the process of earning my PhD, which has occupied roughly twenty-seven percent of my entire life, has been a roller coaster ride, would be a drastic understatement. The personal challenges and financial hardship I've endured would surely have prevented me from finishing my program and my dissertation, were it not for the following individuals whose help was absolutely indispensable to this achievement.

Professor James Walters, whose encouragement and faith in my ability not only brought me into the School of Theology but helped me to stay there.

Professor Elisabeth Bell, my German tutor, who taught me the most difficult language I've ever struggled to learn, and whose humor and patience made the experience a pleasant one. Without her tutelage, I would likely have had to quit the PhD program.

Professors Robert Allan Hill and Jennifer Wright Knust, my dissertation readers, who constantly supported me through this process by encouraging me never to quit, and by assuring me that I had the potential be a good scholar.

The Rev. Dr. R. Preston Price and Mrs. Jean Price, whose scholarship funds in the name of the late Rev. Preston P. Price, were the only thing that made it financially possible to remain in the PhD program in the last semester of my dissertation writing.

Dr. Eli Lizorkin-Eyzenberg, whose kindness in hiring me to teach The Jewish Background of the New Testament online opened up a new world for me in the identity of the first-century Jesus movement as a solidly Jewish sect.

Finally, no words can possibly express the thanks I owe to my parents, Donna and Hans Troost; and to my daughters, Isabella and Helena.

ACKNOWLEDGMENTS

Without them, this work would have remained a dream that I would have regretted never realizing for the rest of my life. Although it would be impossible for me to repay all of their sacrifices of time, finances, and energy to help me see this through to the end, I can only hope that somehow, in some way, God will make a way for me to put to good use the scholarship that has resulted in this book.

Abbreviations

Ant.	*Antiquities* (Josephus)
Apoc. Ab.	*Apocalypse of Abraham*
2, 3 Bar.	*2, 3 Baruch*
Bar	Baruch
Barn.	*Epistle of Barnabas*
1 Clem.	*1 Clement*
Congr.	*De congressueru ditionis gratia On the Preliminary Studies* (Philo of Alexandria)
Contempl.	*De vita contemplativa On the Contemplative Life* (Philo of Alexandria)
DSS	Dead Sea Scrolls
1, 2 En.	*1, 2 Enoch*
Frg. Tg.	*Fragmentary Targum*
Gen. Rab.	*Genesis Rabbah*
Her.	*Quis rerum divinarum heres sit Who is the Heir of Divine Things?* (Philo of Alexandria)
Jos. Asen.	*Joseph & Asenath*
Jub.	*Jubilees*
J.W.	*Jewish War* (Josephus)
L.A.B.	*Liber Antiquitatum Biblicarum* (Pseudo-Philo)

ABBREVIATIONS

Leg.	*Legum allegoriae* Allegorical Interpretation (Philo of Alexandria)
Lev. Rab.	Leviticus Rabbah
LXX	Septuagint
1, 2, 3, 4 Macc.	1, 2, 3, 4 Maccabees
m.	Mishnah
Mek.	Mekilta
Midr.	Midrash
Migr.	*De migratione Abrahami* On the Migration of Abraham (Philo of Alexandria)
Mos.	*De Vita Mosis* Moses (Philo of Alexandria)
Pirqe R. El.	Pirqe de Rabbi Eliezer
QE	*Quaestiones et solutiones in Exodum* Questions and Answers on Exodus (Philo of Alexandria)
QG	*Quaestiones et solutiones in Genesin* Questions and Answers on Genesis (Philo of Alexandria)
Sacr.	*De sacrificiis Abelis et Caini* On the Sacrifices of Abel and Cain (Philo of Alexandria)
Sib. Or.	Sibylline Oracles
Sir	Sirach/Ecclesiasticus
Somn.	*De somniis* On Dreams (Philo of Alexandria)
Spec.	*De specialibus legibus* On the Special Laws (Philo of Alexandria)
Tg.	Targum
Tg. Neof.	Targum Neofiti
Tg. Ps.-J.	Targum Pseudo-Jonathan
T. Isaac	Testament of Isaac
Wis	Wisdom of Solomon

1

Introduction to this Study

MANY SCHOLARS OF JOHN have examined this Gospel's theme of Jesus as the temple, a motif woven throughout the fabric of John's grand Christology.¹ While some, such as M. A. Daise and most notably Mary Coloe, contend that the Gospel represents Jesus as the temple only during his earthly life, and that at the cross the community of his followers became the temple, others agree that, from the Fourth Gospel's perspective, the person of Jesus continued to be the locus of worship after his resurrection, in keeping with the sense particularly of John 2:19, 21 (τοῦ ναοῦ τοῦ σώματος αυτοῦ) utilizing the term employed to reference specifically the Holy of Holies, ναός, and present also in 1:14 (Jesus, the λόγος σὰρξ ἐγένετο, "tabernacled among us," the verb ἐσκήνωσεν harking back to the Exodus tabernacle that housed God's divine Presence/Glory); 1:31 (the Glory/Presence is made known to Israel in Jesus); 1:50–51 (with references to Jacob's dream at Beth-El, the "house of God," meeting-place of heaven and earth); 18:12–20, 38 (Jesus claims to be equal to the Father, indicating that he is the Father's own Presence/Glory); and the entire passion and resurrection narratives, as we will see.² In John 2:19, Jesus tells the Ἰουδαῖοι in the temple complex that should they destroy "this temple," Jesus himself would raise it in three days. Verse 21 identifies "this temple" that will be raised up as "the temple of [Jesus'] body," indicating that Jesus' body—not the community—remains

1. For detailed discussions of this theme, see, among other works, Brown, *According to John (i–xii)* and *(xiii–xxi)*; Coloe, *God Dwells*; Coloe, *Household*; Daise, "Ritual Transference"; Hoskins, *Fulfillment*; Kerr, *Temple*; Kinzer, "Temple Christology"; McCaffrey, *House*; Moloney, *Text and Context*; Schneiders, "New Temple"; Um, *Temple Christology*; Umoh, "Temple."

2 See e.g., Coloe, *God Dwells*, 23–27, 31–63; Kinzer, "Temple Christology," 447–49, 451–53, 457; Koester, *Dwelling*, 102–6; Lee, "Spirit of Truth"; Neyrey, "Spaces and Places," 60–74; Schneiders, "New Temple"; Umoh, "Temple." See also Brown, *According to John (i–xii)*, 1013–14.

"this temple" even after the resurrection.³ As Sandra M. Schneiders observes, if the risen body of Jesus is the temple, and if Jesus abides with his faithful forever, then it follows that those faithful are (not the temple but) *Israel*, in the midst of which God's Glory dwelt in the temple's prototype, the tabernacle.⁴

What does it mean, though, to say that Jesus is "the temple"? Since the purpose and function of a temple in antiquity was to provide a locus of worship in the form of sacrifice, the argument of this thesis is that the motif of Jesus as temple is entirely based upon the idea that he is a sacrifice—indeed, that he is *the* sacrifice that fulfills all the functions of the Jerusalem temple's sacrificial institution in the post-70 CE absence of that institution.⁵ Given that worship (both Jewish and polytheistic) in first-century Palestine and the wider Roman world was defined by sacrifice, the issues of temple and sacrifice are symbiotically connected and a picture emerges in the Fourth Gospel of Jesus fulfilling the temple's functions *as* the locus of sacrifice. Hence, the very reason why John portrays Jesus as the temple is because John claims that Jesus is a sacrificial offering. In order to illustrate this, John pits geographical regions against each other in order to craft the Gospel's unique theology upon the framework of the ancient rivalry between the northern and southern kingdoms of Israel and Judah.⁶ This rivalry is the basis of the Gospel's use of the term Ἰουδαῖοι, as a marker that designates Judeans from those the Gospel terms "Israelites." The former refers to those without temple and sacrifices; the latter, to those who have Jesus as sacrifice and temple.

At this point, a succinct review of scholarship will be helpful in assessing the differing viewpoints on the presence (or the lack thereof) of a sacrifice theme in the Fourth Gospel. After summarizing the work of scholars who agree that John presents Jesus as sacrifice, we will overview relevant scholarship that argues the opposite. We will then preview the main points of the argument of this thesis: corollaries from the Dead Sea Scrolls, specific references to sacrifice in John and their parallels to Philo and rabbinic

---

3. See Kinzer, "Temple Christology," 448, 454, 457. While Kinzer acknowledges that Jesus is portrayed as the temple in John, he does not dismiss the interpretation of the community as temple: in Kinzer's view, Jesus is the heavenly temple, while the community of believers constitutes the new earthly temple. The present study will argue that the Gospel's audience is not temple, but Israel with the temple of the risen Jesus in its midst.

4. Schneiders, "New Temple," esp. 347, 351.

5. See Umoh, "Temple," esp. 318.

6. See Ashton, "Identity and Function," 73–74.

texts, John's presentation of Jesus as locus of worship as "protest literature" providing an alternative to Roman polytheist worship structures, and the relation of the debated term Ἰουδαῖοι to John's worship theme.

Scholars such as Bruce H. Grigsby, Paul M. Hoskins, P. Grelot, J.D.M. Derrett, Frédéric Manns, Rainer Metzner, J. T. Nielsen, and Dennis R. Lindsay have noted a sacrifice theme running strongly through John that displays Jesus not only *making* sacrifice, but *being* sacrifice. These scholars base this perspective chiefly on the Gospel's passion narrative and on the "bread of life" discourse in John 6 (indeed, this thesis will argue that the Bread of Life Discourse is one of several clear prolepses of the passion), as well as rabbinic material that interprets the Passover lamb as a sacrifice of atonement connected to the binding of Isaac.[7] In order for this connection to apply to John, we must examine whether there is "Isaac typology" (or "Akedah typology") in the Gospel. Two scholars, Bruce H. Grigsby and Paul M. Hoskins, may be taken as respective examples of this viewpoint. Both agree that John "contains a Passover typology" that underlies the entire Gospel; indeed, Hoskins claims that this typology is not incidental to the Gospel's Christology but is its very foundation and essence.[8] For Hoskins, John's theme of deliverance, of transference from darkness to light, is centered in the first-century concept of the Passover lamb as the instrument of deliverance from the death of the firstborn recorded in the book of Exodus; John reinterprets this deliverance as deliverance from the death resulting from the effects of sin. There are indications that Passover was associated with the self-offering of Isaac: Grigsby cites several rabbinic texts that view Isaac's willingly offered blood as the blood that redeemed Israel when the destroying angel smote the firstborn of Egypt; hence, Isaac was associated with the Passover lamb, which was viewed in rabbinic writings such as *Gen. Rab.* 22 and many others as a sacrifice of atonement.[9] As Frédéric Manns notes, *Tg.* Lev 22:27 even go so far as to claim that the whole system of animal sacrifice in Jewish worship was intended to atone for Israel's sin by animals' blood reminding God of the shed blood of Isaac.[10] Therefore, if the Passover was associated with the Akedah, and if there are parallels between Jesus and Isaac in John, then the Gospel's

---

7. The appropriateness of referring to rabbinic texts when interpreting the sacrifice theme in John will be discussed below.

8. Hoskins, "Deliverance," 285–99.

9. Brown, *Death of the Messiah*, 2:1440; Grigsby, "Cross"; Manns, "Binding of Isaac."

10. Manns, "Binding of Isaac."

portrayal of Jesus as paschal victim connects him to Isaac traditions and portrays him as a sacrificial offering.

Although John's themes of Jesus as temple and Jesus as sacrifice have been treated at length in previous works, these identifications deserve revisiting. To say that Jesus is the temple and leave the matter there is simply to raise the question of *how* Jesus can be the temple; and to say that Jesus is sacrifice and leave the matter there merely directs us to ask *why* the Gospel portrays him as such. This thesis suggests that the answer to that *why* is this: John is only able to claim that Jesus is temple because that Gospel's primary claim is that Jesus is sacrifice.

There are, of course, scholars who argue not only that Jesus is *not* portrayed as a sacrifice in John, but also that this Gospel is not concerned with sacrifice at all. Most recently, Daniel C. Ullucci has made this claim. Though others have preceded him, Ullucci's argument is made in a particularly forceful manner.[11] At the same time, part of Ullucci's argument is helpful for the present study: he asserts that post-70 CE Christians eschewed animal sacrifice because 1.) there was no longer a temple in Jerusalem in which to legitimately perform it, and 2.) Jesus-believers, as adherents of a Jewish sect, could not sacrifice in existing polytheist Roman temples.[12] I agree on these points; and though Ullucci makes use of them to argue otherwise, I believe these insights can be valuable in understanding *why* John portrays Jesus as temple and sacrifice: post-70 CE Jesus-believers were suddenly without a worship space. The famous conversation of Jesus with the Samaritan woman at Jacob's well in John 4 particularly expresses the Gospel's concern to define the appropriate location for worship (which, as stated above, meant sacrifice). Should God's people worship at the temple on Mt. Zion in Jerusalem? At the rival Samarian temple on Mt. Gerizim? Neither, the Fourth Gospel answers: God's people should worship "at" or "in" the resurrected body of Jesus (harking back to John 2:21). John locates the temple in/as Jesus precisely in the quest to find a locus of sacrificial worship, reinforcing a post-70 CE date for the Gospel's composition (but placing it closer to 70 than recent scholarly consensus has held). John is in fact saturated with sacrificial imagery for this very reason: flesh, blood, water, even an altar (in the form of the cross, as we will discuss in chapter 3 below). Ullucci posits that the absence of a depiction of Jesus participating in the sacrificial Passover meal in John is evidence of a corresponding

---

11. Ullucci, *Animal Sacrifice,* esp. 89. See also Painter, "Sacrifice and Atonement."
12. See Ullucci, *Animal Sacrifice,* 69–74, 101.

absence of concern about sacrifice,[13] however this view raises two concerns: 1.) it seems not to take into consideration the Gospel's temple theme, for temple indicates worship and worship is sacrifice; and 2.) an absence of concrete sacrificial description does not necessarily constitute the absence of sacrificial ideas, especially when we are dealing with what is quite likely the most highly symbolic of the Gospels.[14] Hence, the very absence of overt sacrificial scenes and events can more plausibly be interpreted as a demonstration of the Gospel's concern to define the appropriate location for sacrifice—namely, the temple that is Jesus' body. The manner in which Jesus is bound at his arrest, the fact that he is led to a priest immediately after this binding, the timing of Jesus' death to coincide with the slaughter of the Passover lambs, and the manner in which the spear is thrust into his side on the cross, all place the locus of sacrifice in him. Temple imagery continues with the resurrection narrative, whose garden motif bears a similarity to contemporary Jewish texts that speak of the temple as the Garden of Eden.

Corollaries in the Dead Sea Scrolls

While the scope of this study will not allow a thorough investigation of the long-debated relationship between John and the Qumran literature (henceforth DSS), a focused comparison relating specifically to the concept of temple replacement is helpful for this thesis. The existence in the DSS of ideas that the Jerusalem temple institution was somehow deficient or indeed corrupted indicates that John's Gospel was not unique in making a similar claim. While the differences between the Fourth Gospel and the DSS in this particular regard are equally informative, the chief difference being that the DSS defines the community as the temple whereas John defines the temple-sacrifice as Jesus, the common basic expression of dissatisfaction with the Jerusalem temple may indicate that the opposition to the temple institution found in the DSS reflected or even provided the basis for an anti-temple milieu that formed the background for John's ideas.

Essential to the claims of the Qumran community is the conviction that its members are the only ones who perform correct worship practice. The rest of the people of Israel, who do not belong to this elect community,

---

13. Painter, similar to Ullucci, claims that there can be no atonement theme in John because the Gospel displays no overt "atonement vocabulary" (Painter, "Sacrifice and Atonement," 290–91).

14. Umoh, "Temple," 315.

do not perform correct and acceptable worship, due to the fact (according to the DSS) that the temple upon which their worship stands is not acceptable in the sight of God. In a similar way, John delineates two groups in relation to correct/acceptable worship: those who have the wrong temple (the group titled Ἰουδαῖοι), meaning the institution in Jerusalem; and those who have the proper temple (the group titled Ἰσραήλ/Ἰσραηλίτης, meaning the person of Jesus.

References to Sacrificial Worship in John

The reason for the Gospel's use of abstract sacrificial language in reference to the person of Jesus is precisely that Jesus embodies in his person all of the temple's functions. The sacrificial offering of Jesus' body demonstrates that God's Presence/Glory is located in the person of Jesus in the same way that it had been housed in the wilderness tabernacle/Jerusalem temple; and the fact that Jesus offers himself indicates that he also fulfills the function of the priesthood, which is responsible for maintaining God's presence through sacrificial worship praxis.[15] All of these functions are revealed simultaneously in the Fourth Gospel's crucifixion scene, which is set on a stage evoking temple worship complete with altar (the cross), sacrificial victim (Jesus and the blood that pours forth from his side in 19:34), and officiating priest (indicated by the water that pours forth from Jesus' side, also in 19:34). Jesus' title "Lamb of God" (John 1:29, 36) and the timing of his death during the slaughter of Passover lambs in the temple connect his death to the traditions of the Akedah and the willingly shed blood of Isaac, portrayed in rabbinic texts as the precursor and true meaning of the Passover lamb and (in some sources) providing atonement for Israel's sin.

There is a connection to a different sacrifice as well: the *tôdāh* thank-offering of bread and wine that expressed gratitude to God for rescue from danger and return to life and safety.[16] The *tôdāh* may be in view in the famous Bread of Life Discourse in John 6. Laporte and Lindsay separately note that the *tôdāh* offering was related to the Passover, and particularly to the sacrificial Passover lamb, in that the Passover observance was commonly viewed in early Judaism as a thank-offering for the rescue of the Israelites from slavery in Egypt and the safe passage through the Red

---

15. John's identification of Jesus as priest will be discussed in chapters 2 and 3 below.
16. See esp. Lindsay, "Todah," 86–87.

Sea.¹⁷ Additionally, Frédéric Manns notes that rabbinic texts connect the *tāmîd*, the daily morning and evening atonement offering of a lamb upon the temple altar, to the sacrifice of Isaac.¹⁸ Hence, the *tāmîd* also carries undertones of the Passover, and vice-versa. These associations may help to explain John's identification of Jesus-as-Passover-lamb simultaneously as Jesus-as-bread-from-heaven: if the offering of lambs in the *tāmîd* as well as in the Passover was linked to the Akedah, and if the Passover itself was viewed as a thank-offering similar in meaning to the *tôdāh* that employed an offering of bread and wine, then we can begin to see more clearly that the Fourth Evangelist does not illogically conflate or confuse the ideas of bread sacrifices and flesh sacrifices. Rather, the author operates within culturally current categories to claim that Jesus is at the same time sacrificial bread and sacrificial lamb, in order to demonstrate the overall concept of Jesus as sacrifice, and thereby, as locus of worship.

There are two possible candidates for the priest who officiates the Jesus-sacrifice: Jesus, who lays down his life of his own will and by his own power, or—continuing the Akedah connections—God, who by offering his son acts in the same role in which Abraham had acted in offering Isaac. The present study favors the former interpretation. Several texts within John identify Jesus as the one who consecrates and offers himself. Chief among these are 10:11, 17–18 ("I lay down my life") and especially 17:19 ("I consecrate myself"). Additionally, several actions that Jesus performs, and physical phenomena associated with him, support this interpretation. The water on which Jesus walks immediately preceding the Bread of Life Discourse (6:16–21) indicates his priestly purification before proclaiming the offering of the "flesh and blood" of 6:32–58, the materials with overtones of the bread and wine of the Lord's Supper observance, which in turn evoke the *tôdāh* offering as noted above. In 19:34, the water that issues from Jesus' pierced side after he dies on the cross also signifies priestly washing: Jesus has sanctified himself as priest in order to offer the sacrifice of himself as paschal lamb. We will see that John does not abrogate sacrifice, but operates within contemporary understandings of space to re-locate sacrificial worship from the Jerusalem temple institution to the person of Jesus.

---

17. Laporte, "Philonic Models," 77–78.
18. Manns, "Binding of Isaac," 62–64.

The Jesus-Temple as Anti-Roman Polemic

In Ullucci's words, George Heyman's book *The Power of Sacrifice* claims that the sacrificial overtones of early Christian martyr texts express "conflict with Roman imperial discourse."[19] While Ullucci counters Heyman's argument by stating that sacrifice differs from discourse because sacrifice is an action, an argument could be made that in many cases action can be and is used as discourse. When we combine Heyman's association of martyrdom and sacrifice as anti-imperial discourse with John's sacrificial and temple themes, a most intriguing possibility emerges: that John's temple and sacrifice theme reflects not only a historical Israel/Judea rivalry, but also an anti-Roman polemic. Camillus Umoh suggests that one of the purposes of John's sacrifice theme is to provide an alternative to the religious and political structures of the Roman Empire and especially to the role played by the Jerusalem temple and its cultic personnel in perpetuating those structures.[20] In *John and Empire*, Warren Carter similarly argues that the whole of the Fourth Gospel is coded anti-Roman polemic. While it may be a stretch to claim that this was the entire purpose of the Gospel's composition, Carter makes a compelling case that an anti-Roman theme does appear in John. The claims of the Fourth Gospel seem therefore to coalesce into one sweeping view that not only do the Gospel's "Israelites" have a temple in the resurrected person of Jesus, whereas the Judeans' temple is no more; but also that Rome is not a viable alternative. "We have access to God in a place of sacrificial worship," the Gospel's "Israelites" seem to say, "even in the absence of the Jerusalem temple and while keeping ourselves from the idolatrous temples of Rome."

The Fourth Evangelist concretizes the identification of Jesus as appropriate locus of sacrifice, i.e., temple, by imposing onto the person of Jesus a number of sacrificial images, objects, and practices that function as a collection of "proofs" offered in service to the claim that Jesus completely and perfectly performs the sacrificial functions of the temple. The most significant of these proofs are the Passover lamb, *tāmîd* offering, *tôdāh* (thank-) offering, and water of purification. Taken together, these demonstrate that Jesus-as-sacrifice provides the basis for his identification as sacrificial offering.

---

19. Ullucci, *Animal Sacrifice*, 127.
20. Umoh, "Temple," 326–29.

INTRODUCTION TO THIS STUDY

An Essential Translation Problem: The Temple and the Ἰουδαῖοι in John

The thrust of this study's argument, that John presents Jesus' resurrected body as the correct locus of sacrificial worship in the absence of a temple in which Jesus-believers could offer proper worship to the God of Israel, has implications for a significant and long-standing difficulty in the interpretation of John: how are we to translate the term Ἰουδαῖοι? English translations persistently render this word as "Jews," but in recent decades scholars have engaged in vigorous debate over the accuracy and advisability of this translation. The debate gained impetus especially as a result of post-Holocaust awareness: Because there is no question that the Ἰουδαῖοι of the Fourth Gospel are spoken of as Jesus' deadly enemies in the very vast majority of the term's occurrences, the crime of deicide has all too often throughout history been laid at the feet of "the Jews." While the scope of this thesis cannot fully engage the complex history and implications of this ethnic-theological issue, our argument is that John's Ἰουδαῖοι should be translated not as "Jews" but as "Judeans," since the geographical territory of Judea and the persons and parties affiliated with the temple institution in Jerusalem have direct implications for John's worship theme.[21]

It would appear that the historical division between "Jews" and "Christians" that much scholarship has seen in the Fourth Gospel relies heavily on the "Johannine (Christian) Community" hypothesis advanced by J. Louis Martyn, embraced and adjusted by Raymond Brown, and taken up in various forms by later scholars, including C. K. Barrett and Francis Moloney. We shall begin with Martyn, who proposed a series of stages for the Fourth Gospel's development that essentially traced an initial "Jewish" context through a "Jewish" persecution of "Johannine Christians" that resulted in an official expulsion of the latter from their synagogue communities, until in the final phase of the Gospel's composition/redaction the rejected "Johannine Community" had formed its own identity entirely separate from its parent "Judaism." According to this view, this expulsion was a result of the *birkat ha-minim*, or the infamous "Benedictions Against Heretics." In Martyn's vision of the "Johannine Community," that group's unique identity when fully separated from the synagogue was characterized by a solidly "high Christology" and evidence of the community's history can be mined

---

21. An exhaustive overview of the scholarship in this area would be beyond the scope of this thesis. Here, a brief overview of the scholars whose work this study will principally engage will suffice.

in John in such passages as John 9, the healing of the "Man Born Blind." Martyn claimed that the uniquely Johannine word ἀποσυναγῶγος reflected the community's quite literally being "cast out of the synagogue" due to its rapidly developing "high Christology," itself a development of increasingly Gentile presence. Hence, Martyn attributed a "low Christology," in which Jesus was merely the prophet-Messiah, to the original "Jewish" context, and the later "high Christology," depicting Jesus as possessing more divine characteristics, to a "Gentile" context.

After Martyn, Brown correctly observed that the term Ἰουδαῖοι nearly always "has a hostile connotation" in John. He based this on his argument that the Gospel was written "against a background of Jewish-Christian hostility" similar to Martyn's scheme of a "Johannine (Christian) Community" development over time, with some adjustments to the timeline and to the events that would have characterized each stage. Essentially, however, the idea of an original "Jewish" context, a persecution of "Johannine Christians," and a resulting independent "Christian" community with a "high Christology" remained from Martyn's work.[22] Additionally, Brown asserted that the term Ἰουδαῖοι—remaining translated as "Jews"—was a *symbolic* term. It did not represent "actual" Jews in John's Gospel, but "Jews" as a symbol of unbelief, rejection of God, and the living in darkness that such unbelief and rejection brings. Brown argued that the "Jewish" rejection of Jesus was exemplified in John 9, indicates their "breaking of the covenant whereby God or his Messiah was Israel's king," and therefore signifies that, in the context of an envisioned first-century "Christians vs. Jews" conflict, the "Jews" as a whole have "renounced their status as God's people."[23] Francis Moloney, Brown's student, will adhere to this essential identification.

Before we examine Moloney, however, the work of C. K. Barrett is significant. Barrett called the Fourth Gospel an essentially Jewish text, as its feature of messianic identity in particular is "a question appropriate to Palestine," yet specifies the Gospel's character as a *Hellenistic* Jewish work by virtue of its "metaphysical" portrayal of Jesus as a divine being who descended to earth.[24] This being the case, Barrett claimed that the Fourth Evangelist's self-awareness as a Christian was expressed in the Gospel by a

---

22. Brown, *According to John (i–xii)*, 312, 341, 403. Brown's reliance on the *Dialogue with Trypho* as evidence that "your law" was used also in John as polemic is inappropriate, since it depends on the interpretation found in an apologetic interpretation, not on the Gospel of John itself.

23. Brown, *According to John (xiii–xxi)*, 894–95.

24. Barrett, *John and Judaism*, 10.

supplanting of Judaism: in this case, the Gospel's author "wished to press home upon the Jews the fact that the truth of the Christian position was substantiated by their own historical documents"—hence, "your law" (in John 8:17; 10:34; 18:31).[25] This is not unlike Brown's suggestion that "your law" may function rhetorically in a sense of "the law that you yourselves accept."[26] Barrett argued that the designation of Nicodemus as a "teacher of Israel" in John 3:10 marks that figure as a teacher of the people of God *as opposed to* the group styled Ἰουδαῖοι; however, this is with Barrett's understanding of "Jew" and "Israelite" as specifically religious terms, where "Israelite" is synonymous with "Christian," distinct from "Jew."[27] Following immediately on the Nicodemus dialogue is the dialogue with the Samaritan woman and Jesus' assertion that "salvation is from the Ἰουδαῖοι" (John 4:22). Barrett claimed that this phrase indicated that salvation comes from this particular people, having been the unique recipients of God's revelation throughout history.[28] He also argued that these words reflected a phase in the "Johannine Community's" development indicating a mission that the latter group perceived to lead the world to salvation; but he follows this by stating that when "Israel" facilitated this salvation its privileged position as God's people would "be dissolved."[29] Hence, the "eschatological salvation" that proceeds from "the Jews" is "in the person of Jesus in process of realization and the Jews are losing their position to the church."[30] For Barrett, Jesus is indeed a Ἰουδαῖος but only in a national/political/ethnic sense. However, "Israel" in John is broader than this and believing Samaritans are included in it, as the Samaritans themselves attest when they report that "we know that this is truly the savior of *the world*" (John 4:42).[31] While the Ἰουδαῖοι have been the historical recipients of God's revelation, the revelation that Jesus brings (does not surpass but) widens that original group.[32] This has the effect of defining "Israel" as a mixed group of ethnic Israelites and ethnic non-Israelites, with Ἰουδαῖοι signifying the group that refuses

---

25. Barrett, *According to St. John*, 384.
26. Brown, *According to John (i–xii)*, 341, 403.
27. Barrett, *According to St. John*, 211. See also Brown, *According to John (i–xii)*, 442–43.
28. Moloney, "The Jews," 32.
29. Barrett, *According to St. John*, 237; see also Barrett, *John and Judaism*, 70–72, 75.
30. Ibid.
31. Ibid. Emphasis mine.
32. Ibid.

to "believe in" Jesus and thereby rejects God—the group that ends up still being referred to as "Jews."

Barrett viewed the famous pericope of the healing of the Man Born Blind in John 9 as a legal "trial of the man [born blind], and of Jesus through the man, and of the Jews through Jesus."[33] As in Martyn and Brown before him, Barrett relied on the "Johannine Community" hypothesis in which the "Johannine Christians" were officially expelled from the synagogue, going so far as to claim that this rejection in John indicates that the entirety of Israel has "abdicated its own unique position under the immediate sovereignty of God," giving way to the church (as discussed above).[34] While Barrett notes that the Johannine use of the term Ἰουδαῖοι typically refers to the Jerusalem temple authorities, affiliated with the center of hostility toward and rejection of Jesus, he also argues that John negatively portrays the temple authorities, and Jerusalem, in order to signify the end of Judaism's legitimacy as a religion, the "supplanting" of Judaism by Christianity.[35] Hence, in no case does it "seem that John means 'the Judeans' (as distinct from the Galileans)."[36] For Barrett, John makes a decisive separation of Christianity from Judaism; they are two distinct religions by the time the Gospel is written.[37]

Moloney argued similarly, influenced by not only Brown but also by Severino Pancaro's work on John's use of the terms Ἰσραήλ, Ἰσραηλίτης, λαός, and ἔθνος. Moloney argued that John's use of the term Ἰσραήλ denotes the "people (λαός) of God," which believers in Jesus constitute.[38] Shadows of the "Johannine community" and *birkat ha-minim* theory appear in this argument, to the extent that the Fourth Evangelist was reacting "against mainstream Judaism, now a synagogue-centered community, which

---

33. Barrett, *According to St. John*, 361.

34. Ibid., 546. Adele Reinhartz similarly argues that the Fourth Gospel portrays the Jewish people as being "expelled" from God's covenant, shown especially in John 8:31–59, where the Ἰουδαῖοι claim covenant membership by virtue of their descent from Abraham only to have Jesus respond that they are descended rather from "the devil" and thereby outside of the covenant. Reinhartz, "Grammar of Hate," 422–24.

35. Robert Kysar claims that "the message of Jesus is everywhere presented as superior to the *religion* of the Jews"; the same goes for the superiority of Jesus' "message" over the temple. "The conclusion is inescapable that the text of the narrative nurtures a negative mentality toward Jews and Judaism" (Kysar, "Anti-Semitism," 117). Emphasis mine. See also Ruether, "Theological Anti-Semitism," 192.

36. Barrett, *According to St. John*, 171–72.

37. Barrett, *John and Judaism*, 70–72. See also Brown, *Community*, 25–88.

38. Moloney, *Text and Context*, 20–35.

claimed anyone who believed that Jesus was the Christ no longer belonged to Israel."[39] Here, the "people of God" is not limited to a specific nationalistic or ethnic identity, but now encompasses all nations by means of Jesus (similar to Barrett, as seen above). Hence, the terms Ἰσραήλ, Ἰσραηλίτης, λαός, and ἔθνος are set against the term Ἰουδαῖοι because the latter term connotes a limited membership in the "people of God." Ἰσραήλ, then, refers to the community that embraces Jesus. This is similar to the argument of the present thesis: that the Fourth Gospel's use of the term Ἰσραήλ refers to those who accept Jesus. At the same time, Moloney's evocation of a "mainstream Judaism" is an anachronism that, if accepted, contributes to a sense of diametrical opposition between "Judaism" and "Christianity." In turn, this separation prevents any understanding of John as a first-century Jewish text, addressing uniquely Jewish concerns, framing its points in distinctly Jewish terms in order to answer the question of how to worship in a Jewish manner. This thesis will propose that the acceptance of Jesus as sacrifice and temple must specifically be of the Johannine Jesus *re-locating* Jewish worship—not *replacing* it—in the absence of the Jerusalem temple institution after 70 CE. John's displacement of worship from the Jerusalem temple and relocation of worship in Jesus is entirely in line with contemporary Jewish worship concepts and practices, and *continues* Jewish worship rather than ends it.

As a representative example of Moloney's view, we may take his interpretation of John 1:47. Nathanael's incomplete faith—that Jesus is merely "king of Israel" when he is actually very much more, as expressed in the Prologue—is, for Moloney, the result of Nathanael's incorrect understanding of what "Israel" is. Nathanael uses the term "Israel" in the narrow sense of the national/political entity of the Ἰουδαῖοι, and frames his own messianic concept within the framework of the national/political Davidic messiah expected by that entity.[40] Nathanael's mistake is in a failure to see that "Israel," the "people of God," encompasses *all* nations (including, but not limited to, the Ἰουδαῖοι). Indeed, Moloney claims, Ἰσραήλ is not always used in a positive sense: Nathanael's usage demonstrates misunderstanding, as does the identical usage of the crowds that greet Jesus as "king of Israel" as he enters

---

39. Moloney, "The Jews," 18. See also Brown, *Community*, 13, 48, 56, 173.

40. Moloney, "The Jews," 22. Brown (*Community*, 26, 38, 44) similarly suggests that John's Christology does not envision Davidic Messiahship as the ultimate end of Jesus' identity.

Jerusalem in 12:13.⁴¹ There is a similar issue in 11:50, when Caiaphas claims that "it is more expedient that one man die for the people (λαός) than that the whole nation (ἔθνος) should perish": the narrator immediately adds that Caiaphas' words possess a double meaning. The implication, according to Moloney, is that Caiaphas meant "people" and "nation" in the limited national/political sense, synonymous with Ἰουδαῖοι; but the deeper and true meaning of those terms went beyond Ἰουδαῖοι to encompass all nations in the "people of God," signified by the narrator's assertion that Jesus would die to "gather into one the scattered children of God" (11:52).⁴² While the latter is frequently interpreted to refer to the Diaspora, the phrase "children of God" harkens back to 1:12–13, which claims that the "children of God" are those whom God has empowered to be his children through "belief in" Jesus' "name."⁴³ These are not found only within the Ἰουδαῖοι, as 10:16 clarifies when Jesus, employing the metaphor of the Good Shepherd, states that there are others who must be brought into the sheepfold.⁴⁴ This universal character of the "people of God" becomes explicit when the Pharisees complain that "the world has gone after" Jesus (12:19) and when, only one verse later, Gentiles ("Greeks") arrive asking to "see Jesus" (12:20–21).⁴⁵ To the request of these "Greeks," Jesus responds that his "hour" of glorification has arrived: for Moloney, this can mean nothing other than that Jesus' death will gather the universal "people of God," comprising nations beyond the Ἰουδαῖοι: "When I am lifted up from the earth, I will draw all (πάντας) to myself" (12:32)—*all*, not the narrow national/political entity of Ἰουδαῖοι that the Gospel's characters have been envisioning.⁴⁶

Moloney differs from Pancaro in that the latter claims that the "people of God" established by Jesus' death supplants the "people of God" defined as Ἰουδαῖοι; Moloney argues that the Ἰουδαῖοι are *included* in this reconstituted "people of God."⁴⁷ Hence, while the Gospel's characters have used the terms "Israel," "the nation," and "the people" with the limited scope of the national/political entity of the Ἰουδαῖοι, the evangelist makes these same terms mean something different than the characters intend, turning "Israel," "the

---

41. Moloney, "The Jews," 23.
42. Ibid., 24.
43. Cited in ibid., 25.
44. Ibid.
45. Ibid., 26.
46. Ibid., 26–27; Moloney, *Text and Context*, 31–33.
47. Moloney, "The Jews," 28.

people," and "the nation" into descriptors of an unlimited, universal "people of God." This "people" takes shape in the form of the Beloved Disciple and Jesus' mother at the cross.[48] For Moloney, John's vitriol towards the Ἰουδαῖοι has nothing to do with ethnic identity or even geographical location, but "has everything to do with the definitive rejection of Jesus as the revelation of God," a claim that places us squarely at the beginning of our inquiry into the meaning of the term Ἰουδαῖοι: because Moloney uses the term "Jews" to translate every occurrence of Ἰουδαῖοι, his argument ultimately means that "Jew" is the term for rejecting God.[49]

Moloney's view is seriously flawed, for two reasons: 1.) it does not sufficiently account for his assertion that there are "good Ἰουδαῖοι" in the Gospel; 2.) it does not consider the tradition of "righteous Gentiles," or of the fact that Gentiles associated themselves with synagogues as either "God-fearers" or as full proselytes, especially in Diaspora settings; 3.) it operates on the assumption that there are Davidic overtones in John.

There is no evidence of Davidic messianic expectations anywhere in John. The closest we find is at John 7:42, where in a debate about Jesus' origin the "crowds" suggest that the Messiah is to come from Bethlehem. However, there is no evidence that the term Ἰσραήλ has any Davidic connotation; in fact, quite the opposite is true. "Israel" as the Northern Kingdom had historically rejected Jerusalem's claim to authority both monarchic and spiritual. When Nathaniel calls Jesus the "king of Israel" in John 1:49, he is not expressing a Davidic hope but showing himself to be one of those who accept Jesus as the temple—a member of "Israel" which has the temple and the Glory in its midst, as opposed to Judea, which does not possess the Glory despite the presence of the temple institution. When the crowds at Jesus' entry into Jerusalem hail him as "king of Israel," they are not operating on concepts of "king" from Samuel-Kings-Chronicles but from the Torah (especially, for example, Lev 23). John has no interest in a Davidic expectation, except perhaps to show that such an expectation is misguided. The Gospel's interest is rather to draw a distinction between two groups: Ἰσραήλ (equivalent to the ancient Northern Kingdom), which possesses the dwelling of the Glory in Jesus, and the Ἰουδαῖοι (equivalent to the ancient Southern Kingdom), who do not. By making this distinction, John continues the north's historical rejection of the temple in Jerusalem.[50]

48. Ibid., 28–29.
49. Moloney, *Text and Context*, 40.
50. Lizorkin-Eyzenberg, *Jewish Gospel*, 63–64.

This thesis follows Malcolm Lowe and others in arguing that Ἰουδαῖοι should be translated as "Judeans" in nearly every occurrence in John. As many scholars have noted, Judea in the south is the place of hostility and opposition to Jesus in the Gospel, while Samaria and Galilee in the north are the places of safety and acceptance.[51] The characters who continually look for ways to thwart Jesus and even kill him universally hail from Judea and hence are "Judeans." There is an excellent reason for this geographical distinction: the temple institution was located in the territory of Judea. In accord with the Gospel's identification of Jesus as locus of worship, those with a vested interest in the Jerusalem temple institution reject, oppose, and finally destroy Jesus as a rival temple. Thus, the Gospel does not pit the *religions* of "Judaism" and "Christianity" against each other. To claim that John records this rivalry (as do, for example, Moloney and Martyn) is to make a distinction that the Gospel's own internal logic does not support.[52] Galileans shared with Judeans the same basic faith in the God of Israel and the same scripture tradition, and prior to the temple's destruction in 70 CE, journeyed to Jerusalem to worship when means and opportunity allowed. The difference between the two regions was that the temple was located in Judea and not in Galilee. That is the entire essence of the identity of those to whom John refers as Ἰουδαῖοι. *The essence of the Judean-Israelite debate in John is the appropriate location of worship, which is defined by the appropriate place of sacrifice.*[53] The translation of the term Ἰουδαῖοι is dependent upon the Fourth Gospel's worship concern: because this term occurs over against Ἰσραήλ in John, and due to the fact that the Jerusalem temple institution is located in the geographical territory belonging to the Ἰουδαῖοι, the latter term in practically every occurrence possesses the sense geographic/political "Judeans," not ethnic/religious "Jews."[54]

This study posits that the Fourth Gospel's "Israelites" include both Galileans and Samaritans, and that this designation represents a conscious

---

51. E.g., Charlesworth, "Exclusivism"; Lieu, "Explanation and Hermeneutics"; Lieu, "Worlds"; Lizorkin-Eyzenberg, *Jewish Gospel*, 127; Martyn, *History and Theology*, 73; Tolmie, "Ioudaioi."

52. For this claim, see e.g., among other works, Brown, *Community*; Moloney, "'The Jews'"; Moloney, *Text and Context*; Martyn, *History and Theology*.

53. The prime layout for this debate is found in John 4:1–42, where, as many scholars have noted, the answer to the question, "Should one worship on Mt. Zion or on Mt. Gerizim?" is "One should worship 'in' the person of Jesus."

54. This contrast between Ἰουδαῖοι and Ἰσραήλ, and the Christological ramifications thereof will be more fully addressed in chapter 5 of this thesis.

strategy by the Fourth Evangelist to bring to mind the ancient Northern Kingdom,[55] while the Ἰουδαῖοι are of course associated with the Southern Kingdom and the people of Judean extraction who returned to the land after the Babylonian Exile.[56] This identification is brought home in the Gospel's clear and literal geographical distinction between south and north. In the same way that the ancient Israelites possessed the portable tabernacle as the locus of God's presence or "Glory" (δόξα) during their wanderings in the wilderness, the audience of the Fourth Gospel possesses the locus of the divine Shekhinah/Glory in its midst in the form of the resurrected Jesus. The Fourth Gospel operates on a concept of worship space as fluid and able to be re-located, rather than fixed and static in location.[57] We will therefore follow Schneiders' argument that the community, with the Jesus-temple in its midst, corresponds to *Israel* with the wilderness tabernacle of Exodus in its midst,[58] in contrast to the positions of Coloe and Daise (discussed briefly above) that the "Johannine Community" is the temple.

The claim to have a temple (indeed, *the* temple, the only really efficacious one) sets apart "Israel" from "Judea" in John. Although each respective group lays claim to the ancient faith of Israel, in John's terminology Ἰουδαία/Ἰουδαῖοι denotes those Israelites who have fallen away; but this is not unlike what we find in the Old Testament prophets who railed against the ethical wrongdoings and cultic infidelities of their own people; nor does it differ significantly from the ideas of the Qumran sect, more contemporary with the Gospel. Ἰσραήλ/Ἰσραηλίτης, on the other hand, denotes the group in John that renders worship faithfully, similar to the "remnant" concept also found in the prophets, particularly in Isaiah, Jeremiah, Ezekiel, and Hosea. At the same time, the claim to possess the true place of God's dwelling, and thereby the true place of worship, sets apart John's audience from the wider *Roman* society. If, as most scholars agree, John was written after the Jerusalem temple's fall in 70 CE, John's audience[59] would have

55. In agreement with Lizorkin-Eyzenberg, *Jewish Gospel*, 63–64, 117, 173, 193.

56. In agreement with Ashton, "Identity and Function," esp. 73–74.

57. We will discuss this in detail in chapter 4 below.

58. Schneiders, "New Temple," 338, 346–47, 351. See also Kinzer, "Temple Christology," 447.

59. I intend to use the term "audience" throughout, rather than the term "community" conventionally employed when discussing John. Recently, some scholars have challenged the very idea that a "Johannine community" even existed (we will discuss this further in chapter 4 below, which deals with spatial worship in John). I wish to avoid the particulars of this debate as the scope of this thesis cannot address it in detail. However,

found itself without any location in which to worship—that is, in which to offer sacrifice. Obviously they could not worship in Jerusalem since that institution was no more; nor would they, as Jesus-believers, worship in any temple dedicated to any deity of the Roman pantheon. By claiming their own temple in the form of the resurrected Jesus, in whom, they asserted, God's very Glory dwelt, the Fourth Gospel's audience would in the same breath issue a challenge to the imperial authority of the Roman world in which they lived.

Methodology

This is an exegetical study that takes a synchronic approach to the text of the Gospel. Our exploration of the temple-sacrificial theme will be broadly historical-critical and employ spatial theory, with an eye toward the Christological implications of John's claim that Jesus is temple because he is sacrifice.

Chapter 2 will address the question of *why* and *how* John presents Jesus as sacrifice (and thereby as worship space): he is temple solely because he fulfills the Jerusalem temple's sacrificial functions in that institution's absence. The Gospel's use of specific sacrificial practices, namely the Passover and its connections to Akedah traditions with the *tôdāh* and *tāmîd* offerings, will be examined, as well as the Gospel's portrayal of priesthood.

This chapter will also address parallels between John's portrayal of Jesus as sacrifice and certain rabbinic texts, especially those dealing with the connection between the Akedah, Passover, and the temple sacrifices *tāmîd* and *tôdāh*. Given that major rabbinic texts, including those we will discuss in this thesis, postdate the composition of the Fourth Gospel, a word must be said regarding the use of this literature for the present study.

Rabbinic associations of *tāmîd*, *tôdāh*, and Passover with the Akedah can be shown to preserve earlier traditions, as seen by appealing to strands of Akedah interpretation in pre-rabbinic texts such as *Jubilees*, 4Q225/4QpsJub^a, *2 and 4 Maccabees*, *Wisdom*, *Sirach*, Philo, Josephus, Pseudo-Philo, *1 Clement*, and Melito's *Peri Pashas*, all of which contain similarities to the later rabbinic writings.[60] Pre-dating the Mishnah's

---

that there would have been people who heard and/or read John, and that the evangelist wrote his Gospel in order that it would be read, is hardly to be doubted.

60. See, e.g., Brown, *Death of the Messiah*, 2:1437–38; Derrett, *Victim*, 165; Fitzmyer, "Sacrifice of Isaac"; Huizenga, "Aqedah," 106, 108–9; Manns, "Jewish Liturgy," 61. Brown

identification of the Akedah with Passover, *Jubilees* "reveals how the Genesis story [of the offering of Isaac] was being understood in the second pre-Christian century in Palestinian Judaism."[61] *Jub.* 18:13 identifies Mt. Moriah, the location of Isaac's offering, with Mt. Zion, the location of the Jerusalem temple, making an association by extension between the offering of Isaac and the temple rites and sacrifices; Josephus later makes the same identification in *Antiquities* 1.224, 226.[62] Further, *Jub.* 18:15-18, 19 directly identifies the seven-day Passover festival with the Akedah by characterizing Passover as an anniversary remembrance of that event; specifically, Isaac was bound at the same time that the Passover lamb was sacrificed.[63] (Similarly, a tradition developed that the *tāmîd* had been instituted on the same date.[64]) The *Liber Antiquitatum Biblicarum* of Pseudo-Philo (henceforth *L.A.B.*) stresses that Isaac went to the altar willingly (*L.A.B.* 18:5; in common with 4 *Macc.*), that his blood had atoning power (also in 18:5), and that the Gentiles would recognize Isaac's self-offering as the only true, valid sacrificial offering (*L.A.B.* 32:3).[65] Philo's *Abr.* 170 predicates a priestly function of Abraham in the Akedah, as one who offers sacrifice. Although *1 Clement* is a Christian text, "its early date (the end of the first century CE) and conspicuous reference to a willing Isaac without any Christological exploitation confirms that early Christians knew of the willing Isaac as a well-developed and fully Jewish datum."[66] This text too asserts that Isaac went to his sacrifice willingly (31:3) and suggests that Isaac died on the altar (10:7).[67]

Against scholars who have argued that influence goes in the opposite direction, and that it was John that provided source material for the rabbinic writings,[68] it can be shown that the rabbinic texts we will discuss in

---

argues that Pseudo-Philo preserves ideas that were present "just before or just after AD 70" (Brown, *Death of the Messiah*, 2:1437-38).

61. Fitzmyer, "Sacrifice of Isaac"; Huizenga, "Aqedah," 131.

62. Fitzmyer, "Sacrifice of Isaac"; Huizenga, "Aqedah," 131; Huizenga, "Battle," 39.

63. Other traditions also agree. See Brown, *According to John (xiii-xxi)*, 917; Brown, *Death of the Messiah*, 2:1438, 1440; Daly, *Christian Sacrifice*, 178; Fitzmyer, "Sacrifice of Isaac"; Huizenga, "Aqedah," 128-29; Huizenga, "Battle," 38-39, 41-42, 44; Manns, "Jewish Liturgy," 59.

64. Manns, "Binding of Isaac," 63.

65. Huizenga, "Aqedah," 112, 116-17.

66. Huizenga, "Aqedah," 131-32.

67. Ibid., 132-33.

68. E.g., Reinhartz, "Introduction," 155.

the present study have parallels with literature pre-dating or roughly contemporary with the Fourth Gospel. The chronology is roughly as follows:

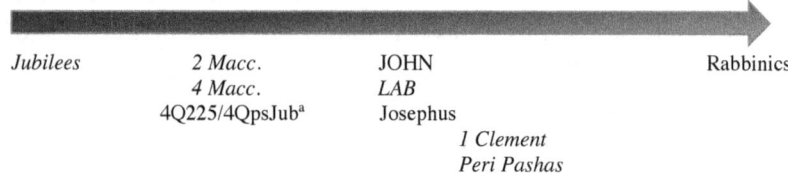

Jubilees	2 Macc.	JOHN	Rabbinics
	4 Macc.	LAB	
	4Q225/4QpsJubª	Josephus	
		1 Clement	
		Peri Pashas	

Figure 1

Along the timeline of composition of the texts relevant to the development of Isaac/Akedah traditions, John sits at the midpoint. The interpretations of the binding of Isaac pertinent to this thesis do not appear for the first time in John; rather, we see that certain traditions pre-date the Gospel and that the earliest texts containing these traditions form one "bookend," with the rabbinic texts forming another. The Isaac/Akedah traditions that concern us here were in development prior to the composition of the Fourth Gospel, which therefore represents a moment in the development of those traditions. Since, therefore, parallels to the later rabbinic texts appear *earlier* than John, those parallels cannot originate with the Fourth Gospel. The later rabbinic texts therefore are not dependent upon John, but represent the natural continuation of Isaac/Akedah interpretations, whose momentum had been building across the time of the Gospel's composition.

Since, therefore, Akedah traditions linking that event to Passover and the temple sacrifices, and assigning an atonement character to the Akedah, were in place by the time both John and the rabbinic texts under discussion were composed, the later rabbinic writings reflect not a sudden interpretation arising in the third century CE, but the culmination of ideas that had long been developing: "The haggadah on the Akedah contained a fairly well-developed soteriology" by the time of the writing of the New Testament.[69] This "haggadah" had been developing along a trajectory of understanding the Akedah in a way that connected that event to Passover,

---

69. Daly, *Christian Sacrifice*, 180–81. Daly's work here and in *The Origin of the Christian Doctrine of Sacrifice*, cited elsewhere in this thesis, is instrumental in tracing Akedah traditions prior to the composition of the New Testament texts, thereby showing that the rabbinic texts do not represent late (2nd or 3rd century CE) developments, nor did the early Jesus-sect invent Akedah sacrifice worship/liturgy typology. See also Knöppler, *Sühne*, 181.

atonement, and temple sacrifice for a long time prior to, and across the time frame of, John's Gospel, reaching crystallization (not invention) during the era in which the rabbinic texts were compiled.[70]

Since the rabbinic literature we will examine in this study can therefore be shown to continue earlier traditions, these texts will help to inform our discussion of sacrifice traditions that lay in the cultural/theological background of the Fourth Gospel's composition.[71]

Chapter 3 will examine John's Passion Narrative as the climax of the Gospel's worship theme, pursuing a close reading of these crucially important chapters. As this scene encapsulates and explicates the entire temple and sacrifice concept of the Gospel in a single event, the Passion deserves to be treated in its own chapter. Chapter 3 will function as a summation of the thesis to this point, just as the Passion account itself functions as a summation of John's temple and sacrifice themes.

Chapter 4 will survey evidence of the first-century phenomenon of relocation of sacred space, including first-century temple opposition movements. Spatial theory as well as ancient ritual theory will be utilized to examine the Fourth Gospel's relocation of sacred space to the person of Jesus, and to challenge scholarship that claims that 1.) John *eradicates* the necessity of physical worship location; that 2.) John portrays the separation of "Judaism" and "Christianity" as two separate religions, claiming the end of the effectiveness and relevance of Jewish worship tradition and praxis; and that 3.) the community, not Jesus, is the temple in John.

This chapter will include an exploration of the Gospel's identification of worship place and practices as a strategy of resistance to Roman imperial oppression. This will help to situate the Fourth Gospel's temple and sacrifice themes in a cultural context of reaction and response to conditions directly affecting the Gospel's audience. Taking all of these points together, chapter 4 will therefore examine how John's relocation of worship to the person of Jesus would have functioned as a coping strategy for an audience cut off from conventional forms of worship that pervaded their world and to which they had likely been accustomed prior to the destruction of the Jerusalem temple and/or their entry into the Jesus-movement.

Chapter 5 will address John's portrayal of the Gospel's Jesus-believing audience as Ἰσραήλ (those who represent the north, Samaria and Galilee) over against Jesus' opponents, the Ἰουδαῖοι (those who represent the south,

---

70. See Huizenga, "Aqedah," 117–18, 133; Huizenga, "Battle," 41.
71. See Thomas, "Rabbinic Judaism," 181–82.

Judea). This establishes the framework within which the Fourth Gospel builds its temple and sacrificial themes, casting proper worship as a rivalry between two geographical regions with the north/Israel possessing the true house of God's Glory in the form of the person of Jesus, just as Israel of old had possessed the house of God's Glory in the wilderness tabernacle.

Finally, Chapter 6 will conclude by summarizing this study's findings and discussing its contributions to the field of Johannine studies, including the Christological implications and the potential for this thesis to contribute to renewed dialogue regarding the translation of Ἰουδαῖοι in John.

2

The Johannine Jesus Fulfills the Functions of the Temple

WORSHIP IN THE ANCIENT Near East, continuing into the time of the Roman Empire and encompassing the areas of the world over which that empire held sway, was defined by sacrificial praxis.[1] While particular forms of observance varied, the basic concept that the god/s must be honored through sacrificial offerings was a constant throughout Mediterranean cultures of the first century CE. Worship in the Jerusalem temple shared this concept in common with its Ancient Near East neighbors and with its Roman conquerors. Worship was sacrifice: the two could not be separated. Therefore, when discussing temple, one must also discuss sacrifice. Indeed, the temple in Jerusalem would have been "inconceivable" without the atonement sacrifices practiced within it, according to the Priestly canonical tradition.[2] In this chapter, we will first examine the associations of the *tāmîd*, *tôdāh*, and Passover sacrifices with Akedah traditions, particularly as the (near-) sacrifice of Isaac in Genesis 22 was interpreted in some rabbinic circles representing a long development of interpretation across the time of the Fourth Gospel, and explore that Gospel's correlations to these interpretations in its identification of Jesus as the one who fulfills and performs the functions of those sacrifices. We will then examine the concept that John is able to identify Jesus as worship locus because Jesus is the priest who performs, in his person, the functions of the *tāmîd* and *tôdāh* sacrifices. After establishing this, the chapter will conclude by demonstrating that the Fourth Gospel's identification of Jesus as *tāmîd* and *tôdāh* depends on clear Passover references within the Gospel text.

1. See, among other works, Boustan, "Confounding," 265–87; Daly, *Christian Sacrifice*; Heyman, *Power*; McClymond, *Beyond*; Petropoulou, *Animal Sacrifice*.

2. Knöppler, *Sühne*, 247, 249.

The scope of this study cannot allow for a detailed discussion of the meaning of sacrifice in general, not only due to the vast kinds and purposes of sacrifices performed in the Jerusalem temple of the first century CE but also because only three of those will occupy our attention in this thesis: *tāmîd*, *tôdāh*, and Passover. Neither are we able here to examine the many and varied interpretations of even those three, nor of the wide-ranging understandings of temple priesthood as these developed throughout history and scripture, and how they were interpreted in various circles in the same period. Rather, the question that must specifically occupy our attention in this chapter is: does John portray Jesus as a sacrifice, and if so, what manner of sacrifice?

Worship is Sacrifice; Sacrifice is Worship

Evidence for the identification of worship as sacrifice even in the absence of a temple is on display most pertinently in first-century Diaspora communities and in the Qumran sect that produced the Dead Sea Scrolls (henceforth DSS). Far removed geographically from the Jerusalem temple—the only temple in which they could legitimately worship—Diaspora communities did not completely abandon sacrifice for lack of a building in which to perform it, but developed their own sacrificial worship practices as a way of participating long-distance in the praxis of the Jerusalem institution. Steven Fine has shown that it was not uncommon for first-century Diaspora synagogues to be regarded with the same degree of holiness possessed by the Jerusalem temple and accordingly observed purity practices similar to those observed at that locus of worship.[3] There is some evidence that Diaspora communities would have participated in the Jerusalem temple rites, even at a distance, through payment of the annual temple tax, prayer, almsgiving, Torah study, and ethical conduct. These would have been concrete ways in which those removed geographically from the temple maintained ties with that worship cultus.[4] Indeed, since these forms of worship were

---

3. Fine, *Holy Place*, esp. 28–32. See also Eisenbaum, *Not a Christian*, 156–57; Klawans, "Interpreting," 1–17, esp. 13.

4. For Diaspora worship practices as sacrificial in nature, see the following: Bowker, *Jesus*, 68; Daly, *Christian Sacrifice*, 160; Fine, *Holy Place*, 28–32; Gruen, *Diaspora*, 121; Hogeterp, "Paul's Judaism," 89–90, 94–95, 103; Poirier, "Purity," 247–65; Quarles, "New Perspective," 39–56; Roetzel, "Sacrifice," 415–16; Williams, "Being a Jew," 8–18. It is worth considering that such practices as "place-holders" for temple sacrifice, allowing "distance participation" in temple sacrifice, may have provided a framework for

already in place within Diaspora communities, they may have provided a "road map" for the continuation of Jewish worship and identity after the destruction of the Jerusalem temple institution in 70 CE. Diaspora community worship therefore demonstrates that even at a distance from, or in the absence of, the physical temple, worship would have continued to involve, and to be defined by, sacrificial practices.[5]

It is well-known that the Qumran sect viewed and defined itself as a temple-community, a kind of "place-holder" for the locus of God's presence/the divine Glory in the world until God brought about the full redemption of Israel and restored proper worship to the Jerusalem temple.[6] Similar ideas are found in the writings of Paul, although no specifically anti-temple views are found in the undisputed letters and there is no indication there that Paul anticipated any change in the temple institution.[7] Both the DSS and the Pauline epistles share the characteristic of the community's performance of temple-less sacrifice by means of prayer and ethical behavior. The DSS adds to these communal ritual purity regulations and adherence to the community rule; Paul adds financial support of the poor, especially in the form of the monetary offerings (modeled on the temple tax) that he collects for the Jerusalem Jesus-community.[8]

Following the scholarly consensus that the Gospel of John was composed in its final form after 70 CE, during the time when the Jerusalem temple was no longer available for worship, we may interpret the Gospel's

---

subsequent rabbinic development after the temple's fall, since the Diaspora practices had long been in place.

5. See Heyman, *Power*, 146–47. While Heyman acknowledges that "sacrificial rhetoric" continued to inform worship, he also claims that, post-70 CE, such rhetoric "spiritualized" and indeed "dematerialized" worship "to challenge the efficacy of material rituals." The present study will argue that the Fourth Gospel does not "dematerialize" worship, but rather locates worship in the material reality of the risen Jesus.

6. See, e.g., Daly, *Christian Doctrine*, 45, 67–69; Köstenberger, "Destruction," 219–20.

7. Troost-Cramer, "De-centralizing."

8. Many scholars use the term "spiritualization" to refer to this process of developing forms of sacrifice in the absence of a temple in which to worship. I eschew this terminology, as it removes sacrifice to the realm of the utter abstract. At the same time, Daly (*Christian Doctrine*, 76) qualifies this term by defining "spiritualization" as more of a "Christologization," particularly in the context of John 4, which we will examine below. Elsewhere, Daly writes, "Philo has a thoroughly spiritualized idea of sacrifice; not in the sense, however, of rejecting material, cultic sacrifice, but of insisting that the true oblation . . . is the devotion of a soul dear to God" (Daly, *Christian Sacrifice*, 397). For Paul's view of the collection as an expression of worship, and the possibility that Paul modeled his collection on the temple tax, see n. 7 above.

presentation of worship as providing an alternative way of sacrificial worship in the temple's absence. While the Jerusalem temple and its rites ceased to exist after 70 CE, Jews, Jesus-believers, and interested Gentiles did not instantly remove worship to the abstract by claiming that worship must be conducted without ritual or sacrifice. The language of sacrifice and temple carried on for decades: as rabbinic Judaism developed after 70 CE, worship was framed in terms of sacrifice so that prayer, almsgiving, ethical behavior, and atonement practices became the new form of maintaining relationship with God by means of sacrificial worship.[9] Additionally, there were expectations in some circles that the Jerusalem temple would be rebuilt (as is evident from coins minted after the Bar Kochba rebellion in 135 CE); accordingly the adoption of prayer, alms, etc. as sacrifice would have been viewed in these circles as a temporary measure, a "place-holder" until the time of the temple's restoration. For the author of the Fourth Gospel too, worship continued to be framed in terms of temple and sacrifice, but with the difference that sacrifice did not take the form of prayer, almsgiving, or ethical behavior but *the person of Jesus*.[10] Since Jesus was the ultimate and perfect sacrifice, there was still a temple in which to worship, and this temple was not a stop-gap until a new building could be constructed and the old rites reinstated. The Jesus-temple was eternal by virtue of Jesus' resurrection to a life that could no longer be subject to destruction. Some post-70 CE apocalyptic literature, roughly contemporary with John, attempts to cope with the destruction of the Jerusalem temple by emphasizing the superiority of the cosmic temple, God's abode in heaven, which cannot be razed by human armies as Rome had razed the temple in Jerusalem.[11] As part of that same quest to define the new manner and place of worship, the Fourth Gospel finds the locus of worship not in a heavenly or earthly building but in the person of Jesus. As we will discuss in chapter 5 below, the group called Ἰσραήλ in the Gospel possesses this correct temple; the group called Ἰουδαῖοι have the wrong temple.

Given that worship continued to be viewed as intrinsically involving sacrifice even during this post-temple time, the Fourth Gospel poses three specific former temple sacrifices with which to identify Jesus, and with

---

9. See esp. Biale, "Blood," 45.

10. For the phenomenon of various Jewish groups continuing to "defin[e] themselves with reference to the temple," see Köstenberger, "Second Temple," esp. 226, 231.

11. E.g. *4 Ezra*; *Sib. Or.* 4 4:8-11; *2 Bar.* 4:2-6; 51:7; 75:7-8, 15-16; 84; 85:3; *3 Bar.* See Koester, *Dwelling*, 74.

which the Gospel's audience would likely have been familiar: the twice-daily *tāmîd*, the *tôdāh* thank-offering, and the annual Passover observance. John legitimates this identification by also portraying Jesus as the new priest who offers sacrifice, performing the functions of the now-absent Jerusalem temple priesthood.[12] We will examine each of these in turn.

The *Tāmîd* Offering

The Association of *Tāmîd* with Akedah and Passover

Some rabbinic texts connect the morning and evening offering of a male, unblemished lamb in the twice-daily *tāmîd* offering to the story of the binding of Isaac in Genesis 22. We will examine the Passover connections in detail below; for the moment, we will focus on interpretations of the *tāmîd* as a twice-daily commemoration of the Akedah, with the *tāmîd* victim, a lamb, as a representation not of the ram miraculously provided to Abraham as a substitute for his son Isaac, but as a representation of Isaac himself. The *tāmîd* was interpreted in some rabbinic circles as a practice necessary to keep the Akedah constantly before the eyes of God, with the lamb representing the original pure and willing sacrificial victim, Isaac. The significance and power of the *tāmîd* to atone for Israel's sin was based on its character as a twice-daily recollection of the lamb sacrificed for the Passover deliverance in Exodus 12, a topic that we will discuss further below.[13] These rabbinic writers suggested that when God looked on the temple's altar and saw the offering of the *tāmîd*, it was the self-offering—and in some cases, the actual shed blood—of *Isaac* that he saw and remembered.[14]

---

12. Kinzer discusses Jesus' cosmic priesthood (and claims that John was written from a perspective of "priestly mysticism"), but claims that this priesthood as portrayed in John supersedes the Jerusalem priesthood by "bringing to fulfillment that which the Temple and priesthood represent" (Kinzer, "Temple Christology," 461–63). The use of the term *fulfillment* is unclear here: it is difficult to ascertain whether Kinzer means something like "fullest embodiment" or the traditional "replacement." While the present study agrees with Kinzer's basic claim about Jesus' portrayal as priest in John, we will argue that this portrayal does not supersede the temple and priesthood in the sense of replacing Jewish worship, but rather that the Johannine Jesus stands as sacrifice, temple, and priest in the aftermath of the Jerusalem temple institution's destruction, thereby *continuing* Jewish worship.

13. See Hoskins, "Deliverance," as noted above.

14. See esp. Grigsby, "Cross," 51–80; Manns, "Jewish Liturgy," 62–64.

Several rabbinic texts demonstrate the association of Jerusalem temple sacrifices with the Akedah. According to *Mek. R. Ishmael* (*Pisḥa* 7:78–82), the Exodus account should be read directly in the light of the near-sacrifice of Isaac.[15] This rabbinic text claims that when God assured the Israelites that their firstborn would be spared from death when God saw the blood of the slaughtered lamb on their doorposts (Exod 12:13), the blood that God "saw" (that is, recalled) was actually the blood of *Isaac*:

> *And When I See the Blood.* I see the blood of the sacrifice of Isaac. For it is said: "Abraham called the name of that place Adonai-jireh. Likewise it says in another passage: "And as he was about to destroy, the Lord beheld and He repented Him," etc. What did He behold? He beheld the blood of the sacrifice of Isaac, as it is said: "God Himself will see the lamb," etc.[16]

The Passover lamb, therefore, recalls and represents the Akedah, with Isaac as the "lamb." In his exposition of this passage in the *Mekhilta*, Manns writes: "The sacrifice of the Passover lamb reminded God of Isaac's perfect self-oblation and invoked his merits. ... The saving virtue of the Passover lamb came from the merits of that first lamb, the son of Abraham, who offered himself upon the altar."[17] It seems that the text quoted above carries on an earlier tradition regarding the power of Isaac's blood, which we find in Pseudo-Philo's *L.A.B.* 18.3; 32.3; 40.2 (possibly 18.5).[18] How, though, are we to reconcile these interpretations, which refer to Isaac's blood, with the fact that Gen 22:12–13 clarifies that Abraham did not actually slaughter or, apparently, even wound his son?

The scope of the present study prevents us from concerning ourselves with particulars of the canonical text of Genesis 22. We must focus our

---

15. See Brown, *According to John (xiii–xxi)*, 917; Manns, "Jewish Liturgy," 60.

16. Lauterbach, *Mekhilta*, 56; Hammer, *Classic Midrash*, 57. See also Manns, "Jewish Liturgy," 60.

17. Manns, "Jewish Liturgy," 60. See also Daly, *Christian Doctrine*, 48, 49, 52. There has been some debate on whether this text possesses any reference to Isaac's "merit," as expressed recently by Lauterbach (*Mekhilta*, 57n7) and by Joseph A. Fitzmyer in agreement with him (Fitzmyer, "Sacrifice of Isaac"). I agree, however, with Daly and Manns that the application of Isaac's merit to his descendants is in view, because of the clear association of the Passover liberation with Isaac's self-offering and because what God is described as "seeing" is the "lamb," i.e., Isaac.

18. Daly, *Christian Doctrine*, 49; Daly, *Christian Sacrifice*, 177, 180; Fitzmyer, "Sacrifice of Isaac"; Huizenga, "Aqedah," 109–13. Fitzmyer agrees that *L.A.B.* 32.3 and 40.2 refer to an atonement factor for Isaac's descendants, but disagrees with Vermes that 18.5 holds the same meaning.

attention instead on the *interpretations* of this biblical passage that were likely current at the time of the Fourth Gospel's composition and that accordingly provide a significant correlation to the Fourth Gospel, contributing to a cultural and theological situation in which John's Christology could take form. In the *Tg. Neof.* Genesis 22, Abraham offers the following prayer "in the name of the Memra of the Lord" when the ram appears as a substitute offering for his son Isaac:

> And now, when [Isaac's] sons are in the hour of distress you [= God] shall remember the Binding of their father Isaac, and listen to the voice of their supplication, and answer them and deliver them from all distress, so that the generations to arise after him shall say: "On the mountain of the sanctuary of the Lord [= Mount Moriah, location of the temple] Abraham sacrificed his son Isaac, and on this mountain the glory of the Shekinah of *the* Lord *was revealed to him.*"[19]

This targumic passage is packed with terms significant for John's Christology, particularly *Memra* and *Shekinah*. John clearly identifies Jesus as the divine Glory, as we will see; and the "Memra of the Lord" was a rabbinic term equivalent to the concept of λόγος, with which Jesus is also identified in John 1:1, 14. Of course, "the glory of the Shekinah" had been housed in the Jerusalem temple on Mount Moriah. This will assist us later in forming a picture of the Fourth Gospel's argument for a worship location centered in Jesus.

Note that the text quoted above affirms that Abraham "sacrificed his son"—not that he "*almost* sacrificed his son." Once again, although the knife did not touch Isaac, he was *reckoned* as actually sacrificed, by virtue of his free acceptance of, and willing participation in, the offering of his own life. The idea that Isaac had died on the altar seems to predate the rabbis, as in addition to the *L.A.B.* passages on Isaac's blood mentioned above, possible allusions to Isaac's death in the Akedah event are found in *4 Macc.* 13:8–12 and in *1 Clem.* 10:7.[20] Two rabbinic texts show the development of this concept by asserting that Isaac died on his father's altar: the first, *Pirqe R. El.* claims that Isaac "died of terror while bound upon the altar, and that

---

19. McNamara, *Targum*, 119. The identification of Moriah as the site for the later temple is repeated in *Gen. Rab.* 22.12, but had been made long before the composition of these texts, as demonstrated by a comparison with *Jub.* 18:13 (Fitzmyer, "Sacrifice of Isaac").

20. Huizenga, "Aqedah," 123–24, 132–33.

he was revived by the heavenly voice that told Abraham not to proceed with the slaughter."[21] The second, *Tg. 1 Chr* 21:15, offers the shocking image of Isaac's ashes actually lying on the altar.[22] Though these views were in the minority among the rabbinic writings, and "the idea of the death and resurrection of Isaac was generally rejected by rabbinic Judaism,"[23] they need not be in the mainstream in order to find currency within "fringe" groups.

Judging by the presence of similar concepts in the *L.A.B.*, *4 Macc.*, and *1 Clem.*, as discussed above, interpretations of the Akedah that included Isaac's actual death circulated widely enough to provide a fertile theological soil in which early Jesus-believers grappled with the meaning of Jesus' life, death, and resurrection. The followers of Jesus may well have appealed to Akedah traditions in an attempt to understand and articulate their own faith experience; and this process may be in evidence in John's portrayal of Jesus as sacrifice, in terms similar to those used of Isaac.

Mek. R. Simon II.II.2 goes so far as to claim that Isaac's blood was actually shed on the altar at Abraham's hand, and that this bloodletting was the reason why God brought about the Passover deliverance from Egypt generations later:

> R. Joshua says, "'And God spoke to Moses': "the Holy One, blessed be He, said to Moses, 'I am trustworthy to pay the reward [for the devoted action of] Isaac son of Abraham, from whom departed a fourth [of a *log*] of blood on top of the altar. And I said to him, "Because of your great strength, those condemned to death will be retrieved." "But now, as the [obligation to fulfill] the oath [that I swore to your forefathers] to bring the Children of Israel out from Egypt is incumbent upon me, and I am requesting [of you] to bring them out—you say to me, "Make someone else Your agent!""[24]

Here, we may understand "Isaac" as the representative of the collective people Israel, identified as a whole with Isaac as their ancestor: when God says that he is going to "reward Isaac" he means that he is going to save Isaac's descendants, Israel, from bondage in Egypt for the sake of Isaac's actual shed blood. The instrument and facilitator of that salvation, the blood of

---

21. Quoted in Rosenberg, "Jesus, Isaac," 387.
22. See Daly, *Christian Doctrine*, 48, 49; also Daly, *Christian Sacrifice*, 180.
23. Rosenberg, "Jesus, Isaac," 388.
24. Nelson, *Bar Yoḥai*. See Manns, "Jewish Liturgy," 60; Manns, "Targum," 78. Recall that the rabbinic association of the Passover with the Akedah of Isaac finds precedent in *Jubilees* (Huizenga, "Battle," 44–45).

the Passover lamb, thereby recalled the blood of Isaac; therefore Isaac was the prototype of the Passover lamb.[25]

Other interpretations do not depict Isaac being sacrificed, but suggest that he was regarded by God as having been sacrificed, as in Philo's *Abr.* 177.[26] Rabbinic texts continued this tradition as well: in *Midr. Rab. Gen.* (56.9), we read that when Abraham was about to sacrifice the ram that God had sent as a substitute offering in place of Isaac, Abraham uttered this prayer:

> "Sovereign of the Universe! Look upon the blood of this ram as though it were the blood of my son Isaac; its *emurim* as though they were my son's *emurim*," even as we learned: When a man declares: This animal be instead of this one, in exchange for that, or a substitute for this, it is a valid exchange. R. Phineas said in R. Banai's name: He prayed: "Sovereign of the Universe! Regard it as though I had sacrificed my son Isaac first and then the ram instead of him," as in the verse, *And Jotham his son reigned in his stead.*[27]

The last two lines, dealing with the term *instead*, clarify that Abraham prayed not that the ram be regarded as sacrificed in Isaac's place, but *following upon* a sacrifice of Isaac.[28] In this interpretation, Abraham wants God to consider that Isaac had really been sacrificed *in addition to* the ram. Hence, although Isaac was not literally sacrificed, he was *considered to have actually been* sacrificed.[29] The merit of being a sacrificial victim was applied to Isaac; in this rabbinic interpretation Isaac was also said to have been aware at the time that this same merit would be applied to his descendants in the form of the Passover/Exodus event.[30]

Mek. R. Simon links Akedah and Passover elsewhere as well:

---

25. Manns, "Jewish Liturgy," 60.

26. Daly, *Christian Sacrifice*, 178. C. H. Dodd *(Interpretation)* recognized the affinities between John and some of Philo's writings.

27. Freedman and Simon, *Midrash Rabbah*, 499.

28. Ibid., 499n4.

29. Daly, *Christian Doctrine*, 48, 52; Daly, *Christian Sacrifice*, 177–80; Huizenga, "Aqedah," 131.

30. Manns, "Targum," 77–79. See also Daly, *Christian Doctrine*, 48; Daly, *Christian Sacrifice*, 177–80; Huizenga, "Battle," 44–45. L.A.B. 32.12–13 also refers to a mighty act of God on behalf of Isaac's descendants, perhaps an oblique reference to the Passover; although it is not Abraham's or Isaac's actions in the Akedah that cause this deliverance but "the memory of God" (Huizenga, "Aqedah," 113–14, 116).

> Let the [one] sword held in hand come and offset [the other] sword held in hand. Let the sword held in hand [by Abraham on Mount Moriah]—"And Abraham stretched out his hand, etc." (Gen 22:10)—offset the sword held in hand [by Pharaoh], as Pharaoh said, "The foe said, ('I will pursue, I will overtake, I will divide the spoil ... I will bare my sword ...')" (Exod 15:9). [And let the sword held in hand by Abraham] suspend the sword held in hand by Pharaoh, who said, "I will bare my sword, my hand shall subdue them" (Exod 15:9). (XXI:V.2)[31]

In this passage, the merit gained by Abraham in obeying God's command to raise a "sword"/knife to offer up his son is applied to Israel generations later in the Exodus event; it is Abraham's merit that effects Israel's liberation from the oppression of the Pharaoh and renders Pharaoh's own sword ineffective against them.

> R. Banyah says, "[God said,] 'For the merit of the commandment that Abraham did will I split the sea for them'—And he split the wood" (Gen 22:3). (XXIII:I.8).[32]

Here, Abraham's splitting of the wood on which Isaac's body is to be burned as a whole burnt-offering (*tāmîd*!) is interpreted as a foreshadowing of God's division of the Red Sea that allowed Israel to escape permanently from Pharaoh's army.

> At the morning watch, (the Lord looked down upon the Egyptian army from a pillar of fire and cloud, and threw the Egyptian army into a panic) (Exod 14:24): He brought forward on their behalf [the merit of]: Abraham's morning—"And Abraham rose early in the morning, etc." (Gen 22:3) ... (XXV:II.1)[33]

These brief lines associate the morning of the Red Sea crossing with the morning on which Abraham prepared to sacrifice Isaac.

The meaning and effect of the Akedah as an atoning sacrifice may be applied not only to the first Passover but to each subsequent Passover observance. Most important for this thesis, the association of the Passover with the Akedah indicates that the Passover lamb was viewed as a sacrificial

---

31. Nelson, *Bar Yoḥai*. As discussed above, the identification of Mt. Zion as Mt. Moriah had existed at the time of the writing of *Jubilees*; hence, this rabbinic text can be seen to continue and further interpret an earlier tradition, which would have been in place at the time of the Fourth Gospel's composition.

32. Ibid.

33. Ibid.

offering (specifically as an offering of atonement) due to its association with the Akedah, and both carried the same or a similar meaning.[34]

The Function of *Tāmîd* and Passover as a Sacrifice of Atonement Recalling the Akedah

As a twice-daily recollection of the Akedah, the *tāmîd* possessed the same associations and functions as the Passover. This association was so strong and so entrenched in late Judaism that "all the ideas predicated of the most varied sacrifices in which lambs could be used came also to be associated in one way or another with the Paschal lamb."[35] While this may be overstated, it is certainly true of the texts we will discuss in this chapter, which directly associate the Akedah and Passover with the twice-daily *tāmîd* sacrifice in the temple. Significantly, the *tāmîd* included an offering of bread (*minḥâ*), enhancing its Passover association.[36] In these texts, Isaac is seen as the pure lamb, indeed as the prototype of the Passover lamb. These texts show that the attributes of a "lamb," most particularly those of a sacrificial lamb, could be, and were, "transferred" to a person; this is of great importance to our study of Jesus as "lamb" in John and will figure vitally in our discussion of worship space in chapter 4 of this thesis.[37]

The sources under consideration categorize the Passover among the sacrifices of *atonement*. Several canonical texts (Deut 16; 2 Chr 30; 1 Cor 5:7), apocryphal writings (e.g., *Jub.* 49), and Josephus's *Ant.* 1.224, 226, display the same characterization, and show that such an understanding of Passover existed at the time of the New Testament.[38] The very location of the Jerusalem temple on Mount Moriah, where according to tradition the Akedah had taken place, is significant for understanding the association of

---

34. "The fact that the Passover was a sacrifice is seldom contested" (Daly, *Christian Doctrine*, 39)—at least at the time of Daly's writing. See also Daly, *Christian Sacrifice*, 197–98, 201.

35. Daly, *Christian Doctrine*, 39; Daly, *Christian Sacrifice*, 204.

36. McClymond, *Beyond*, 73, 77.

37. Hasitschka, *Befreiung*, 61. Hasitschka refers specifically to *Neof. Gen.* 22:8.

38. Fitzmyer, "Sacrifice of Isaac"; Metzner, *Verständnis*; see also Knöppler, *Sühne*, 233, 238, 244. I must disagree with Fitzmyer that "the identification of Mount Moriah with the Temple Mount is a minor detail and of little significance for the developing doctrine of the Aqedah," as I will argue further that some traditions, not least of which the Fourth Gospel, identified that event as determinative for the selection of the correct locus of sacrificial worship.

temple worship with the Akedah as well as the Akedah's associations with Passover.[39] A most intriguing parallel arises with the assertion in the *Frg. Tg.* that one of the benefits of Isaac's blood sacrifice was divine pardon for moral sin: "Remember on their behalf the Akedah of Isaac their Father, forgive them their sins and free them from all anxiety."[40] We will see below that Philo's association of Passover with liberation from sin resonates strongly with the Fourth Gospel's identification of Jesus as Passover lamb, whose death liberates God's people.[41]

In *Tg.* Gen 22, we read that during Abraham and Isaac's trek up Mount Moriah, when Isaac asks his father "where is the lamb for the burnt offering?" Abraham replies: "From before the Lord has he prepared for himself a lamb for the burnt offering; *otherwise you will be the lamb of the burnt offering.*"[42] These exact words are echoed in *Gen. Rab.* 56:4; both texts were preceded in the concept of Isaac as "burnt-offering" in *L.A.B.* 18.5; 40.2–4.[43] In all three texts, equivalents are drawn between Isaac, the burnt-offering *tāmîd*, and the Passover lamb. *Lev. Rab.* 2.11 explicitly interprets the twice-daily *tāmîd* as a remembrance of the Akedah:

> Of the ram it says, "And he shall kill it on the side of the altar northward (ẓafonah) before the Lord." The Sages said: When Abraham, our father, bound Isaac his son, the Holy One, blessed be He, instituted the sacrifice of two he-lambs, one in the morning and one in the evening. Why did He do this?—When Israel offer up the daily sacrifices on the altar, and read this verse, viz.

---

39. Brown, *Death of the Messiah*, 2:1438; Daly, *Christian Doctrine*, 48. See also Fitzmyer, "Sacrifice of Isaac"; Huizenga, "Aqedah," 131. It is worth repeating that the rabbinic sources that connect Passover/temple sacrifice with the Akedah are preceded in this interpretation by earlier sources, such as *Jubilees*, as we have discussed.

40. Fitzmyer, "Sacrifice of Isaac"; Manns, "Targum," 78–79. These words are echoed in the Roman Catholic liturgy after the praying of the Lord's Prayer: "Deliver us, Lord, from every evil, graciously grant peace in our days, that, by the help of your mercy, we may be always free from sin and safe from all distress." The mid-twentieth century translation from the Latin rendered "distress" as "anxiety."

41. It will not be my intention to attempt to prove direct dependence of John on Philo. Rather, as the two are roughly contemporary, their similarities may indicate culturally current ideas that may have influenced the development of John's Christology, possibly quite independent from Philo's writings specifically.

42. McNamara, *Targum Neofiti I*. Emphasis mine. See Manns, "Targum," 69–80; Daly, *Christian Doctrine*, 48.

43. Daly, *Christian Sacrifice*, 179–80; McNamara, *Targum Neofiti I*, 117n6.

'Ẓafonah before the Lord, the Holy One, blessed be He, remembers the binding of Isaac.[44]

This text associates the binding of Isaac with the binding of the lamb of the *tāmîd*.[45] The passage is also significant for the location and purpose of the Jerusalem temple. The geographical situating of this worship locus was by no means arbitrary: according to *Jub.* 18:13, *Tg.* Gen 22 and *Gen. Rab.*, the reason why the temple stood on Mount Zion was because Zion was identified with Moriah, and only in the location where Isaac had been offered on the altar could any other sacrifice be acceptably performed.[46] The *tāmîd*, as the twice-daily offering of a lamb on the temple's altar, not only recalled but *reenacted* Isaac's sacrifice. We might even say that Abraham created the prototypical temple by his action of offering up Isaac, and that Isaac was the prototypical sacrifice. I will argue below that the Fourth Gospel, by evoking the Akedah/Passover/*tāmîd* in order to identify Jesus as sacrifice, is actually claiming that Jesus functions not as the Jerusalem temple institution but as that first, perfect "Temple of Abraham."[47]

The *tāmîd* was therefore, for some rabbis, a twice-daily recollection and a kind of repeated "abbreviated" Passover. Since Isaac was linked to the Passover lamb, and since the twice-daily *tāmîd* offering of a lamb was intended to remind God of Isaac's self-offering for the benefit of Isaac's descendants, there is a symbiotic connection of Passover and *tāmîd*.

Tāmid as Atonement

Some sources assign the atoning function of the Akedah to Isaac's willingness, even eagerness, to be sacrificed at his father's hand. An early indication of this appears in the brief statement in 4Q255/4QpsJub^a (2.ii.4), in which Isaac issues the simple request, "B[ind me fast]."[48] This interpretation was apparently widespread: *L.A.B.* 40.2 interprets Isaac as agreeing cheerfully to the proceedings; *4 Macc.* 16:20 asserts that Isaac "did not flinch" from Abraham's knife; and Josephus (*Ant.* 1.13.4) claims that Isaac, a grown man at twenty-five years of age, *ran* to the altar with a sense of eagerness,

---

44. Freedman and Simon, *Midrash Rabbah*, 31. See Manns, "Jewish Liturgy," 62.

45. Brown, *Death of the Messiah*, 2:1435.

46. See Daly, *Christian Sacrifice*, 175, 179; Fitzmyer, "Sacrifice of Isaac"; Manns, "Targum," 70–71.

47. This will be addressed in our discussion of worship space in chapter 4 below.

48. Fitzmyer, "Sacrifice of Isaac."

even of joy (*Ant.* 1.232).⁴⁹ Pre-dating both Josephus and the rabbinic texts, *Jub.* 16:15–18 places Isaac's age at twenty-three at the time of this event. In all of these interpretations, Isaac is an adult and thereby an informed, willing participant/victim.⁵⁰

Later, the Palestinian Targum continued the tradition of a willing Isaac by portraying him as thirty-seven years old at the time of the Akedah. Other rabbinic texts follow suit. *Sipre Deut.* 32 records: "R. Meir says: Scripture says, *Thou shalt love the Lord, thy God, with all thy heart.* Love Him with all your heart, as did your father Abraham . . . *And with all thy soul*, as did Isaac, who bound himself upon the altar."⁵¹ *Tg. Ps.-J., Tg. Neof. I, Frg. Tg. 17,* and *Gen. Rab.* 56.8 respectively assign to Isaac a degree of anxiety not that his father is going to slaughter him, but that he might inadvertently fight his father and thereby render the sacrifice invalid; hence Isaac asks Abraham to bind him especially tightly (an apparent echo of 4Q255/4QpsJuba, cited above). *Lev. Rab.* 2.10 states that Isaac in fact "cast himself before his father as a lamb that is to be sacrificed."⁵²

These views of Isaac's free offering of his own life find a corollary in ideas of *martyrdom* as vicarious atonement for sin in some traditions, most prominently on view in 2 and 4 *Macc.*⁵³ The latter in particular tells of the righteous Judeans whose opposition to Hellenization under Antiochus Epiphanes resulted in their surrender of their lives, which according to the text's interpretation accomplished atonement for the sins of the whole people.⁵⁴ (By extension, there is the idea that the people's sin was to blame for the atrocities of Hellenization to begin with.⁵⁵) Several passages within 4 *Macc.* refer to the example of Isaac in the Akedah as a willing sacrifice, "the model of everyone who paid for the Sanctification of the Name with

---

49. Brown, *Death of the Messiah*, 2:1438; Huizenga, "Aqedah," 109, 123–24, 129–30; Manns, "Jewish Liturgy," 61; Manns, "Targum," 72–73. See also Daly, *Christian Sacrifice*, 179.

50. See Fitzmyer, "Sacrifice of Isaac"; Huizenga, "Aqedah," 106, 108–9, 111–13, 118, 120, 122, 124, 128, 130–33; Manns, "Jewish Liturgy," 61; Manns, "Targum," 72. See also Daly on Pseudo-Philo's *L.A.B.* in *Christian Sacrifice*, 177–78; Brown, *According to John (xiii–xxi)*, 917.

51. Hammer, *Sifre*. Emphasis mine. See Manns, "Targum," 72–73.

52. Ibid., 71n5, and 72–73. See also Grigsby, "Cross," 59.

53. See Derrett, *Victim*, 47–48; Huizenga, "Aqedah," 124–25.

54. See Huizenga, "Aqedah," 120, 124–25, 127.

55. See Ibid., 125–26. 4 *Macc.* presents vicarious suffering for the sins of Israel's leaders, and vicarious atonement from the martyrs.

his life," as in 13:12 ("Isaac offered himself to be a sacrifice for the sake of uprightness") and 16:20 ("Isaac did not withdraw when he saw the knife lifted against him by his father's hand").[56] The death of a just person as atonement for the sins of his people/nation is found especially in *4 Macc.* 4:19–22; 6:28–29 ("Cause our chastisement to be an expiation for them. Make my blood their purification and take my soul as an expiation for their souls") and 17:21–22 ("They have become as an expiation for the sin of our nation, and by the blood of these righteous men and the propitiation of their death, Divine Providence delivered Israel").[57] This is not unique to only one text tradition, however, as similar concepts appear in Josephus's *Antiquities* and in the *L.A.B.*, which both respectively preserve a sense that willing self-offering possesses a character, indeed a power, of atonement on behalf of others.[58]

Concerning the relation of this tradition to the Akedah, "If the blood of martyrs is viewed by God as an expiatory sacrifice the self-offering of Isaac atoned for the sins of his descendants."[59] Likewise, *L.A.B.* claims that "Isaac was conscious of the merits of his self-offering for his sons."[60] The evidence suggests that "in a very real sense, Rabbinic thought recast Isaac as the 'Lamb of God' who takes away sin."[61] Recall the words of *Tg.* Gen 22 that attest to Isaac's readiness to offer his life on the altar, and his anxiety to ensure that the validity of his self-offering will apply merit to his descendants (in the form of the Passover/Exodus).

The texts under study here clearly interpreted Isaac as a "sacrificial lamb" whose free self-offering atoned for the sin/s of his descendants. The lamb offered and consumed in the annual Passover observance was viewed in these texts as a remembrance of Isaac's self-offering and thereby

---

56. Brown, *Death of the Messiah*, 2:1438–39; Daly, *Christian Sacrifice*, 178–79; Fitzmyer, "Sacrifice of Isaac"; Huizenga, "Aqedah," 109, 120; Manns, "Targum," 73.

57. Huizenga, "Aqedah," 122–26; Manns, "Targum," 73.

58. Daly, *Christian Doctrine*, 49, and *Christian Sacrifice*, 179. In the former, Daly claims that Isaac's willingness to offer up his life for the sake of his descendants "[overcame] the great internal weakness of Old Testament sacrifice as an act of religion"; it cannot be argued that those who actually practiced sacrificial worship would agree with this statement. The sacrifices of the Jerusalem temple institution were intended as a remembrance of Isaac's self-offering; the two were symbiotically connected. Hence, in its own context the sacrificial rites were a manner of participation in Isaac's self-offering. See also Huizenga, "Aqedah," 109–11, 116.

59. Daly, *Christian Doctrine*, 76. See also Grigsby, "Cross," 59–60.

60. Manns, "Targum," 74. See also Daly, *Christian Sacrifice*, 180.

61. Grigsby, "Cross," 60. See also Daly, *Christian Sacrifice*, 179–80.

as a sacrifice of deliverance and of atonement.[62] We may notice similar overtones to the figure of Jesus in John if we can determine whether the Fourth Gospel evokes Isaac in relation to Jesus, an undertaking we will pursue below. For the moment, it is necessary to continue establishing the significance of the sacrificial offerings associated with the Akedah and the Passover.

The *Tôdāh* Offering

Several scholars have noted that the *tôdāh* offering, as a thanksgiving for deliverance, especially associated with deliverance from death, was linked to Passover in the first century CE insofar as it recalled the praise and thanks offered to God by the Israelites for their deliverance from the plague of the death of the firstborn at the first Passover in Egypt. The *tôdāh* expressed gratitude for the salvation that God had in the past provided for the people with whom he was in covenant relationship, as well as hope for present and future salvation based on past salvation exemplified by the Exodus. It was specifically associated with salvation from imminent death.[63] As Hartmut Gese writes:

> When someone is rescued from death, from an illness, or from persecution that poses a threat of death, then the divine deliverance is celebrated by a worship service built on a thank offering as a new foundation for the person's existence. Here he confesses God as deliverer (*jd*[*h*] hiph) in a thank offering (*todah*) . . . In the thank offering the focus is . . . on the bringing of well-being out of a state of trouble. It is not ordinary sacrificial worship, but a service of worship in which by a sacrifice Yahweh is praised and acknowledged as the deliverer . . . the one rescued can begin his life anew in the sacred meal.[64]

Hence, as an expression of praise and gratitude for deliverance from the death that results from sin,[65] the *tôdāh* carried Passover associations and the annual Passover had the character of a *tôdāh*.

---

62. Grigsby, "Cross," 59–61; Knöppler, *Sühne*, 233, 237; Rosenberg, "Suffering Servant," 388.

63. Gese, "Origin," 117; Laporte, "Philonic Models," 72; Lindsay, "Todah," 86–87; Nielsen, "Lamb," 235, 239.

64. Gese, "Lord's Supper," 129.

65. Lindsay, "Todah," 132.

By the first century CE, the *tôdāh* was no longer among the daily rites performed in the Jerusalem temple. It is significant for this thesis that, like the *tôdāh*, the Passover was also largely a domestic ritual, although linked to temple sacrifice as well. Also significant is the fact that the *tôdāh*—like the *tāmîd*—included a bread offering accompanied by a libation of wine (*reaḥ minḥâ*).[66] We will see below that the association of the *tôdāh* with Passover, along with the association of that festival with *tāmîd* as discussed above, folds into the Fourth Gospel's portrayal of Jesus as Passover lamb and allows John's Jesus to function as lamb, bread, and wine at the same time and without contradiction, because like the *tāmîd*, the *tôdāh* also recalled the Passover.

The *Tôdāh* Wine and the Priesthood of Jesus: John 2:1–11

Both elements of the *tôdāh* offering, bread and wine, are found in the Fourth Gospel. Unlike the Synoptics, which locate the bread and wine at the Passover meal that takes place on the evening before Jesus' arrest and subsequent death, John re-locates the bread to the famous "Bread of Life Discourse" of chapter 6 and the wine to the scene of the wedding feast at Cana in chapter 2.

The Fourth Gospel does not include a Passover meal. In John 13:4 we read that "Jesus rose from supper," suggesting that he and the disciples had been eating; and the scene is set "before the feast of Passover" (John 13:1). We are not told, however, what Jesus and the disciples are eating (nor do we see them eating at all; apparently the action takes place after the "supper" was over). However, food and drink each make a respective appearance elsewhere in the Gospel. Bread appears in John 6:22–59, and wine in John 2:1–11. We will begin with the latter passage, as this establishes the themes of sacrifice and priesthood integral to this thesis.

In John 2:6, we are told that at the Cana wedding "there were six stone water jars . . . for Jewish (Ἰουδαίων) ceremonial washings." In chapter 5 below we will see that Ἰουδαίων in this passage (as in the vast majority of occurrences in John) should be translated as "Judeans," so we will employ that translation here: the water jars in this scene would be used for "*Judean* ceremonial washings." This implies that the ceremonial washings in question would be connected to the same kind of ceremonial washings that occurred

---

66. Ibid., 130–31; McClymond, *Beyond*, 95.

in the temple in Judea/Jerusalem.⁶⁷ This would not be unusual, as we have seen that purity and worship practices were observed beyond Judea (as in the Diaspora). Because of this implicit reference to the temple and its rites, the "ceremonial washings" in John 2:2–11 should be understood as a reference to the "*ritual* washings" undertaken by the temple priests, lustrations necessary for their purification prior to offering sacrifice.⁶⁸ Therefore, when Jesus orders that the jars be filled with water, he is acting in a priestly role, having water prepared for ritual purification. It is no coincidence that the "Temple Incident" (2:14–25) follows immediately upon the Cana wedding, since the wedding contains overtones of purification and priesthood and the Temple Incident displays Jesus as a rival temple.⁶⁹ Knöppler rightly characterizes 2:21 as a "soteriological statement with atonement character," especially in light of the fact that the term ναός, typically designating the temple building containing the Holy Place and, most significantly, the Holy of Holies, is used to refer to Jesus' body in 2:19, 21. This identifies Jesus' function as dwelling of God's presence (Glory) and, as was the function of God's dwelling, the place of sacrifice.⁷⁰

Contrary to the argument of Raymond E. Brown, the elements of water and wine can be said to possess significance in and of themselves.⁷¹ We have established that water was integral to priestly purification as well as to the washing/rinsing of the sacrificial victims; and wine was a libation offering that accompanied the sacrifices of *tāmîd* and *tôdāh*, which were both associated with Akedah and Passover.

---

67. Lizorkin-Eyzenberg suggests that the presence of the water for "Judean" purification indicates that Cana may have been "one of those places which was considered to be under Jerusalem's religious control and under the influence of the *Ioudaioi*" (Lizorkin-Eyzenberg, *Jewish Gospel*, 13, 38).

68. See Thomas, "Rabbinic Judaism," 164–65; Um, *Temple Christology*, 20.

69. See Kinzer, "Temple Christology," 455.

70. Knöppler, *Sühne*, 247. See also Frühwald-König, *Tempel*, 232–33. While Knöppler acknowledges that the term ναός designates Jesus as temple, he also claims that this means that Jesus abolishes the Jerusalem temple institution and renders the institutional sacrificial cult obsolete as the place of God's presence. I agree that John pits Jesus against the Jerusalem temple, but I do not agree that this renders the sacrificial cult obsolete. As I will argue in chapter 4 below, sacrifice is not abrogated in John, but relocated. Köstenberger additionally notes that in the aftermath of the first destruction in the sixth century BCE, "the presence of Yahweh himself . . . served as a substitute for the loss of the Jerusalem temple," and cites Ezek 11:16 in this connection (Köstenberger, "Second Temple," 218–19).

71. Brown claims that the water and wine themselves possess little to no significance in *According to John (i–xii)*, 103–4.

Wine libations would have been poured out over the surface of the altar of sacrifice, an important aspect of worship for our thesis.[72] *Tg.* Gen 35:9ff. interprets that canonical verse to state that Jacob poured water and wine on his stone pillow after seeing the vision of the stairway to heaven, as a precursor or rubric for the Feast of Tabernacles.[73] First, we cannot help but recall John 1:51, in which Jesus famously attributes to himself the features of the Beth-El scene.[74] Secondly, and more pronounced, John 7 (particularly vv. 37–38), which depicts Jesus at the Feast of Tabernacles, possesses a strong priestly association with both water and wine. A high point of this feast was the ritual in which the priest poured water from the Pool of Siloam, whence water for temple use was drawn (another uniquely Johannine feature) into one bowl atop the altar of sacrifice, poured wine into an adjacent bowl, and removed stoppers from the vessels so that the water and wine flowed in separate streams: "the wine into a special receptacle, the water through sluices under the altar to the 'Stone of Foundation' which was in Hebrew legend the first solid thing created by God, the navel of the world from under which flows life-giving water to the whole earth."[75] Hence, the Johannine account of Tabernacles (possibly having in the background traditions surrounding *Tg.* Gen 35:9ff.) is a prolepsis of the crucifixion, at which blood (paralleled with wine) and water flow from the pierced side of the dead Christ on the cross, marking the cross as an altar. Christ is, thereby, the priest who makes the offering of his own life. We will return to this in our discussion of the Johannine passion narrative in chapter 3 below.

Water and wine therefore possess strong worship associations. Returning to John 2:2–11, Jesus asks others to provide water in order to create the wine. Why is this the case? Surely John's Jesus, through whom "all things came into being" (John 1:3), could have simply made wine appear in the jars; it is significant that he requires water as a base for creating the wine. In this case, why was there not already water in the jars? The fact that the jars intended for ritual washings have to be filled "to the brim" by the servants (2:7) indicates that they were initially empty—how, then, did the

---

72. McClymond, *Beyond*, 96.

73. Ibid.

74. See Kinzer, "Temple Christology," 447–48; Köstenberger, "Second Temple," 236.

75. Daly, *Christian Doctrine*, 76–77; Daly, *Christian Sacrifice*, 290–92. See also Kinzer, "Temple Christology," 449; Moloney, *Text and Context*, 196–97.

guests purify themselves?⁷⁶ They did not. This scene, therefore, portrays an absence of purity which only the divine Glory itself can restore.

The priestly class is shown to engage in purifying rites involving water in canonical texts, such as Exod 29:4; 30:17; 40:30ff, Lev 16:4, 24; Num 8:5–22, as well as various apocryphal texts such as *Jos. Asen.* and *T. Isaac*.⁷⁷ Marianne M. Thompson has argued convincingly that Jesus' changing of water into wine at Cana "effect[s] an appropriate purity."⁷⁸ Jesus' action indicates not replacement or supersession (as much scholarship, which is well known and need not occupy us here, has historically and unfortunately argued), but rather represents "messianic *fullness*," which naturally "entails messianic cleansing."⁷⁹ Once again, this fits the theme of temple purity established in the Temple Incident immediately following Cana and placed close to the Gospel's beginning as an indication that the rest of the text is going to present Jesus as temple.⁸⁰ Placed in close proximity as they are, the Temple Incident and the Cana miracle are intended to emphasize the purity theme and the role of Jesus as priest in achieving purity. This will be clarified further when Jesus washes his disciples' feet in John 13:1–11; in 15:3 Jesus states that his word cleanses them.⁸¹ Hence, Jesus as priest performs the purifying function that the Jerusalem temple had previously performed.

In the Cana scene, Jesus takes water, the element of priestly ablutions, to indicate that he consecrates himself as priest before offering wine, one of the elements of the *tôdāh*, just as the priest in the Jerusalem temple would have ritually purified himself before offering sacrifice.⁸² The bread portion

---

76. Lindars claims that "the artificial, and to some extent allegorical, nature of the story forbids us to ask such awkward questions as: Were the jars empty? Would it be necessary to drain them off first?" (Lindars, *Gospel*, 130). Aside from the oddity of claiming that scholarship is forbidden to ask anything at all, I would argue that the allegorical nature of this scene is precisely the feature that demands we ask its meaning.

77. Um, *Temple Christology*, 20.

78. Thompson, "Reflections," 266.

79. Ibid.

80. Ibid. See also Brown, *Community*, 118.

81. Thompson, "Reflections," 266.

82. Lindars (*Gospel*, 130), Brown (*According to John (i–xii)*, 105, 107), and Moloney (*Text and Context*, 68) have noted that the wine in this passage also indicates abundance or superabundance, especially associated with the messianic age and the messianic banquet; we will examine this in a later chapter in light of Warren Carter's argument that the miraculous production of wine at Cana is part of John's overall rhetoric of resistance: where the Roman Empire creates a lack of resources for those most in need, Jesus displays the abundance of God's kingdom.

of the *tôdāh* will appear in John 6: 22–59, the "Bread of Life Discourse." In the meantime, at Cana, the priest, Jesus, *creates* the wine of the offering from the water of priestly purification. The implication is that Jesus' authority to offer sacrifice comes from his ontological nature as priest, an idea that will resume in the Johannine passion narrative. This is why Jesus initially declines his mother's subtle request that he create wine for the wedding feast: "My hour has not yet come" (John 2:4): it is only in John's crucifixion scene that Jesus is fully revealed as priest (as well as sacrifice and temple); if he creates libation wine prior to that event, he is revealing his priesthood before the appointed "hour." When, however, he does create the wine at Cana, the event is a revelation of "his glory" (John 2:11). The Greek translated as "glory" here is δόξα, the same word used of the Shekinah in the LXX of Exod 24:16; 33:18; 40:34 (where the Glory descends upon the newly-finished Tent of Meeting); Ezek 10:4, 18, 19; 11:22–23 (the progression of the Glory away from the temple due to the uncleanness of Jerusalem); and Ezek 44:4 (the Glory returns and fills the restored temple). We are meant to recall the identification of Jesus as "Glory" in John 1 and other passages. This is why the final verse in this passage states that the Cana sign pointed to the "Glory."

The clear ritual aspects of the Cana scene indicate that we should understand the water and wine of this passage in a ritual context: these elements being present at Cana, and the Cana wedding being immediately followed by the Temple Incident, which puts Jesus forward as a rival to Jerusalem's temple institution, it cannot be the case that the water and wine themselves are accidental. Rather, the water and wine in John 2:1–11 possess the characteristics of *sacerdotal* and *sacrificial* elements.

Priesthood and λόγος in Philo

Some examples from the works of Philo of Alexandria may be helpful at this point in illuminating the Fourth Gospel's portrayal of Jesus as priest. We will further engage Philo below in our discussion of Passover models contemporary with the Fourth Gospel.

In *Somn.* I.215, Philo portrays the λόγος as the high priest of the cosmic/heavenly temple; on earth, the high priest of the Jerusalem temple reveals the λόγος in his attributes of absolute righteousness and in his position standing between humanity and God.[83]

---

83. Daly, *Christian Sacrifice*, 406–7. See also Fuglseth, *Johannine Sectarianism*, 108–10.

> For there are, as is evident, two temples of God: one of them this universe, in which there is also as High Priest His First-born, the divine Word (θεῖος λόγος), and the other the rational soul, whose Priest is the real Man; the outward and visible image of whom is he who offers the prayers and sacrifices handed down from our fathers … which is a copy and replica of the whole heaven, the intention being that the universe may join with man in the holy rites and man with the universe.[84]

What does the λόγος offer as high priest? *His own self*:

> And, when the happy soul holds out the sacred goblet of its own reason, who is it that pours into it the holy cupfuls of true gladness, but the word (λόγος), the Cupbearer of God and *Master of the feast*, who is also none other than *the draught which he pours— his own self* free from all dilution, the delight, the sweetening, the exhilaration, the merriment, the ambrosian drug … whose medicine gives joy and gladness? (*Somn.* II.249)[85]

The identification of the λόγος as one of the "temples of God" indicates that the λόγος is, in Marianne M. Thompson's words, "the visible manifestation of the deity."[86] Philo's identification of the λόγος as the "master of the feast" pouring himself as a libation offering for the health of the soul is quite similar to the Cana scene in John 2, where Jesus consecrates himself with water as would a priest, then creates wine, the second element of the *tôdāh* offering, an action which reveals the Shekinah and points toward Jesus' offering of his own blood at the crucifixion.[87] It is worth noting that the Suffering Servant of Isa 53, whose associations with both Jesus and Isaac we will discuss further below, was said to have "poured out his life" as an offering for "many."[88] This image also has associations with the well scene in John 4, where Jesus offers himself as living water as discussed above.

Jesus as λόγος/priest may also be in view in John's depiction of the soldiers' gambling for Jesus' robe as the latter hangs on the cross in John 19:23–24. Philo interprets the garments of the high priest as symbolic of the universe itself:

---

84. Philo, *On Dreams*. See Laporte, "Philonic Models," 81.
85. Philo, *On Dreams*. Emphasis mine.
86. Thompson, "Reflections," 276.
87. Laporte, "Philonic Models," 82, 85.
88. Brown, *Death of the Messiah*, 2:1180.

> For it expresses the wish first that the high priest should have in evidence upon him an image of the All, that so by constantly contemplating it he should render his own life worthy of the sum of things; secondly, that in performing his holy office he should have the whole universe as his fellow-ministrant. And very right and fit it is that he who is consecrated to the Father of the world should take with him also that Father's son, the universe, for the service of the Creator and Begetter. (*Spec.* I.84–97) [89]

John 19:23–24 does not describe the appearance of Jesus' robe, but it is the only Gospel that mentions this garment. It is worth considering whether this robe in John may possess priestly significance. We will discuss this further in the next chapter.

The *Tōdāh* Bread: John 6:22–59

This passage, the Bread of Life Discourse, simply brims over with Passover references and imagery. The first and most obvious occurs in verses 30–31: "What sign are you going to give us then, so that we may see it and believe you? What work are you performing? Our ancestors ate the manna in the wilderness; as it is written, 'He gave them bread from heaven to eat.'" In verse 32, Jesus responds: "It was not Moses who gave bread from heaven, but my Father who gives the true bread from heaven." Jesus then goes on to identify himself as that true bread provided by the Father, and to claim that eternal life depends upon his disciples' consuming his flesh, which is real food; and his blood, which is real drink (vv. 53–56).[90] Significant for this thesis is Philo's characterization of the Exodus manna as the soul's nourishment: "*the word of God*, which can satisfy all our needs."[91]

---

89. Philo, *Special Laws*.

90. Moloney contends that this is merely figurative, picturesque speech indicating that one must come to Jesus in order to obtain life. It is misunderstood by the "Jews," who, according to Moloney, have no choice but to misunderstand because they are irrevocably "locked within a closed religious system" and cannot grasp "higher" spiritual concepts (Moloney, *Text and Context*, 44). Moloney's approach muddles the issue by essentially claiming that Ἰουδαῖοι does not mean ethnic Jews, that "Israel" is the "new people of God" that includes ethnic Jews and non-Jews, and that "Jews" is the term for rejection of God (*Text and Context*, 40), even though there were "Jews" within the group that the Fourth Gospel terms "Israel." As will become clear, I strenuously disagree both with Moloney's identification of Ἰουδαῖοι and his assertion that the Fourth Gospel is not interested in ritual worship.

91. Laporte, "Philonic Models," 74. Emphasis mine. For an extended discussion of

> The souls, therefore, that have indeed already had experience of the word, but are not able to answer the question, inquire of one another "What is it?" ... In the same way then the soul, when it has been gladdened, is often unable to say what the thing that gladdens it is. But it is taught by the hierophant and prophet Moses: he will tell it, This bread is the food which God hath given to the soul, for it to feed on His own utterance and His own word; for this bread, which He hath given us to eat, is "this word." (*Leg.* III.173)[92]

The word (λόγος) of God is food for the human soul. This is consonant with views of the wilderness manna as a figure for the spiritual nourishment the Torah gave.[93] Consider also the following, in which Philo refers to the manna as God's word and as instruction:

> The one extends his vision to the ether and the revolutions of the heaven; he has been trained also to look stedfastly [*sic*] for the manna, which is the word of God, the heavenly incorruptible food of the soul which delights in the vision. (*Her.* 79)[94]

> One should not desire anything that is beyond one's capacity ... Wherefore in another passage sacred Scripture (orders) the measuring of the spiritual food that came down from heaven like a spring and was called "manna" by the Hebrews, that it might not be too much for anyone or too little. For it is necessary that teaching should be more abundant for the intelligent man, and less for the foolish man because of the fine equality of proportion. (*QG* IV.102)[95]

We cannot help but think here of the Johannine identification of Jesus as λόγος in John 1:1, 14, and as "bread of life" throughout John 6. In an intriguing parallel to Philo's identification of λόγος as bread of life, the Fourth Gospel equates Jesus as λόγος with Jesus as bread of life; the reference to Eucharist bringing Christ to his people recalls traditions in which the wisdom brought by Torah descended to the congregation on the Sabbath.[96]

---

the similarities between Philo's interpretation of manna and the Fourth Gospel's portrayal of Jesus as bread of life, see Borgen, *Bread*, esp. 62.

92. Philo, *Allegorical Interpretation*.

93. Borgen, *Bread*, 114; Brown, *According to John (i–xii)*, 262; Moloney, *Text and Context*, 178–81; Thompson, "Reflections," 271.

94. Philo, *Who is the Heir*.

95. Philo, *On Genesis*.

96. Borgen, *Bread*, 114, 154–58.

When imagining a scene in the family of Jacob in *Leg.* III.179, Philo puts these words into Jacob's mouth: "the foods which nourish the soul are various forms of knowledge."[97] So too the Fourth Gospel insists upon knowledge of Jesus, both "bread" and "word," as necessary for what the Gospel calls eternal life.

> He was in the world . . . yet the world did not know him. (1:10)

> I myself did not know him; but I came baptizing with water for this reason, that he might be revealed to Israel. (1:31)

> Anyone who resolves to do the will of God will know whether the teaching is from God or whether I am speaking on my own. (7:17)

> You will know the truth, and the truth will make you free. (8:32)

> Sanctify them in the truth; your word (λόγος) is truth. (17:17)[98]

According to John 8:32, the function of the truth is to make free or to deliver, the precise actions of God for which the *tôdāh* expressed praise and gratitude. Throughout the Bread of Life Discourse, Jesus makes clear that the deliverance he brings is a deliverance from death to life:

> Very truly, I tell you, it was not Moses who gave you the bread from heaven, but it is my Father who gives you the true bread from heaven. For the bread of God is that which comes down from heaven and gives life to the world. (6:32–33)

---

97. Philo, *Allegorical Interpretation*.

98. Brown's claim that the "true bread from heaven" is Jesus' teaching is questionable on the grounds that Jesus identifies himself, not just the words he speaks but his very person, as the true bread that descends from heaven. Jesus himself, as λόγος, is the wisdom of God and the truth one must know. In consuming Jesus, John 6 recalls wisdom traditions, the most familiar being Wisdom's invitation to partake of her banquet in Prov 9:5. Most striking, however, is the direct echo of *Sir* 24:21 ("Those who consume me") in John 6:57 ("The one who consumes me"), indicating that to consume Jesus as bread of life is to consume the divine Wisdom and, hence, to consume the Torah itself. Brown, *According to John (i–xii)*, 262, 264; see also Borgen, *Bread*, 155, 186.

Brown (*According to John (i–xii)*, 262, 264) is correct that the Synoptics (Mark 8:14–21 and Matt 16:5–12) portray Jesus' teaching as bread; but that is not the Fourth Gospel's portrayal. Moloney (*Text and Context*, 182) similarly argues that there is "nothing Eucharistic" in John 6 when Jesus tells the crowd that he himself is the "bread of life," Jesus is simply using picturesque speech to emphasize that life is obtained by coming to him. The "Jews," characteristic of their function according to Moloney's overall argument, misunderstand because they remain stuck in their insistence on a literal, materialistic ritual system and cannot rise to the spiritual level on which Jesus is speaking.

> I am the bread of life. (6:34, 48)
>
> This is indeed the will of my Father, that all who see the Son and believe in him may have eternal life; and I will raise them up on the last day. (6:40)
>
> Your ancestors ate the manna in the wilderness, and they died. This is the bread that comes down from heaven, so that one may eat of it and not die. I am the living bread that came down from heaven. Whoever eats of this bread will live forever; and the bread that I will give for the life of the world is my flesh. (6:49–51)
>
> Those who eat my flesh and drink my blood have eternal life, and I will raise them up on the last day; for my flesh is true food and my blood is true drink ... Just as the living Father sent me, and I live because of the Father, so whoever eats me will live because of me ... not like that which your ancestors ate, and they died. But the one who eats this bread will live forever. (6:54–58)[99]

So strong are the parallels between Philo's interpretation of the Exodus manna and the Fourth Gospel's portrayal of Jesus (the λόγος as bread of life that can be consumed in quite a physical manner in the Lord's Supper) that Peder Borgen has argued that John 6 is a midrash on Exod 16, making extensive use of haggadic elements.[100] According to this view, since "Philo, John and the Palestinian midrash all paraphrase words from an Old Testament quotation by means of haggadic traditions," Bultmann's suggestion that John 6:58 was a later interpolation is highly unlikely.[101] John 6 fits too well into its own religio-cultural milieu, in which haggadic traditions were being built upon to form homiletic interpretations of Old Testament passages, to be attributed to a later, "more Christian" period and redactor. In fact, John lifts whole words and phrases directly from Exodus 16, at times substituting certain words or phrases as an exegetical/homiletic

---

99. Jesus' words in this passage find an echo in John 11, when Jesus assures Lazarus' sister Martha: "Those who believe in me, even though they die, will live, and everyone who lives and believes in me will never die" (11:25–26). Jesus then proceeds to prove his words by restoring life to the four-days dead Lazarus.

100. Borgen, *Bread*, 155, 186. I cannot agree, however, with Borgen's assertion that the Fourth Evangelist was writing in "a 'school' of a church after the break with the synagogue had become a definite fact," as this assertion repeats the scholarly error of drawing too hard (and anachronistic) a line between "Christianity" and "Judaism." Nor can I accept Borgen's argument that John "reflects a Gnosticizing tendency" (ibid., 3).

101. Ibid., 25, 38.

technique for the sake of the midrash.[102] John 6:49–57 employs the word φαγεῖν, which evokes haggadic fragments dealing with the Exodus manna; in John 6:52–58 φαγεῖν is used in a discussion that very likely refers to eucharistic traditions of the early Jesus-movement.[103] It would seem therefore that the evangelist employs both haggadic and eucharistic traditions in order to put forward Jesus as bread of life. In this way, the evangelist connects λόγος to manna in a way strikingly similar to Philo's approach. At the same time, John adds the term ὁ τρώγων in vv. 57–58, indicating that the "bread" that is Jesus' "flesh" (σάρξ, 6:55) and the "wine" that is his "blood" (αἷμα, 6:55) are to be actually consumed, as were the sacrificial offerings of *tôdāh* (consisting of bread and wine offerings) and the Passover lamb. Aileen Guilding has observed that John 6 can be seen as a eucharistic discourse by virtue of the term εὐχαριστήσας, uniquely from the Synoptics, which employ εὐλόγησε in their parallel accounts of the Feeding of the Multitude.[104] Additionally, Jesus' assertion that his σάρξ must be consumed would correspond to the Israelites' demand for κρέα to eat in the wilderness in Exod 16:3, 8, 12 and Num 11:4, 13, 18, 21, 33 (LXX).[105] Hence, John 6 in its eucharistic tenor is a Passover scene—or rather, since it is a Passover scene, it forms a link between Passover and Eucharist. Eucharist can then be said to fulfill the function of Passover, according to the Fourth Gospel.

A difficulty for this understanding lies in John 6:63, where we read that "it is the spirit that gives life; the flesh is useless." Keeping in mind that John 4:7–26, Jesus' dialogue with the Samaritan woman, has by this time established Jesus as the physical location of sacrificial worship,[106] we must ask whether a surface reading that abstracts worship from the physical realm is appropriate for understanding the words of 6:63.

In 6:63b, Jesus states that "the words I have spoken to you are spirit and life." As David Biale has shown, Jesus defines the words of his teaching, not the flesh of which he speaks earlier in the same chapter, as "spirit

---

102. This includes use of elements from eucharistic tradition as well as the Old Testament. A parallel approach can be seen in 1 Cor 11:27–29. Ibid., 90–93, 95, 97.

103. A similar approach can again be found in Philo. Additionally, the fact that John 6:51–58 employs this technique in identical fashion to the rest of the discourse militates against that passage's being a later interpolation. Borgen, *Bread*, 95–96. See also Evans, "Feeding," 38, 131.

104. Borgen, *Bread*, 59.

105. Ibid., 61–62.

106. We will discuss John 4:7–26 in detail in chapter 3 of this thesis, as this passage possesses vital significance for John's identification of Jesus as sacrifice.

and life."[107] Simon Peter reiterates and confirms this in 6:68 ("You have the words of eternal life"). Hence, the implication is that Jesus' teaching imparts spiritual life; whoever accepts the teaching he has just given *about* his flesh and blood will receive this spiritual life. The "bread that came down from heaven," however, is Jesus himself (6:41), not his words. Likewise, his "flesh" and his "blood" are not said to be the words that he speaks, but are described as "true food" and "true drink" (6:55). 6:62 places this in context by dealing with Jesus' return to the Father, which would indicate that Jesus is here referring back to his assertion that he "came down from heaven" (3:13; 6:41, 51).[108] Jesus returns to the Father in order to give life to his disciples (3:15, 16, 36; 4:14, 36; 5:21, 24, 29; 6:39), so that they in turn may be "born from above" (as Jesus had referenced in the dialogue with Nicodemus, 3:3). "The availability of the life-giving spirit (6:62: τὸ πνεῦμα ἐστιν τὸ ζῳποιοῦν)—as the Holy Spirit, the Paraclete and the Spirit of Truth—for the next generation is conditioned on Jesus' departure (16:7), the uplifting of the Son of Man (3:14), his ascent (3:13, 6:62) and the glorification of Jesus."[109] The reference to the "spirit that gives life" in 6:63, then, is more a reference to Jesus' spoken indications of his return to his place of origin, to his disciples' being "born of spirit" (3:6, 8), and to the coming promises of the Farewell Discourse than to the characteristics of Jesus' flesh and blood to be consumed by his disciples. The separation between spiritual and material found in much Christian tradition (and particularly stemming from the Enlightenment) is an artificial one and, indeed, would not have been in view in the time of the Fourth Gospel's composition. The very identification of Jesus as Lamb in John, with all of the material sacrificial connotations that accompany this term, speaks to this orientation toward the physical.[110] A complete rendering of "flesh" to the abstract would also render invalid the crucifixion, which is entirely material, including the outpouring of blood and water from Jesus' pierced side.[111] An abstraction

---

107. Biale, "Blood," 53. While Biale makes this point, he applies the identification of Jesus' words as spirit to also identify his "flesh" and "blood" as his words/teaching. Our argument is that they are not the same: the identification of Jesus' words as spirit does not imply the identification of his flesh as his words. I therefore agree with Biale that the "spirit" in 6:63 is identified with Jesus' words, but disagree on the extension of that identification to Jesus' teaching.

108. See Kinzer, "Temple Christology," 454–57.

109. Buch-Hansen, *Spirit*, 347–49.

110. Murphy, "Devouring," 51–62, 53–56.

111. Ibid., 54.

of "flesh" would also require us to deal with the assertion in 1:14 that the λόγος "tabernacled among us" (an idea integral to John's temple theme, as we have seen) precisely by becoming "flesh." Therefore, there is nothing in John 6:63 to preclude an understanding of the "bread of life"/manna that is Jesus' flesh, and the command to consume his blood, in a manner consistent with the material sacrifices of Jewish worship offerings, specifically in connection with the bread and wine offered at Passover and in the *tôdāh* and the wine libations of *tôdāh* and *tāmîd*, as we have thus far discussed.

A further identification of Jesus as manna may lie in a subtle association between John's Prologue and the timing of the manna's appearance to Israel in the wilderness wanderings. The Book of Numbers states that the manna fell at night; John 1:5 identifies Jesus as "the light [that] shines in the darkness," which the darkness has not and cannot overcome.[112] Jesus also famously identifies himself as "the light of the world" (8:12). As is well known, the contrast between darkness/night and day/light is a prominent theme in John, and as such is not separate from the central theme of the Gospel: namely, Jesus as temple and sacrifice. In John 6, Jesus' comparison of himself with the manna that came at night to sustain Israel in the desert identifies him as the light that comes into the terrifying darkness of Passover night in order to give himself as the atoning sacrifice "for the life of the world" (6:33). Light was also a prominent feature of the Tabernacles festival rites; as we will see, John 7 applies much Tabernacles imagery to Jesus, including light, water, and wine libations.[113] Therefore, the association of manna with light evokes Tabernacles and its rituals and symbolism; chapter 6 therefore alludes to temple worship by looking forward to the Tabernacles scene in chapter 7.[114] Through this association, John's Jesus as manna is the bread that delivers from death, just as the Passover manna in Philo is a thanksgiving for deliverance from bondage in Egypt. Just as the Passover/Exodus event marks a deliverance from slavery to passion and a progression towards virtue (as in Philo), similarly in John we find Jesus as the bread that marks a passage of deliverance away from death and toward eternal life.[115] In these ways, John's Jesus fulfills the function of the *tôdāh*.

There is, at this point in our argument, very little to prevent us from seeing a cultic intention in John's depiction of Jesus. The bread/manna

---

112. Prosic, *Development*, 99–101.
113. See Kinzer, "Temple Christology," 448–49, 457–58.
114. Moloney, *Text and Context*, 201–2.
115. See Metzner, *Verständnis*, 158, 355.

whose life-giving function Jesus embodies in John 6 is portrayed as a concrete "food" by the use of the term φαγεῖν, followed by the term ὁ τρώγων in vv. 57–58. To consume the bread/manna is to consume Jesus, the divine λόγος, in a very real sense.[116] This would speak to the probability that the Fourth Gospel is referring to an actual practice performed by the early Jesus-believers that would have been viewed as sacrificial—namely, the Lord's Supper—made possible by Jesus' own sacrificial death, in a way very similar to the Passover having been made possible by the willing self-offering of Isaac.

Models of Passover as a Thanksgiving Sacrifice in Philo and Josephus

In his discussion of Philo's interpretations of the thank-offering, Jean Laporte observes that Philo "literally interprets the Passover as a gesture of thanksgiving for the deliverance of the people of Israel from Egypt and the crossing of the Red Sea."[117] For Philo, the "Passover" was "less the passage of the angel of death . . . than the passage of the people of Israel from Egypt to the Holy Land. . . . In this context of thought, the lamb of Passover becomes a symbol of progress, as suggested by the coupling of the substantive *probaton* (sheep) with the verb *probaino* (to step forward)."[118]

Philo claims that the specific progression facilitated by the Passover was that of the Israelites' journeying from "the bondage of the passions" (signified by Egypt) to "the acquisition of virtue" (signified by Canaan, the land promised them by God's covenant with Abraham).[119] So essential is this aspect of passage from one spiritual state to another that Philo calls the Passover "the Crossing-feast" in *Spec.* II.145.[120] Philo assigns the purpose of *thanksgiving* to this act of "crossing" in *Mos.* I.180 and *Contempl.* 87. In both works, he describes the Israelites' song of thanksgiving at the far side of the

---

116. Borgen, *Bread*, 187–92.

117. Laporte, "Philonic Models," 77.

118. Ibid., 78; see also Daly, *Christian Sacrifice*, 395. Cf. Philo: "The sheep is 'progressive,' as the name itself shows, being so called in accordance with the progress of the soul, and it indicates improvement" (Philo of Alexandria, QE I.3). See also Nielsen, "Lamb," 226–27, 237. A discussion of Passover as "positive change" is found in Prosic, *Development*, 82.

119. Laporte, "Philonic Models," 78. See also Nielsen, "Lamb," 237.

120. Philo, *Special Laws*.

Red Sea after it had been crossed and Pharaoh's army had been swallowed up by its waters. Elsewhere, Philo claims that the purpose of all sacrifice is the rendering of thanks to God: the first-fruits offering is a thanksgiving for possessing the Promised Land (*Somn.* II.72–76) as well as for the possession of the natural, material senses (*Congr.* 96); characterizes the whole burnt-offering, thank-offerings, and sin offerings as thanksgivings (*Spec.* I.195–197); and defines sacrifice in general as "expressions of *gratitude* as religion demands" (*Spec.* I.224).[121] Especially significant for this thesis, Philo assigns a thanksgiving ("*tôdāh*") character to the *tāmîd* sacrifice, which as we have seen was linked to both the Passover and the Akedah, stating that one of the purposes of the *tāmîd*, occurring at the boundaries of day and night, is to express gratitude "for respectively the benefactions of the day time and the night time."[122] Clearly, thanksgiving was a—if not the—primary purpose and function of sacrifice in Philo's interpretation.[123]

The view of the Exodus event, specifically the Red Sea crossing, as a progression from sin to God's service appears in three other passages in particular:

> For thou art required also, when making it thy study to cross over from the passions and when sacrificing the Passover, to take the forward step, whose symbol is the lamb, not without measure, for he says, "each man shall reckon what suffices for him as a lamb." (*Leg.* III.165)[124]

> For we also find that when he that sees God is studying flight from the passions, the waves become fixed as if frozen, that is to say the rush and growth and vainglory of the passions; "for the waves became solid in the midst of the sea, in order that he that seeth Him that IS might pass beyond passion. (*Leg.* III.172)[125]

> For we are bidden to keep the Passover, which is the passage from the life of the passions to the practice of virtue, 'with our loins girded' ready for service. (*Sacr.* 62)[126]

---

121. Ibid. See Daly, *Christian Sacrifice*, 404. Emphasis mine.
122. Tamara Prosic, *Development*, 102.
123. Laporte, "Philonic Models," 72; Lindsay, "*Todah*," 87, 88 (referencing Gese).
124. Philo, *Allegorical Interpretation*.
125. Ibid.
126. Philo, *Abel and Cain*.

Thus, in Philo, the *tôdāh/eucharistia* was associated not only with Passover in general but especially with the Passover lamb, and the whole Passover observance functioned as a *tôdāh* for the salvation from bondage in Egypt. Not only do the Passover meal's bread and wine function as *tôdāh*, but the paschal lamb functions as *tôdāh* also, representative as it is of the Israelites' liberation. As discussed above, Philo had interpreted the *tāmîd* as an atonement offering. As Laporte notes, in Philo "the sacrifices which fulfill a purpose of thanksgiving are the sacrifices of salvation."[127]

There is additional evidence that the Passover offering was viewed as a sacrifice in or close to the first century. Josephus, for example, does not interpret Passover as a *tôdāh* but refers to the Passover as the feast "at which they sacrifice from the ninth to the eleventh hour" (*J.W.* VI.422).[128] Philo also identifies the Passover as a sacrifice and views the Exodus event as the initiation of the Israelite priesthood: God made the whole people Israel a nation of priests at the first Passover, when God "permitted the nation ... to prepare with their own hands and to slaughter the sacrifice of the so-called Passover (as) the beginning of good things" (*QE* I.10), hence not only allowing but ordering families in private homes to perform a priestly function before the official priesthood was established.[129] In *Spec.* II.145, Philo again states that the people as a whole are "raised for that particular day to the dignity of the priesthood" because "the festival is a reminder and a *thank-offering* for that great migration from Egypt ... in obedience to the oracles vouchsafed to [the Israelites]."[130] Here, we see clearly that Philo assigns to the Passover the function of a sacrifice of thanksgiving, effectively equating it with the functions of both *tôdāh* and *tāmîd*.[131]

---

127. Laporte, "Philonic Models," 72.

128. Josephus, *Jewish War*.

129. Philo, *On Exodus*. See Daly, *Christian Sacrifice*, 410–11; Laporte, "Philonic Models," 78.

130. Philo, *Special Laws*. Emphasis mine. A similar idea predates Philo in *Jub*. 18, which attributes the obedience of the Israelites to the obedience exhibited by Abraham (not by Isaac, although he is here portrayed as consenting to the sacrifice). Huizenga, "Battle," 46. See also *Spec*. II.163: "the Jewish nation is to the whole inhabited world what the priest is to the State. For the holy office in very truth belongs to the nation because it carries out all the rites of purification and both in body and soul obeys the injunctions of the divine laws." Laporte discusses Israel's high priest as priest of all peoples and nations by virtue of the sacrifices he performs in thanksgiving not only for Israel but for the whole created universe. Laporte, "Philonic Models," 81.

131. Laporte, "Philonic Models," 80.

Jesus/Isaac

Whether the Fourth Gospel makes use of Isaac typology in its portrayal of Jesus is a matter of debate. For example, Martin Hasitschka argues *against* the presence of Isaac typology in John on the following bases:

- The designation of Jesus as "the only beloved son" is not enough to form a solid association with Isaac, who was also called "the only beloved son" of Abraham.
- Abraham's role in the Akedah and the role of God in the sacrifice of Jesus are quite different; there is no direct parallel between Abraham and God.
- The Fourth Evangelist casts Jesus' death in terms of one and only one image from the Old Testament: that of the bronze serpent (Num 21:8–9; John 3:14–15). Hasitschka poses the rhetorical question: "If John had wished to express an Isaac typology, wouldn't he have done so clearly, as in the case of the Bronze Serpent?"[132]

Hasitschka is partially correct on the first point: while the "only beloved son" connection is present in John, this alone would certainly not be enough as evidence for Isaac typology. This point, however, in no way precludes the Fourth Gospel from employing Isaac typology *by other means*. To address the second point: God does not sacrifice Isaac in Gen 22, or in any of the extra-biblical or rabbinic interpretations of the Akedah; Abraham performs that role. In John, Jesus is portrayed as performing the sacrifice of his own life (John 10:17–18). This would fit better with the depictions of Isaac running to the altar, throwing himself upon it, etc., as discussed above. Thus, John's Jesus is compared chiefly to Isaac, not to Abraham or even to God (insofar as his self-offering is concerned). Hasitschka's third point suggests that the author of John would have been as clear in a comparison to Isaac as to that of the bronze serpent if the evangelist had wished to evoke Isaac; however, this is quite an assumption, especially when dealing with what is arguably the most symbolic/metaphorical of all the Gospels. John often makes oblique references, hints more than explains, and draws parallels by way of images.[133] It is by no means necessarily the case that a lack of clearly stated verbal references

---

132. Hasitschka, *Befreiung*, 60–61. Translation by author.
133. See Köstenberger, "Second Temple," 215–16.

to Isaac eliminates the possibility that John is evoking Isaac by means of certain imagery, phraseology, and subtle allusions.

If the Fourth Evangelist draws subtle, ironic comparisons between Jesus and Isaac, it is in order to cement the idea that *Jesus is sacrifice* and hence the place of worship (temple). If the Akedah provides a picture of the prototypical temple, then portraying Jesus in light of the Akedah shows him as the consummation of that prototype.

If the "glory of the Shekinah" was revealed to Abraham on Moriah by virtue of Isaac's self-offering, then Jesus' own self-offering on the cross in John reveals "the glory of the Shekinah." Indeed, the Glory is identified as the person of Jesus himself in John 1:14; 2:11; 7:18; 11:4, 40; 12:23, 41, 43; 17:5, 22, 24. If Jesus consummates the prototype established by and in the Akedah, then Jesus' self-offering would effect atonement for future generations just as Isaac's self-offering did. Along with the concept of one's own descendants, however (as in Isaac's case), there may have been an early tradition extending the atoning power of Isaac's self-offering to the Gentiles as well, attested in *L.A.B.* 32.3.[134] Thus, Isaac-typology in John would suggest that Jesus' sacrifice applies to all nations, bringing the Abrahamic Covenant to fruition.

Several scholars have noted that the Fourth Gospel draws clear parallels between Isaac and Jesus. In the first instance, recent scholarship has unearthed an early Christian tradition that Jesus died on the cross on the anniversary of his conception, which may have corollaries in traditions surrounding Isaac's conception and birth related to the Akedah and to Passover.[135] *Jub.* 16:12–13 expands on the canonical Gen 18:9-15; 21:1–2 to set calendar dates for Isaac's conception and birth, placing the latter at Pentecost. Later, *Exod. Rab.* 15.11 appears to continue and comment upon this interpretation by placing the Akedah on the anniversary of Isaac's birth ("In this month was Isaac born, and in this month he was bound").[136] It appears, then, that in the cases of both Isaac and Jesus, tradition assigns the purpose of the victim's birth as his eventual self-offering.[137]

---

134. Huizenga, "Aqedah," 116–17.

135. Grigsby, "Cross," 75n87; Manns, "Jewish Liturgy," 60; McGowan, "December 25," 46–48, 57–58.

136. Freedman and Simon, *Exodus Leviticus*, 173. See also Manns, "Jewish Liturgy," 60. Recall too that Isaac's binding at the time of the Passover lamb's sacrifice was written in *Jubilees* (Huizenga, "Battle," 42, 44).

137. Of course, direct dependence or even influence cannot be proven (and it is not my intention to make the attempt), but the parallels are intriguing and there is a

As is well known, John is the only Gospel to claim that Jesus carried the cross by himself (John 19:17), an image that may intend to evoke Isaac shouldering the wood that would soon consume him on the altar his father had constructed (Gen 22:6).[138] In John 3:16, God is described as giving up his only son to a sacrificial death just as Abraham had; and that son, Jesus, went to that death willingly, offering up his own life to destruction for the sake of his "friends" (John 15:13) just as Isaac in the rabbinic texts had gone to his death knowing that his sacrifice would accrue merit to his descendants.[139] In the "Good Shepherd Discourse," Jesus assures his disciples that he lays down his life for the benefit of his "sheep": "For this reason the Father loves me, because I lay down my life in order to take it up again. No one takes it from me, but I lay it down of my own accord. I have power to lay it down, and I have power to take it up again" (10:17–18).[140] As for the "taking up" of his life "again," we have seen above that some rabbinic texts suggested that God had restored Isaac to life, and an early form of this tradition may also be recorded in Heb 11:19, which refers to the Akedah as a prefigurement of Jesus' death and resurrection.

Against Bruce H. Grigsby's argument that the Fourth Evangelist not only shows "an interest in *how* the death of Christ was redemptive," but indeed places Christ in a "role as the new Isaac,"[141] our argument is that, similarly as the Fourth Gospel evokes Moses in order to show that Jesus is not a *new* Moses but surpasses him (as Wayne Meeks has shown[142]), John evokes the Akedah not in order to identify Jesus as Isaac but to show how Jesus consummates the Akedah's prototypes of sacrifice and temple, as discussed above, and adds a new factor. Where some of the Akedah interpretative traditions asserted that it was God who restored life to Isaac—whether by substituting the ram or by actually bringing Isaac back from the dead,

---

possibility that there was some interplay between traditions.

138. See e.g., Grigsby, "Cross," 60. Brown (*Death of the Messiah*, 2:1440) and Manns ("Jewish Liturgy," 61) both trace this to Melito's homily *Peri Pashas* (*On the Pasch*).

139. Daly, *Christian Doctrine*, 50; Huizenga, "Battle," 34. Although Hasitschka (*Befreiung*, 63) denies Isaac typology in John, he addresses Jesus' willing self-offering.

140. Daly (*Christian Doctrine*, 77; *Christian Sacrifice*, 292) stresses the voluntary nature of Christ's self-offering; however, he associates this with the selfless, sacrificial way of life expected of believers as expressed in Paul and in Hebrews, rather than with the voluntary self-offering of Isaac.

141. Grigsby, "Cross," 61. Emphasis in original.

142. Meeks, *Prophet-King*.

as we have seen—in John it is Jesus who raises himself from death by his own power.

Since most of the Akedah connections come to the fore in the Johannine passion account, we will resume this argument in chapter 3 below.

Discursus: The Suffering Servant

In John 1:29, 36, John the Baptist famously calls Jesus "the Lamb of God, who takes away the sin of the world."[143] Since Isa 53:7b likens the Suffering Servant of the Lord to "a lamb that is led to the slaughter" (LXX κεκακῶσθαι; MT טָבַח, used of meat slaughtered for consumption[144]), there has been a great deal of debate regarding whether John 1:29, 36 refer to the Suffering Servant of Isa 53, to the Passover Lamb, or to both. Indeed, there is debate as to whether the moniker "lamb" attributed to the Isaianic Servant may be considered an equivalent to the paschal lamb, or whether this Servant-lamb represents something else. The presence of "Servant typology" in John is equally controversial as the presence of Isaac typology.

The Isaianic Servant motif has been applied in different ways to many characters of both canonical and extra-biblical literature, including Joseph; Daniel; Daniel's three friends Shadrach, Meshach, and Abednego; the "righteous man" of *Wis.* 2, 4, and 5; the Teacher of Righteousness in 1QH 4:5–5:4 and 8:35–36; and the seven martyred brothers in *2 Macc.* 7.[145] When we include rabbinic references, the Suffering Servant of the Lord was apparently quite a widespread trope during the time periods in which these texts were composed. In all of these cases, the Servant provides a pattern for "the protagonists in stories about the persecution, exaltation, and vindication of wise courtiers—righteous persons who were spokesmen for God."[146] Given these many examples of alluding to the Servant in post-exilic and intertestamental texts, the early Christian use of Servant imagery to refer to Jesus would hardly be an innovation, and would fit quite well within interpretative traditions preceding, and roughly contemporary with, the Fourth Gospel.

---

143. Significantly, the article accompanying "Lamb of God" in both 1:29 and 1:36 is in the absolute (ὁ ἀμνὸς τοῦ θεοῦ), as are the "ἐγώ εἰμί" sayings throughout the Gospel (Knöppler, *Sühne*, 242).

144. Brown, Driver, and Briggs, *Lexicon*, 370–71.

145. Nickelsburg, "Reading," 244.

146. Ibid., 243.

Murray Rae helpfully defines three hermeneutical approaches in this scholarly debate:

- Determinate meaning: The meaning of a text is fixed according to the author's original intention. Any interpretation that varies from that intention is an illegitimate imposition on the text. The flaw in this approach, of course, is that its rigidity does not allow a text to speak to different situations in different time periods.

- Anti-determinate meaning: A hermeneutic of new, updated interpretations for new times and new situations. The meaning of any text is totally fluid. The pitfall in this approach, however, is that there are no limits to interpretation, allowing the interpreter to make the text mean whatever he or she wants it to mean with no regard for an original intention of author/s and/or redactor/s. Both the determinate and anti-determinate meanings therefore represent opposite extremes in interpretative approaches.

- Underdetermined meaning: Rae borrows this term from Stephen Fowl, but adjusts Fowl's argument. Between the two extremes of determinate and anti-determinate, "an underdetermined hermeneutic ... allows for a measure of hermeneutical diversity, while precluding the absolute freedom that provides no safeguard against error." Whereas for Fowl "the way to achieve that end is to abandon the notion of textual meaning," Rae argues that the meaning of a text in varying times and circumstances is an action of God's Holy Spirit, who endows the text with real meaning applicable to each situation. Interpretation is kept from becoming anti-deterministic "by the fact that Scripture is a witness to the being and acts of God and not something else." Of prime importance in this hermeneutic is "the location of texts within the biblical canon. ... The relation of particular books of the Bible to other biblical books is not merely arbitrary so far as their interpretation is concerned but sheds light on what the individual texts may be said to mean. ... The biblical texts ... are characterized ... by a canonical unity brought about by their shared witness to a common object."[147]

An underdetermined hermeneutic present in John's Gospel would explain not only the Gospel's identification of Jesus as the Servant of Isaiah 52–53,

---

147. Rae, "Texts," esp. 19–20, 41–43.

but would also explain the liberties taken in Akedah interpretations found in the extra-biblical and rabbinic sources we have been discussing. Rae uses as an example of the Book of Daniel, whose author "reappropriat[ed]" the Servant "for his own times and [found] a new subject to bear the title of Yahweh's servant."[148] Here, Rae is referring to passages such as *Sir.* 48:24–25, 4Q161–165, and Dan 12:3, all of which make use of the Servant image in ways very different from the original context of Deutero-Isaiah, in order to address and make sense of their own post-exilic *sitz im leben*. Whereas the text originally very likely intended the Servant as the people Israel, later post-exilic interpretations identified the Servant as an individual redeemer figure.[149]

Grigsby argues that John 1:29 refers only to the Servant, and that there are no Akedah or Passover associations in the Baptist's identification of Jesus as "Lamb of God." Rather, the Akedah motif appears in John 3:16, where Jesus is said to give his life for the sake of "the world" (by implication, as Isaac had offered his life for the sake of his descendants).[150] Daly, on the other hand, sees Akedah connections in John 1:29 as well as in 3:16, with an additional "implicit mention of resurrection" in the latter verse.[151] However, Grigsby also claims that the "lamb" of John 1:29 refers solely to the paschal lamb *without* Isaac typology.[152]

Hasitschka also claims that "the Lamb of God" in John 1:29, 36 is not intended by the evangelist as an identification of Jesus as the *paschal* lamb, but rather as an indication of Jesus' view of his own self-sacrifice and of his meek deportment as he went to that sacrifice freely: like the Suffering Servant of Isaiah 53, Jesus approaches his sacrifice in humble, submissive service to God, of his own free will, and with great dignity.[153] This, according to Hasitschka, is the only meaning of the Isaianic Servant's being called a "lamb" as well as Jesus' only connection to the Servant. Hence, Jesus = Lamb = Servant, but without any overtones of Akedah, the Passover lamb, or any other sacrifice. Against Hasitschka, however, Metzner has shown

148. Ibid., 38.
149. Rosenberg, "Suffering Servant," 385.
150. Grigsby, "Cross," 60.
151. Daly, *Christian Sacrifice*, 182; also Daly, *Christian Doctrine*, 52.
152. In the end, Grigsby allows that "because the Evangelist connects the title with the expiatory function of 'taking away' the world's sin, one is justified in seeing some degree of influence by the 'Akedah' tradition. For in this tradition . . . Isaac's sacrificial death was both expiatory and anticipatory of the Paschal sacrifice" (Grigsby, "Cross," 53, 60).
153. Hasitschka, *Befreiung*, 79–86, 106–8.

THE JOHANNINE JESUS FULFILLS THE FUNCTIONS OF THE TEMPLE

that the application of "lamb" image to Jesus in John 1:29, 36 is not about vulnerability but must be a direct allusion to the Passover lamb, based on Jesus' stated ability in those verses to "remove" or "carry away" (αἴρω) the world's sin. This characteristic is overtly connected with the "lamb of God" as atonement and with sin/darkness as important themes in the Gospel's overall context.[154] The Servant of Isaiah 53 is not said to remove sin, but to "bear" it (53:4, MT נָשָׂא; LXX φέρει); hence, while Metzner identifies the "lamb" in John 1:29, 36 as the Passover lamb he also rejects any identification of Jesus with the Servant, since this figure is not said to remove sin but only to "carry" it, while the term αἴρω in John indicates that Jesus actually takes sin away.[155]

While I agree with Metzner's argument that the "lamb" in John 1:29, 36 is meant to be the Passover lamb, and for similar reasons which we will examine further in the next chapter, we have seen above that several lines of tradition claimed that the paschal lamb had only been possible through its prototype, Isaac, who had offered himself as a "lamb of burnt offering" for the life of his descendants. As we have seen above, Isaac was identified with/as the Passover lamb (and, by extension, with the twice-daily *tāmîd* offering). Hence, if the "lamb" of John 1:29 is the Passover lamb, which was associated with Isaac in rabbinic texts, Isaac is certainly in view in this verse. It is not necessarily the case, therefore, that John portrays Jesus as either the Servant or the Passover Lamb, since some traditions identified the Servant and Passover Lamb with each other. Further, if the identification of Jesus as "lamb" in John 1:29, 36 refers to the Passover lamb, it may also possess Isaac/Akedah associations; and if "lamb" here refers only to the Servant and by extension to Isaac, it may also possess paschal associations. The two are not mutually exclusive—quite to the contrary, they are mutually interdependent.

Some scholars have claimed that the "lamb" in John 1:29, 36 cannot refer to the Servant, or cannot refer to the paschal lamb, on linguistic grounds. An example is provided once again by Grigsby (and shared by others), who argues that the Johannine identification of Jesus as "lamb" does not identify him as the Servant of Isaiah 53 because Jesus is actually *called* a lamb while "Isaiah 53 only offers statements that *compare* the

---

154. Metzner, *Verständnis*, 140, 143, 153, 157. See also Dietzfelbinger, "Sühnetod," 67; Knöppler, *Sühne*, 239, Wick, *Urchristlichen*, 329.

155. Metzner, *Verständnis*, 15–16, 119, 123, 150, 152–53, 156–58. See also Heyman, *Power*, 136.

Servant with a lamb."¹⁵⁶ This seems, however, to split hairs too finely; in fact, it is a false distinction. The Johannine language, "There is (ἴδε) the Lamb of God," is metaphorical while Isa 53:7 employs simile: "Like a lamb led to the slaughter . . . he was silent and opened not his mouth." There is no practical distinction in meaning between the usage in Isaiah and that in the Fourth Gospel; indeed, Grigsby allows "that the evangelist would have juxtaposed the Servant and the Paschal Lamb in his Christology is not unprecedented either in the New Testament or in early Christian thought."¹⁵⁷ On similar grounds, Christian Dietzfelbinger asserts that, in keeping with the connection between the Servant-lamb and the Passover lamb, "Lamb of God" in John 1:29, 36 is taken from "lamb" in Isa 53:7, 12, and both refer to the Passover lamb.¹⁵⁸

While examining linguistic variations can be helpful, we would do better to look at the function of "lamb" in the entire overall context of the Fourth Gospel.¹⁵⁹ The way in which the Fourth Evangelist (and any redactor/s) uses terms such as "Lamb of God" need not directly correspond to the way in which this term was used elsewhere. While an argument can be made against the identification of the Isaianic Servant as "Lamb of God" in the function of removing sin, we must interpret the function of the Johannine ἀμνός through the lens of the *whole* Johannine understanding of sin as an ontological state: while it is true that the Servant of Isa 53 is only compared to a lamb and does not remove the world's sin but only bears it, the Johannine context, made particularly clear in the Passion narrative, uses the Servant-lamb imagery to express the Johannine understanding of sin and to identify Jesus as the Servant-lamb/Passover lamb who does perform atonement.¹⁶⁰ It is also possible that Isa 53:7 does intend to identify the Servant as the Passover lamb, in the sense that the Servant's suffering and death performs the same function as the Passover lamb: the deliverance of his people, specifically a deliverance that takes the form of atonement for sin. This is reinforced when we consider that the Servant is said to be led to the "slaughter," in the MT טֶבַח, a term used of meat slaughtered for

---

156. Grigsby, "Cross," 54.
157. Ibid.; see also Heil, "Unique High Priest," 732.
158. Dietzfelbinger, "Sühnetod," 67. Translation mine.
159. In agreement with Knöppler's approach.
160. Knöppler, *Sühne*, 240–41. It is important to note that while Knöppler agrees with Dietzfelbinger that the concept of Jesus' death as atonement in John was taken from received tradition, Knöppler does not share Dietzfelbinger's view that this received tradition "controls" the Johannine understanding or picture of Jesus' atoning death (242).

consumption, which would fit the Passover lamb. This would not, of course, mean that the Servant is literally to be consumed; but it may draw a parallel to the lamb of the Passover, indicating that the term "lamb" predicated of the Servant is indeed intended to link the Servant to the Passover victim (which is consumed).

We observed above that Philo of Alexandria and some rabbinic texts on Isaac's self-offering interpreted the Passover as an atonement sacrifice. Clearly, the suffering of Isaiah's Servant of the Lord is redemptive for others. The Servant's willing subjection to suffering and death wins deliverance, atonement, and life for his descendants, just as Isaac's self-offering made the Passover/Exodus possible for his descendants. "Lamb" is predicated of all three: the Servant is compared to a lamb, Isaac is portrayed as a lamb, and the Passover of course centers on the sacrifice of a lamb. In *Tg.* Gen 22, "the nature and effect of the Servant's passion are applied to the sacrifice of Isaac so that Gen 22 becomes the story of a just man who offered himself for the benefit of sinners."[161] Such interpretations offer corollaries to the identification of Jesus as "lamb" in the Fourth Gospel, and help to shed some light on whether that identification refers to the Passover lamb, the Servant-lamb, or both.

Rabbinic tradition identifies the "Suffering Servant" of Isa 53 with Isaac in the Akedah.[162] According to Rosenberg, "in Jewish tradition Isaac is the prototype of the 'Suffering Servant' ... described in the midrash as the first to experience 'chastisements' from God, and in *Tg.* Job 3 he is expressly styled 'the servant of Yahweh.'"[163] This parallel is fascinating in its implications for our study of the temple Christology of the Fourth Gospel, as Christian tradition has historically seen the embodiment of Isaiah's "Servant of the Lord" in the life, suffering, death, and resurrection of Jesus. The rabbinic texts we have examined so far associate Isaac with the Servant, particularly in the Servant's characterization as a "lamb" (Isa 53:7) and especially in his giving of his life "as a sin-offering" (Isa 53:10b), "seeing his descendants in a long life" (Isa 53:10c), and "taking away the sins of many" (Isa 53:12d). We have seen above that Isaac in several rabbinic texts embodies all of these characteristics. Hence, roughly contemporary with the

---

161. Although Manns acknowledges the influence of Isa 53:7 on the targumic interpretation of the Akedah, he argues that "the fourth Song cannot be applied to Isaac" (Manns, "Targum," 75–76).

162. See Brown, *According to John (xiii–xxi)*, 917.

163. Rosenberg, "Suffering Servant," 385.

Fourth Gospel, Isaac was identified as the Suffering Servant, as the Passover Lamb that facilitates liberation for his descendants, and as the prototype of the *tāmîd* sacrifice.[164] If Isaac was identified as the prototypical paschal lamb, and if he was also identified with the Servant, then there is a strongly implied identification of the Servant-lamb as paschal lamb.

We have seen above that some sources depicted Isaac's actual death on the altar and subsequent return to life. Raymond Brown sees an association of Jesus' statements that "the Son of Man will be lifted up" (John 8:28; 12:32-34) with the language used of the Suffering Servant in Isa 52:13, and suggests that "the Johannine language for Jesus' laying down his life (ψυχή) in John 10:11, 15, 17-18 stems from Isa 53:10 with its reference to the Servant's giving his life (ψυχή) as an offering for sin."[165] Jesus is revealed as the Servant in being "lifted up" in crucifixion as well as "lifted up" in the sense of being glorified at his resurrection.[166] The subsequent recognitions of Jesus by Magdalene and the disciples once more bring the Servant motif to bear: as Nielsen points out, Jesus' true identity and purpose (as well as the new identity and purpose of his disciples) is revealed in his passion, resurrection, and return to the Father, just as the Servant's identity is only revealed after his suffering is complete and God has exalted him.[167] When this common resurrection motif is seen in conjunction with Jesus as Passover lamb, consummating the prototype that Isaac had provided for that sacrificial victim, Jesus' identification with Isaac in John becomes all the stronger. As Isaac was the lamb offered on the altar of his own free will, Jesus is the lamb who freely offers himself on the altar that is the cross; as Isaiah's Suffering Servant evokes Isaac, Jesus takes on the characteristics of the Servant in the form of his parallels with Isaac and the Akedah.

There is a linguistic clue that may support the connection between the Johannine Jesus and the Servant. Isaiah 52:13 (MT) utilizes three Hebrew terms for the Servant's exaltation: יָרוּם, נִשָּׂא, and גָּבַהּ. The LXX renders one of these terms as συνήσει ("understand") and the other two as ὑψωθήσεται and δοξασθήσεται.[168] Forms of the first verb, ὑψωθήσεται, appear in John 3:14; 8:28; and 12:32, 34, all of which are used to describe Jesus' being

---

164. See Daly, *Christian Doctrine*, 48-49.

165. Brown, *According to John (xiii-xxi)*, 1071-72. See also Nielsen, "Lamb," 244-47.

166. Nielsen, "Lamb," 245. On the resurrection connections, see Rosenberg, "Suffering Servant," 387-88; Ginsberg, "Oldest Interpretation," 25-28.

167. Ibid., 247, 249.

168. Jakovljević, "Ebed," 60.

"lifted up" in his passion and death on the cross.[169] Hence, there is a parallel between the exaltation of Jesus, whose suffering achieves liberation for his descendants, and the exaltation of the Suffering Servant, whose affliction achieves the same, as Isaac's self-offering had done. Although in John Jesus' suffering is his exaltation, the Servant's suffering and exaltation are two separate events (and the second appears to be a reward for the first). Both figures, however, suffer in order to achieve liberation for others, just as Isaac had done in offering his life so that his descendants would, generations later, be liberated from slavery in Egypt. John makes use of the Servant imagery in order to draw a parallel to Isaac, and through Isaac, to the Passover lamb and the other sacrifices associated with the Akedah and Passover: the *tāmîd* and the *tôdāh*.

As mentioned above, just as the Suffering Servant "poured out his life" (Isa 53:12), Philo described the λόγος pouring itself out as a sacrificial offering. There exists, then, a parallel between the Servant and a first-century concept of λόγος such as we see in Philo. Since John identifies Jesus as the λόγος, an intriguing corollary becomes apparent between the Servant who pours out his life as an offering and the λόγος who makes the same offering. Since the Suffering Servant was associated with Isaac, the association of Jesus (λόγος who pours himself out) with Isaac (the Servant who pours himself out) becomes clearer. Recall also our earlier discussion that the atonement effected by Isaac's suffering in rabbinic texts fits with the motif of expiatory suffering in other Jewish intertestamental writings. In 2 and 4 *Macc.*, the prime occurrences of atoning martyrdom in early Jewish texts, God is said to be reconciled to his people "through the death of the martyrs" and "the martyr has become a sacrifice for the purification of the people. God effects this purification through the martyr's blood, just as he effects expiation through the blood of sacrificed animals."[170] With every caution against anachronism, it is worthwhile to consider that later Christian piety prized martyrdom so highly, portrayed martyrdom as a sacrifice, and applied atoning power to a martyr's death, because Jesus himself was seen as the ultimate martyr in the line of the Israelite tradition; thus the later Christian martyrologies may preserve earlier traditions that cast Jesus' suffering and death in the same frame, as a sacrifice of atonement—indeed, as the perfect and therefore the ultimate expiatory death.[171]

---

169. See Moloney, *Text and Context*, 75; Nielsen, "Lamb," 247–49.
170. Young, *Sacrificial Ideas*, 68–69, 227–30. Emphasis mine.
171. See Ibid., 107ff; also Biale, "Blood," 46; Daly, *Christian Sacrifice*, 378–83;

John's Jesus fulfills all of the roles and functions predicated of Isaac in our discussion up to this point. His death, associated with Passover, liberates from darkness, sin, and death in a new Exodus which inaugurates a new covenant.[172] John 1:29, 36 is, in fact, a prolepsis of the cross, as Jean Zumstein has noted: the Johannine "Lamb of God can in fact be associated either with the figure of the Suffering Servant or with the paschal lamb. At any rate, the allusion to the Passion is clear ... the narrative constructs, through the figure of the paschal lamb, a *curve of tension* that places the whole narrative under the sign of the cross."[173]

Summary and Conclusions: Jesus as Sacrifice in John

The Fourth Gospel, far from recommending an end to sacrificial worship after the Jerusalem temple's destruction, envisions the continuation of such worship in the person of Jesus. As early as John 1:29, 36, Jesus is identified as Passover lamb by the article preceding "Lamb of God" (ὁ ἀμνὸς ... ὁ αἴρων), which is in the absolute (just as the ἐγώ εἰμί sayings are in the absolute).[174] The whole phrase utilizes language deriving directly from the Passover tradition and pointing forward to Jesus' death as Passover lamb with atonement functions; and it may be accurately stated that these verses form a "thesis statement" for the whole Gospel.[175] This thesis statement will be reiterated in the Cana scene and temple cleansing, which effectively announce that the rest of the Gospel is going to present Jesus as sacrifice and, because he is sacrifice, he is the place of worship in the absence of the Jerusalem temple and against the temples of polytheistic Rome.

In the rabbinic writings, preserving and expanding upon traditions current in the first century CE, an atoning function was assigned to the Passover lamb and its associated *tāmîd* sacrifice because the atoning sacrifice of Isaac had not only foreshadowed Passover and *tāmîd* but had effectively established those rites and gave them their meaning. The twice-daily

---

Heyman, *Power*, esp. ch. 4.

172. Ceresko, "Rhetorical Strategy," 53–54. See also Grelot, *Les Juifs*, 165; Sloane, "Justice," 12; Zumstein, "L'Interprétation," 2131–32.

173. Zumstein, "L'Interprétation," 2020. Emphasis in original.

174. Knöppler, *Sühne*, 247.

175. Ibid., 242, 244. See also Frühwald-König, *Tempel*, 104: John's Prologue is "a reader's guide" to Jesus' identity as that identity will unfold throughout the Gospel.

atoning *tāmîd* sacrifice in the Jerusalem temple, performed at the boundaries of time, morning and evening, was symbiotically related to both Isaac and the Passover lamb, since, as we have seen, the *tāmîd* was said to have existed to remind God of Isaac's atoning sacrifice. Indeed, Daly does not exaggerate when he claims that "the Akedah had a special causal relationship to the atoning efficacy of all other sacrifices."[176] Considering that kid goats were acceptable paschal victims in addition to lambs, it is significant that John refers to Jesus as *lamb* in particular.[177] The most likely explanation is that the Fourth Evangelist intended to use the lamb image to draw a connection between Jesus, Isaac, and the Passover and *tāmîd* lamb sacrifices that gained their effectiveness from the Akedah. All of this would show Jesus as sacrifice, in particular the sacrifice that performs the function of deliverance from death. In John, that death is the death that results from the darkness of sin.

Lindsay observes that writings of early church fathers such as Justin Martyr and Ignatius of Antioch, as well as late first-century non-canonical texts such as the Didache, the apocryphal Acts of the Apostles, and the Acts of John, universally apply the term *eucharistia* to the practice of the Lord's Supper, the Christian liturgical meal featuring the blessing and consumption of bread and wine as a recollection of and participation in Jesus' death. In this connection, Lindsay discusses the use of the term *eucharistia* in the Greek text of Aquila's references to the *tôdāh* as well as the Septuagint's consistent employment of the phrase "sacrifice of praise" to refer to the *tôdāh*, surmising that "the [meaning/significance of the] Greek *eucharistia* corresponds to the Hebrew *tôdāh*,"[178] and that the Christian meal known in the late first century as *eucharistia* was accordingly viewed as a sacrifice: specifically, as a thank-offering for a mighty act of God delivering the covenant people from death as at the first Passover.[179] The use of the terms φαγεῖν and τρώγων in John 6 indicates that, like the Passover lamb and the bread of the *tôdāh*, the early Jesus-believers would have engaged in the eucharistic consumption of bread and wine as a sacrificial worship event, made possible by Jesus' sacrificial death in a similar way that the Passover sacrifice had been made possible by Isaac's self-offering.

---

176. Frühwald-König, *Tempel*, 180.

177. Ibid., 203.

178. Since the LXX does not render the Hebrew תּוֹדָה as εὐχαριστία but typically as δῶρον, the correspondence would be in meaning rather than in linguistics.

179. Lindsay, "Todah," 92–93; Nielsen, "Lamb," 239.

It is in John's passion account that all of these ideas and the identification of Jesus as Passover lamb, *tāmîd*, and *tôdāh* crystallize in the form of a temple scene that includes all of the elements of Akedah and sacrificial worship that we have so far examined. To that scene we now turn.

3

The Johannine Passion as Sacrifice Event Revealing the Place of Worship

THE FOURTH GOSPEL'S CRUCIFIXION scene illustrates in dramatic fashion the themes discussed in our previous chapter. In John's Passion account, we see a complete temple scene, featuring the *tāmîd* atonement sacrifice, the *tôdāh* thank-offering expressing gratitude for deliverance from death, and the Passover that unites both. Knöppler expresses this admirably when he writes that "The majority of the Johannine atonement statements stand in the context of the narrative of Jesus' crucifixion: the statements in John 19:14a, 29, 33, 36 are determined by their explicit connection to the New Testament-era Passover, belonging to the atonement cult."[1] The Akedah theme is prominent: Jesus is portrayed as the priest who offers the sacrifice of his own life in a parallel with Isaac in the rabbinic texts we have discussed. We must recall also Philo's depiction of the λόγος as high priest of the eternal temple in heaven, the prototype and pattern of the earthly temple in Jerusalem, and as God's "steward" who pours out a libation of self-offering. Because of the association of the Jerusalem temple with Eden, seen in some apocalyptic texts preceding or roughly contemporary with John, the presence of a garden motif also sets the passion and resurrection as a temple scene.

Jesus' Arrest and Trial

We shall begin with John 12:18, the "Triumphal Entry" into Jerusalem, characterized by the crowd's waving of palms, an action associated with

---

1. Knöppler, *Sühne*, 233, 244. Translation mine.

some sacrificial/cultic practices.[2] The temple theme continues with John 18, the Fourth Gospel's version of the synoptics' "Agony in the Garden," though the "agony" aspect is missing in John. This absence may be influenced by the above-discussed traditions in which Isaac did not flee from the sacrificial knife and feared only that he might render the sacrifice invalid by inadvertent struggle. The presence of a garden also recalls that the Jerusalem temple was frequently portrayed as a model of Eden in some OT apocrypha and pseudepigrapha, most notably 1 *En.* and *Apoc. Ab.*, which we will discuss below. Eden had been the location in which humanity and God were in full and harmonious friendship; after the expulsion of Adam and Eve from the garden and the end of this state of friendship, the worship system provided a way in which the relationship between humanity and God could be restored and the temple took the place of Eden.[3] Stephen T. Um discusses at length the connection in Jewish intertestamental literature between the river of Eden and the river that will flow from the restored temple, as in Ezek 47:1–12; several other biblical and extra-biblical texts also "combine the life-promoting water with the eschatological Temple."[4] In Ezek 47:1, the river that enlivens the city, bringing forth lush trees and teeming with fish, "was flowing down from the very presence of God, since it apparently maintained the route which [the Shekinah] had traveled in his return to the Temple" in Ezek 43:1–5.[5] The description of angels worshiping God in the Garden of Eden in *2 En.* 8:8 "suggests that the heavenly abode was a model for the earthly Garden and Temple."[6] The garden motif forms an *inclusio* to the Johannine passion account, for a garden appears both at the beginning of the narrative and again at the resurrection, a detail unique to John among all the Gospels. The garden motif brackets not only the passion and resurrection accounts but the entire Gospel, calling the audience back to the Gospel's first words "in the beginning" (ἐν ἀρχῇ, John 1:1) and to the "word" (λόγος, 1:1) that created all things, echoing the primordial act of creation recounted in Gen 1:1ff. In recalling the λόγος, we are also reminded of the associations of priesthood in Philo's description of the λόγος, as discussed

---

2. Wick, *Gottesdienste*, 330.

3. See Kinzer, "Temple Christology," 455.

4. Um, *Temple Christology*, 54. For Jesus as eschatological temple in John, see also Kinzer, "Temple Christology," 459–60; Koester, *Dwelling*, 25; Lee, "Spirit of Truth," 284.

5. Ibid.

6. Koester, *Dwelling*, 22, 23. See also Barker, *Gate*, ch. 2.

in the previous chapter. In the garden of Jesus' arrest, therefore, a worship setting is firmly established with both temple and priest.

We will return to the garden of the resurrection at the end of this chapter. For the moment, we will concentrate on the aspect of Jesus' arrest most significant for this thesis: his being "bound." John 18:12–13 marks a departure from the Synoptics' passion accounts.[7] In Matt 27:2, Mark 15:1, and Luke 22:54, Jesus is brought to the high priest before he is brought to Pilate; however, in all of these passages Jesus is not "bound" at this point but "seized/arrested" (συλλάβοντες). Luke does not have Jesus being "bound" at all; Matthew (27:2) and Mark (15:1) show him "bound" (δήσαντες) *after* the meeting with the high priest and before being sent to Pontius Pilate. In John, however, Jesus is "bound" (ἔδησαν) and "led" or "taken" (ἤγαγον) directly to Annas, a former high priest.[8] This being "led" or "taken" is also reminiscent of the Suffering Servant, who "was taken away" (Isa 53:8a, MT לֻקָּח; LXX ἤρθη). John emphasizes this by repeating that Jesus remained bound (δεδεμένον) when he was sent (ἀπέστειλεν) from Annas to the current high priest, Caiaphas, in John 18:24. That Jesus is "sent" to the high priest is ironic: as Jesus had been "sent" by God in a number of verses throughout the Gospel up to this point, he is in his arrest described as being "sent" to a sacrificial death, indicating that God had "sent" him for this very purpose.[9] When Caiaphas had said in John 11:50 that it would be more expedient that "one man die for the people than to have the whole nation destroyed," his words contain not only the well-known ironic allusion to Jesus' atoning death but cast that death in sacrificial terms.[10] It is therefore significant that Jesus is "bound" and then led to this very priest, then remains "bound" when led to another priest. Both occurrences of the term "bound" in John's Passion are directly followed by Jesus' being led to a priest. This recalls that Isaac was first led or "taken" (Gen 22:2–3, MT יִקַּח; LXX παρέλαβεν) to the place of ritual slaughter as the sacrificial victim at the hands of Abraham his father, who acted in the capacity and authority of a priest to offer sacrifice, the wood of the altar was placed on his shoulders, and Abraham "bound"

---

7. See Brown, *According to John (xiii–xxi)*, 813; Lizorkin-Eyzenberg, *Jewish Gospel*, 243.

8. See Brown, *Death of the Messiah*, 1:401.

9. Jesus is said to have been "sent" by God in John 3:34; 4:34; 5:23, 24, 30, 36, 37, 38; 6:29, 38–39, 57; 7:16, 18, 28, 29, 33; 8:16, 18, 26, 29, 42; 9:4; 10:36; 11:42; 12:44, 45, 49; 13:20; 14:24; 15:21; 16:5; 17:38, 18, 21, 23, 25; 20:21.

10. Wick, *Gottesdienste*, 329. Wick also claims that Jesus characterizes his own disciples' future deaths as sacrificial in John 16:2.

him (Gen 22:9: MT וַיַּעֲקֹד; LXX συμποδίσας) for placement on the altar.¹¹ As mentioned above, *Jubilees* presents the binding of Isaac as taking place at the time of the sacrifice of the Passover lamb.¹² After Jesus is "bound," his captors "took [him] along" (παρέλαβον, 19:16b) to the priests and the wood of the cross is placed on his shoulders; after Abraham "took" (παρέλαβεν, Gen 22:2-3 LXX) Isaac he placed the wood of the altar on Isaac's shoulder (Gen 22:6) and then bound him.¹³ As mentioned in the last chapter, the binding of Isaac was associated in some traditions with the binding of the *tāmîd* lamb; therefore, the audience of the Fourth Gospel's passion account, in recognizing the Akedah in the binding of Jesus and his being led to a priest, would naturally make the association with the *tāmîd*. John appears to rearrange the sequence of events from Gen 22, possibly to show the Akedah connections to portray Jesus as sacrifice (Passover/*tāmîd*/*tôdāh*) while making it clear that Jesus is not Isaac *redivivus*. The Akedah connection, when combined with Caiaphas' characterization of Jesus' death as a sacrifice, strengthen the allusions to Isaac and thereby to Passover (and to the sacrifices connected with it, *tāmîd* and *tôdāh*).¹⁴

Many scholars have noted that John's Jesus is in total control over the events leading up to his death. He "permits himself to be arrested" knowing full well what is going to happen to him (cf. John 6:64; 13:1, 3; 18:4) and, paralleling Isaac, goes to his arrest and subsequent death willingly.¹⁵ Melito, in his homily *Peri Pashas* (#25: 59, 69), claims that the depiction of Jesus carrying his own cross, which appears uniquely in John (19:17), is remi-

---

11. Michael Theobald argues that Abraham provides the "type of Christ" in John 8:31–59 ("Zeuge," 172); however, Theobald (182) frames this typology in terms of the "Johannine Community" being "fatherless." The sacrificial imagery throughout the Gospel points strongly in the direction of Isaac being a clear type for Jesus in John, even in terms of performing sacrifice. Although Abraham acted in a priestly role in the Akedah, Isaac, as we have seen, was regarded in rabbinic texts as offering himself. The other parallels to Isaac in the Fourth Gospel speak to Jesus performing functions along the lines of Isaac, rather than Abraham. Theobald, "Abraham," 172–82.

12. Huizenga, "Battle," 42, 44.

13. In turn, this harkens back to Exod 12, where the Israelites are commanded by God to "take" a "lamb" for sacrifice. Ibid., 53.

14. See Ibid., 41.

15. Brown, *According to John* (xiii–xxi), 818; Brown, *Death of the Messiah*, 2:1070-71; Lizorkin-Eyzenberg, *Jewish Gospel*, 243. See also Heil, "Unique High Priest," 735; Huizenga, "Battle," 34; Moloney, *Gospel of John*, 483; Vawter, "According to John," 457, 460, 462. Moloney goes so far as to assert that Jesus exercises "domination" over "the events in the garden" (Moloney, *Gospel of John*, 483).

niscent of Isaac carrying the wood that will form the altar on which his life will be offered; *Barn.* 7:2 also associates that altar with the cross of Christ.[16] For Brown, the detail that Jesus carried his cross unassisted indicates the unique Johannine concern, reflected throughout the rest of the Fourth Gospel, that Jesus was "sole master of his own destiny," including of the time and manner of his death (eg. John 10:17–18; 12:32–33); but he allows that the Akedah theme may also lie behind this detail, since "Certainly OT allusions in the Gospel accounts of the Crucifixion are frequent, and the Isaac motif was a popular one in Jewish circles and seemingly in Christian circles as well."[17] Jesus' taking up of his own "altar" also parallels the above-discussed traditions of Isaac's willingness (even eagerness) to be sacrificed. By means of these features—Jesus' being bound and led to priests, and his full willingness to be sacrificed as well as his full knowledge of the effects of that sacrifice—John establishes the Akedah theme at the very beginning of the passion account.[18]

As Isaac was viewed in many rabbinic texts as the prototypical "lamb" of the *tāmîd* and Passover, we are meant to understand by this point in the Johannine passion narrative that Jesus is going to fulfill all of the functions of these offerings as the account of his passion and death unfolds. When the narrator makes the point in John 19:14 that Jesus stands before Pilate and the temple leadership on the "Day of Preparation for the Passover," it is a signal that the sacrifice of the Passover lamb is near; the corresponding nearness of Jesus' own death strengthens his identity as the Passover lamb.[19] When Pilate presents Jesus to the gathered temple authorities, his "behold (ἴδε) the man" (John 19:5) and "behold (ἴδε) your king" (John 19:14) echo the prior words of John the Baptist in 1:29, 36, "behold (ἴδε) the Lamb of God."[20] Therefore, Jesus is presented to the temple authorities as the Passover lamb.

---

16. Brown, *Death of the Messiah*, 2:1070–71; Brown, *According to John (xiii–xxi)*, 818; see also Barrett, *According to St. John*, 548.

17. Brown, *According to John (xiii–xxi)*, 917.

18. See Brown, *Death of the Messiah*, 2:1440.

19. Knöppler, *Sühne*, 238.

20. Ibid., 241.

The Crucifixion

Jesus' Χιτών as Indication of his Priesthood

While Matthew (27:35), Mark (15:24), and Luke (23:34b) all state that Jesus' garments (ἱμάτια) were divided among the soldiers who crucified him, John alone features an additional account of Jesus' "tunic" (χιτών).[21] In John 19:23-24, Jesus' garments (ἱμάτια) are forcibly removed, as in the Synoptics; but following this the soldiers who had crucified him also gamble for possession of his χιτών, the word employed to identify a part of the high priest's vestments in Exod 28:4-5; 29:5 (LXX).[22] Our thesis agrees with Barnabas Lindars that "it is not impossible that John wishes the discerning reader to see a parallel with the long outer robe of blue of the High Priest" in this verse: Josephus describes this priestly vestment as being "woven without seams" (*Ant.* 3.161), and as we have seen, Philo equates the high priest's χιτών with the Logos that holds creation together "in a seamless unity."[23] Additionally, Exod 28:31-32 (LXX) describes the high priest's "robe" (ποδήρη) as "woven work" (ὑφάντου), and John 19:23 tells us that Jesus' tunic was also woven (ὑφαντός) in a single piece (δι' ὅλου).[24] According to Exod 28:31-32, the high priest's tunic was woven in one piece (ποιήσεις ὑποδύτην ποδήρη ὅλον ὑακίνθινον) so as not to allow it to be torn (ἵνα μὴ ῥαγῇ).

Another parallel to Philo lies in the removal of the high priest's vestment. In *Leg.* 2.56, Philo claims that the high priest (as representative of the λόγος, who pours out an offering of the self) removes his full-length robe and "enters the Holy of Holies naked 'to pour out as a libation the blood of the soul and to offer as incense the whole mind to God our Saviour [sic] and Benefactor.'"[25] The image of the high priest removing his garment before offering sacrifice is similar to John's portrayal of Jesus' χιτών being removed before he offers his life on the cross (John 19:23a). Hence, Jesus would not only be a sacrifice, but the priest who offers that sacrifice. The Gospel itself attributes the gambling-away of Jesus' χιτών to Ps 22:19, in which the psalmist laments the distribution of his "garments" or "clothing" (ἱμάτια).

---

21. Lindars, *Gospel of John*, 577; Vawter, "According to John," 461.

22. See Barrett, *According to St. John*, 550; Brown, *Death of the Messiah*, 2:957.

23. Lindars, *Gospel of John*, 578; see also Fuglseth, *Johannine Sectarianism*, 110-12; Vawter, "According to John," 461; Heil, "High Priest," 742.

24. Heil, "High Priest," 742.

25. Petropoulou, *Animal Sacrifice*, 157.

Matthew and Mark both portray Jesus crying out from the cross the famous "My God, my God, why have you forsaken me?" (Matt 27:46; Mark 15:34), a quotation also of Ps 22:1. However, while John utilizes the same psalm a different line is quoted, emphasizing not the psalm's sense of abandonment but its reference to the unjust distribution of the protagonist's garments among his persecutors. John 19:23a uses the term ἱμάτια, the term from Ps 22:19; but verse 23b focuses on the χιτών, using the term that describes the high priest's tunic in every LXX passage in which that particular vestment appears. Clearly, there is an intended difference between Jesus' ἱμάτια and his χιτών. While many scholars have interpreted the seamless, untorn χιτών as a sign of the oneness of the "Johannine Community," formed by the Beloved Disciple and Jesus' mother at the cross, the associations of the χιτών within the context of sacrifice already established in this scene make it much more likely that an identification of Jesus as high priest is in view.[26]

This does not exclude a unity theme, however. The high priest was viewed as a sign of the oneness of God and the unity of God's covenant people.[27] In some English translations, the words describing how the χιτών was woven, ἐκ τῶν ἄνωθεν, are rendered as "from the top down"; but the Greek phrase recalls Jesus' use of ἐκ τῶν ἄνωθεν in his conversation with Nicodemus in John 3:3, 7 as well as his words to Pontius Pilate in 19:11: "You would have no authority over me unless it were given you from above (ἐκ τῶν ἄνωθεν)."[28] Since the phrase ἐκ τῶν ἄνωθεν signifies divine origin/divine authority throughout the Fourth Gospel, the χιτών woven ἐκ τῶν ἄνωθεν is of divine origin, as is the covenant unity of God's people that this priestly garment represents.[29] Hence, while a unity theme may be present, it does not exclude an identification of Jesus as high priest.

Rather than relying on John 19 alone for evidence that Jesus is portrayed as high priest in John, we should assess the theme as it appears

---

26. For the communal unity view, see e.g., Barrett, *According to St. John*, 550; Brown, *Death of the Messiah*, 2:921, 957–58; Lindars, *Gospel of John*, 578; Moloney, *Gospel of John*, 503, 507; Vawter, "According to John," 461–62. While Vawter agrees that Ps 22 is in view, he supports the association with the high priest while noting that some rabbinic texts assign seamless robes to Moses and Adam. Then there is the famous seamless tunic of Joseph in Gen 37:3, a parallel that would identify that patriarch as "a type of Christ . . . one betrayed by his brothers and yet their Savior." See also Heil, "High Priest," 742, where the office and identity of the high priest represented, and was directly connected with, the unity of God's covenant people.

27. Heil, "High Priest," 742.

28. Ibid., 742–43.

29. Heil attributes the significance of this unity to the inclusion of Gentiles. Ibid., 743.

throughout the Gospel. The work of John Paul Heil is quite instructive in this regard. Through a narrative-critical methodology, Heil arrives at the determination that the Fourth Gospel portrays Jesus as *unique* high priest in characteristic use of dramatic irony, weaving the theme of Jesus-as-high-priest throughout the narrative. According to Heil's scheme, Jesus' high priesthood is:

1. Ironic, since none of the characters realize that Jesus is high priest but the Gospel's audience does;
2. "New and different, since Jesus sacrifices himself rather than an animal;"
3. Unique in setting Jesus' high priesthood over against the high priesthood of other characters in the narrative, namely Annas and Caiaphas.[30]

Countering Heil's second point above, Jesus' sacrifice of himself is neither new nor very different: as I have argued in this thesis, the Fourth Gospel evokes interpretations of the Akedah (not new by any means!) in its portrayal of Jesus, an event in which Isaac had willingly offered his own life as a sacrificial "lamb." This embedding of the Akedah in the Gospel is a major part of the portrayal of Jesus as high priest who offers his own life in sacrifice. The sacrificial offering of a person, of his own free will, has established precedent not only in the Akedah and its interpretative traditions, but in Jewish traditions of martyrdom, as we have discussed.

Regarding Heil's third point, the contrast between Jesus and the institutional Jerusalem priesthood as it appears in the Gospel prior to Jesus' arrest and trial, the following are in view:

- Caiaphas utters the famously ironic statement that "it is better that one man should die for the people than to have the whole nation destroyed" (John 11:50) and accuses his own colleagues of not knowing anything (11:49); by contrast, Jesus "knows" his own "sheep" and rather than condemn someone else, he will willingly lay down his life for them (10:14–15). Jesus is the shepherd, in contrast to the "wolf" Caiaphas.[31] This evokes the prophets' censure of the priests and kings of Israel, who were supposed to be good shepherds and instead devoured the sheep. The shepherd/leadership theme comes to fruition in 18:15, when the disciple who "was known to the high priest" brings

30. Ibid., 730.
31. Ibid., 731–45.

Peter into the courtyard. Heil points out that the word for "courtyard" here, αὐλή is the same word used of "sheepfold" in 10:1, 16. Hence, the "courtyard (αὐλή) of the high priest" corresponds to the "sheepfold (αὐλή) of the good shepherd." The implication is that "being known to the high priest" ironically means being known not to the high priest Caiaphas but to the high priest Jesus.[32]

- Jesus sets himself above Caiaphas in his position as teacher of God's word. One of the main functions of the priesthood was to teach the people; when Jesus employs the emphatic ἐγώ during his confrontation with Caiaphas in 18:20, the implication is that Jesus, not Caiaphas, has been in the temple among the people, taking the proper teaching role of the high priest in the absence of the institutional high priest doing his job. By contrast, Caiaphas has hidden himself away from the people, derelict in his duty, plotting secret sessions of the Sanhedrin instead.[33]

My disagreement with Heil lies in his repetition of the supersession hermeneutic that has historically dominated too much scholarship. The present study argues that John's Jesus does take the place of the temple and its functions, including sacrifice and priesthood; but for the sole reason that the Jerusalem temple institution no longer exists at the time of the Fourth Gospel's composition.[34] John does not abrogate sacrifice, but re-locates it in the person of Jesus. The Fourth Gospel does not seek to change the character, purpose, or meaning of Jewish worship, but seeks only to shift the location of that worship.

The overall temple features of the crucifixion scene make it likely that the term χιτών was chosen by the Gospel's author/s and/or redactor/s for a very specific reason: to refer to the high priest's vestment. Hence, in the crucifixion Jesus is the high priest (as was Abraham for the rabbis and the λόγος for Philo) who offers the perfect sacrifice of his own life (as does the λόγος in Philo and Isaac in the Akedah).

---

32. Ibid., 737–38.
33. Ibid., 739–40.
34. See Metzner, *Verständnis*, 135.

The Crucifixion: Passover Associations

John's Jesus is crucified at the time of day when the temple priests slaughter the Passover lambs, and this likely marks a deliberate change by the Fourth Evangelist to the timing of Jesus' crucifixion for the purpose of identifying Jesus as the one who fulfills the Passover lamb's function.[35] While many scholars have argued in favor of the "lamb" indicating either the Passover lamb, or Isaac as sacrificial "lamb," or the Servant-lamb, we have seen above that all three are likely in view in John's identification of Jesus as "lamb," since all three were interrelated in meaning.[36] We have seen in the last chapter that both Passover and Servant are tied to the Akedah and, by extension, to the *tāmîd* sacrifice that kept the Akedah continually before the eyes of God, as a reminder of God's promise to deliver Isaac's descendants due to the merits accrued to them through their ancestor's voluntary self-offering on their behalf. Therefore, to state that the Johannine "lamb" is based on the Suffering Servant *or* the Passover *or* the Akedah, exclusive of any one of these, is to divorce the Servant-lamb and Passover-lamb from the other "lambs" with which they are symbiotically linked.

The report that Jesus' bones remained unbroken, the presence of hyssop, and the blood from Jesus' side function together to associate Jesus' death with the function of the Passover lamb as deliverer from death (and, as Philo had considered, transferred the people from a sinful state to one

---

35. Barrett, *According to St. John*, 545; Brown, *According to John (xiii–xxi)*, 918; Brown, *Death of the Messiah*, 1:847; Derrett, *Victim*, 147; Grelot, *Les Juifs*, 28, 108, 165; Knöppler, *Sühne*, 234; Lindars, *Gospel of John*, 571; Moloney, *Gospel of John*, 496; Nielsen, "Lamb," 252; Wick, *Gottesdienste*, 329; Zumstein, "L'Interprétation," 2120. See also Lizorkin-Eyzenberg, *Jewish Gospel*, 33–34.

36. For arguments that the Johannine "lamb" possesses a single meaning or possibly a combination of two meanings to the exclusion of others, see e.g., Brown, *According to John (xiii–xxi)*, 918, 951, 953; Hasitschka, *Befreiung*, 66; Nielsen, "Lamb," 226–27. Brown claims that "Isaac's symbolism is only one factor in leading us to think that John looked upon Jesus as a sacrificial victim who died at the same hour that the paschal lambs were being slaughtered in the Temple." Nielsen accepts that Passover and Servant associations are in view in John but are nevertheless "not conclusive," and though he is correct in observing that the Passover possessed a function of transferring the people to a sinless state, he argues against any atoning purpose. Nielsen also dismisses any Akedah connection in Jesus' being called "lamb." Hasitschka argues that the Gospel's use in 19:36 of the language of Ps 34:21 indicates that the Fourth Evangelist purposely chose this language to show Jesus as the Servant; but as we have seen above, Hasitschka does not see a connection to Passover.

of virtue).³⁷ Since "death and sin are closely connected," the Servant-lamb who endures affliction for his people's "transgressions" (Isa 53:4–6) is also in view, as is Isaac, whose self-offering served to liberate his descendants from death.³⁸ The assertion in John 19:36 that Jesus' bones were not broken is taken directly from the regulations for the ritual slaughter of the Passover lamb in Exod 12:10, 46 and Num 9:12, which proscribe the breaking of the paschal lamb's bones.³⁹

> The prophecy quoted in [19] v. 36 refers back to the omission of the crucifragium (v. 33). The quotation about the consumption of the Passover lamb from Exod 12:46 (cp. Exod 12:10 [LXX]; Num 9:12) was altered in John 19:36 in light of LXX Ps 33 (34):21. Since the quotation has in view the ritual universality of the Passover lamb belonging to the atonement cult in the New Testament era, and turns this aspect to the crucified Jesus, it once more, according to 19:14a, 29, brings up the theological understanding that the Crucified One is the true Passover Lamb.⁴⁰

As discussed in the previous chapter, the date of the first evening of Passover, Nisan 14, was identified in some rabbinic texts as the anniversary of the Akedah, strengthening the association of Passover as a commemoration of that event and the idea that the Passover was made possible by Isaac's own self-offering as a lamb of burnt-offering (as in *Tg. Gen* 22, discussed above).

Blood and Water

In John 19:34, when a soldier pierces the side of the already-expired Jesus with a lance, both blood and water flow from the wound in a feature unique to John among the four Gospels.⁴¹ So crucial is this passage that Knöppler

---

37. Nielsen, "Lamb," 253.

38. Ibid., 253–54.

39. See Brown, *Death of the Messiah*, 1:35, 847; Heil, "High Priest," 729–45, 732; Knöppler, *Sühne*, 234, 236; Lindars, *Gospel of John*, 590; Metzner, *Verständnis*, 144–48; Moloney, *Gospel of John*, 509; Nielsen, "Lamb of God," 253; Vawter, "According to John," 462; Wick, *Gottesdienste*, 330.

40. Knöppler, *Sühne*, 236–37. Translation mine.

41. "This incident is mentioned elsewhere only in the *textus receptus* of Matt 27:49, where it is undoubtedly due to textual assimilation to this passage in John." Barrett, *According to St. John*, 556.

does not exaggerate in claiming that the Gospel's whole intention can be found in 19:34b.[42]

There is a link here to Zec 12:10 (MT), "They shall look on him whom they have pierced," relating to onlookers at the Crucifixion, who, when they look upon Jesus pierced by the lance—the true Passover lamb—they will be saved by the Passover lamb's atoning merits.[43] This refers directly back to Jesus' reference in John 3:14 to the bronze serpent from Num 21:6–9: just as the Israelites had been saved by looking upon the bronze serpent hoisted upon the pole in the wilderness.[44] We therefore have in the lance-thrust a reference to the covenant people Israel in the wilderness, which the Fourth Gospel casts as the people who possess the true temple and sacrifice in its midst, in contrast to the Ἰουδαῖοι, who claim that God's presence dwells in their institutional Jerusalem temple. As always in John, the point is entirely about the correct location of worship; the Passion narrative places that location squarely in the person of Jesus as sacrifice.

Blood also possesses covenant significance, as the covenants with Israel related in the Hebrew Scriptures were frequently ratified with blood. The ratification of God's covenant with Abraham was effected through blood sacrifices (Gen 15:1–20), and the covenant of Torah at Mount Sinai was also ratified by the sprinkling of the people with blood (Exod 24:3–8).[45] Here, Jesus' earlier command "drink [my] blood" (6:53–56), which had been prefigured in the wine created at the Cana wedding (2:9ff.), comes to its fruition: his blood has been poured out. Daly points out that "early rabbinic attitudes toward sacrifice failed increasingly to distinguish between the technicalities and the ideas associated with particular sacrificial rites. Ideas associated with the blood rite of the covenant sacrifice tended to become associated with the blood rites of any sacrifice, especially where the blood was tossed or thrown."[46] When the Passover lamb was slaughtered in the Jerusalem temple, its blood was dashed against the sides of the altar, thereby possessing "strong covenantal associations. One suspects that the compiler of the Mishnah tractate *Pesahim* considered this sacrificial blood rite to be the most essential part of the Passover observance."[47] When Jesus'

---

42. Knöppler, *Sühne*, 235.
43. Ibid., 237.
44. See Moloney, *Text and Context*, 75–76.
45. See Daly, *Christian Doctrine*, 38.
46. Ibid.
47. Ibid., 39. Daly's point (38) that NT texts frequently disregard the original context

blood pours out after the lance-thrust, an image is created of the lamb's blood tossed onto the altar. Recall also Philo's idea, discussed in chapter 1 of this thesis, that the Jerusalem high priest entered the Holy of Holies naked on the Day of Atonement to sprinkle the sacrificial blood. John does not tell us explicitly whether Jesus was crucified naked; but given that such was the common practice and that the evangelist seems to describe the complete removal of all of Jesus' clothing, it is likely that nakedness is implied.[48] It is difficult not to see a parallel between Jesus, the λόγος made flesh, crucified naked, his side pierced and blood outpoured on the cross as on an altar; and Philo's unclothed high priest, who is a representation of the divine λόγος, bringing a blood offering of atonement into the Holy of Holies. This adds another element to the crucifixion as a temple scene and enhances Jesus' identity as both priest and sacrifice.[49]

The water from Jesus' side has typically been interpreted as a representation of the waters of baptism and/or as the outpouring of the Spirit, in light of 19:30, when Jesus "hands over the spirit" at the moment of his death.[50] While this meaning will not be disputed here, an additional claim will be made that water in this verse also indicates priesthood and thereby completes the temple aspects of the crucifixion scene.

For our purposes, the most significant uses for "water" in the LXX are found in Numbers, Isaiah, and Ezekiel. In the LXX of Num 19:9, 13, 18, 20, 21, the phrase ὕδωρ ῥαντισμοῦ refers to the "water of purification" or "water of sprinkling" by which one who was defiled by corpse-contact was cleansed. Here, the ashes of the red heifer "sin-offering" were mixed with water, and the resulting ὕδωρ ῥαντισμοῦ (MT מֵי נִדָּה), "sprinkling-water," was applied to the defiled Israelite by sprinkling with hyssop and effected restoration to a state of ritual purity. In Num 8:7, ὕδωρ ἁγνισμοῦ designates the water by which the Levites are purified: the Greek "purity water" (or "clean water") here translates the Hebrew מֵי חַטָּאת meaning "sin-offering water."[51] Ezekiel's vision of the restored temple (Ezek 40:38) describes a location in which the sacrificial offerings would be "rinsed" or "washed": the

---

of a passage they quote, as in Heb 9, applies equally to the rabbinic interpretations of the Akedah that we are considering in this thesis.

48. Brown, *Death of the Messiah*, 2:953.

49. See Brown, *According to John (xiii-xxi)*, 920-21; Brown, *Death of the Messiah*, 2:955-58; Metzner, *Verständnis*, esp. 135.

50. See Barrett, *According to St. John*, 554; Lindars, *Gospel of John*, 587; Wick, *Gottesdienste*, 331.

51. Brown, Driver, and Briggs, *Lexicon*, 308-9, 622.

Hebrew דּוּחַ/יְדִיחוּ is repeated in 2 Chr 4:6 with the same meaning, referring specifically to the washing of sacrificial victims.⁵² The term also appears in Isa 4:4, where it indicates a "washing away" of moral guilt.⁵³ The latter passage uses יָדִיחַ to describe a purification effected by means of a "judging spirit and consuming spirit" (בְּרוּחַ מִשְׁפָּט וּבְרוּחַ בָּעֵר). The spirit that Jesus "delivers" from the cross, being represented by the water flowing from his pierced side, is in fact the spirit that judges (John 5:22, 27, 30; 8:16, 26; 9:39; 12:31; 16:8, 11; possibly 19:13) and purifies; therefore, purification is certainly in view in this scene.⁵⁴ Indeed, in the sacrificial system practiced at the Jerusalem temple, priests verified and pronounced purification but only God could effectively bring purification about; hence, purification must be effected not by any high priest, but by the high priest who is also the divine λόγος.⁵⁵

There is some debate as to whether the water from Jesus' side is related to the "living water" of which he speaks at the Feast of Tabernacles in John 7:38–39, chiefly due to some inconclusiveness regarding whether it is Jesus or the believer from whom "living waters" will flow. Considering the ritual imagery permeating the whole crucifixion narrative, however, it is most likely that Tabernacles does look forward to this aspect of Jesus' death.⁵⁶ The work of Stephen T. Um in this regard is helpful. Drawing a linguistic connection with the temple vision in Ezek 47:1, in which life-giving water flows from "under the right shoulder of the temple," Um operates on the basis of the Hebrew מִכֶּתֶף in that passage, which can mean either "from the side" or "from the shoulder" to claim that John "has exploited the possible meaning 'shoulder,'" with the result that "from *below* the shoulder" (of the temple) in Ezek 47:1 renders "'from his breast' (ἐκ τῆς κοιλίας αὐτοῦ)" in John.⁵⁷ Aileen Guilding's views on the "living water" of John 7:38–39 are also worth considering. Considering the *Tosefta*'s (Sukkah III.3) interpretation of Zech 14:8 that predicts waters flowing from the temple in the end

---

52. Ibid., 188.

53. Ibid.

54. Kinzer, "Temple Christology," 455.

55. For purification by the spirit in the Johannine crucifixion account, see Knöppler, *Sühne*, 234–35, 238; Metzner, *Verständnis*, 132.

56. Kinzer, "Temple Christology," 448–49; Moloney, *Text and Context*, 201.

57. Um, *Temple Christology*, 157–58. Brian D. Johnson agrees that the subject from whom living waters will flow is meant to be Jesus ("Salvation," 83–99: 95–96). See also Grelot, *Les Juifs*, 76.

time (as also in Ezek 47:1–12), Guilding concludes that the "belly" out of which the "living waters" will flow in John 7 is Jesus, not the believer.[58]

As discussed in the previous chapter, at a particular point during the Feast of Tabernacles the high priest poured water from the Pool of Siloam into one bowl atop the altar of sacrifice, poured wine into an adjacent bowl, and removed stoppers from each vessel so that the water and wine flowed in separate streams below the altar. In John 9:39, the Pool of Siloam is associated with Jesus' granting of sight to the man born blind, who is harassed by the Jerusalem religious authorities for embracing Jesus—in effect, for embracing a rival temple (the infamous ἀποσυναγῶγος). In essence, this indicates adherence to a temple other than the Jerusalem institution: the healed man "sees" in Jesus an alternative worship location, a rival temple. Siloam therefore links Tabernacles and the healing of the man born blind. When the water pours from Jesus' side in John's passion narrative, the implied connection to Jesus' pronouncement at Tabernacles regarding "living waters" flowing from "his side" calls to mind the Tabernacles ritual water, as well as the healing of the man born blind, which is another scene with temple significance. This is strengthened by the association of Tabernacles with the beginnings of the temple, as noted by Guilding. After King Solomon's temple dedication prayer in 1 Kgs 8:27, seven days of feasting follow, which "can have been none other than the Feast of Tabernacles" as we may discern from its beginning on the fifteenth day of the seventh month (2 Chr 7:8–10), the description of a "closing festival" (cf. Lev 23:36), and the retirement of the people "into their tents" (1 Kgs 8:66).[59] Since Jesus predicates of himself all of the Tabernacles festival's attributes and features, the worship and meaning of that temple festival are found in his person.[60] The Tabernacles image of water and wine pouring to the base of the altar is recalled in the Johannine outpouring of water and blood from Jesus to cast the Passion as a temple scene, with the cross as the altar on which Jesus performs the functions of both priest and sacrifice.

As mentioned in chapter 2 above, in relation to the significance of water and wine as they appear in the Cana event in John 2, *Tg.* Gen 35:9ff. claims that Jacob poured water and wine on his stone pillow after seeing the vision of the stairway to heaven, as a precursor or rubric for the festivities of

---

58. Guilding, *Jewish Worship*, 92. See also Kinzer, "Temple Christology," 448–49; Moloney, *Text and Context*, 201.

59. Guilding, *Jewish Worship*, 95.

60. See e.g., Frühwald-König, *Tempel und Kult*, 214–15.

Tabernacles.⁶¹ This also possesses significance for the identification of Jesus as temple in John, as Jesus refers to this very scripture in John 1:51. During the Farewell Discourse, Tabernacles appears again. Whereas the Tabernacles theme of water predominated in John 7–8 (extending into chapter 9), in the Farewell Discourse the festival's wine libation is emphasized and the community, rather than Jesus, is in view. Also in the Farewell Discourse the Spirit is promised, and as we have seen, the Spirit was referred to in the Tabernacles scene in John 7–8 by the reference to water. Jesus refers to his "hour" at Cana—a clear reference to the crucifixion—and the narrator states that Jesus' turning of water to wine manifested his "glory." Tabernacles and Cana are thus both prolepses of the cross.⁶² We may say, then, that the placement of the temple incident immediately following the Cana narrative is no accident. As Jesus identifies his own body as the temple in a reference to the resurrection at John 2:21, the temple incident also points to the cross and to the cross's atoning function.⁶³ If Jesus' body is the temple, then his death must have atonement function because, as mentioned in chapter 2 above, the Jerusalem temple existed for the sole purpose of atonement sacrifice and was useless without that worship praxis.⁶⁴ As Zumstein points out, the Gospel "is wholly oriented toward the cross" from the very beginning; the Passion narrative is referenced immediately and repeatedly.⁶⁵

Significantly, the blood of the sacrificial victim was applied to the altar or poured out at the altar's base in several temple rites other than Tabernacles, among them the offering of first-fruits, the עוֹלָה, the שְׁלָמִים, the אָשָׁם, and some חַטָּאת observances.⁶⁶ We should also recall our discussion of wine being poured out on the altar of sacrifice in other libation rites, most especially as an accompaniment to the *tôdāh*.⁶⁷ Priesthood is also in view in the outpouring of water and blood from Jesus' side: as discussed in chapter 2, the water of Cana signified priestly purification, and the blood of a sacrificial victim was also sprinkled on priests in the rite of ordination

---

61. Ibid.
62. Zumstein, "L'Interprétation," 2121, 2123.
63. See Brown, *Community*, 118; Grelot, *Les Juifs*, 29, 108.
64. Knöppler, *Sühne*, 248–49.
65. Zumstein, "L'Interprétation," 2126, see also 2128. Translation mine.
66. McClymond, "Spilled Blood," 238; also McClymond, *Beyond*, 115.
67. McClymond (*Beyond*, 95) argues against the old interpretation of wine representing blood.

to the Jewish priesthood.[68] In John 19, just as the Jerusalem temple priests purify themselves before offering sacrifice at the altar,[69] so Jesus purifies himself as priest to offer himself, the "lamb" who, in his identification with Isaac and the Suffering Servant, performs the functions of Passover, *tôdāh*, and *tāmîd*. Because the cross encompasses all of these connections, it is the place where atonement sacrifice is effected.[70]

Another indication that John portrays Jesus as high priest may lie in the burial cloths lying in the tomb at the resurrection. We will discuss this further below; for the moment, let us consider that the cloth that had wrapped Jesus' head was seen by Peter to be "rolled up and lying in a place by itself" (John 20:7).[71]

Timing

In John 6, the importance of the manna had brought the Passover theme to the fore. As Martin Hasitschka notes, the precise time of Jesus' death (the sixth "hour") is significant in that all leaven had to be removed from Jewish homes by that time in preparation for the Passover.[72] Grelot points out that the time of noon, which marks the beginning of the removal of the leaven, corresponds with the time at which Jesus is first brought before his accusers.[73] Though Hasitschka rejects an identification with Passover

---

68. Ibid., 114–15.

69. See Nielsen, "Lamb," 234–35.

70. Knöppler, *Sühne*, 248; Metzner, *Verständnis*, 156–58. See also Dietzfelbinger, "Sühnetod," 67, 75–76. Although Dietzfelbinger recognizes that Jesus' death is portrayed in atonement-sacrifice terms in John, he argues also that this is not the primary concern of the Fourth Gospel ("neither the whole nor the center," 74); more important is the portrayal of Jesus as Way, Truth, Life, Resurrection, etc. In Bultmannesque fashion, Dietzfelbinger claims that the primary meaning of Jesus' death, although atonement significance is present, is that the cross is Jesus' method of return to his heavenly Father. I agree with Dietzfelbinger's arguments in favor of "Lamb of God" as Passover lamb and of Jesus' death as atonement-sacrifice, but I disagree that this is a minor issue; indeed, I wish to argue that this is the overriding theme of the Fourth Gospel, as demonstrated by the "thesis statements" connected to Passover, Suffering Servant, cult, and sacrifice that establish in the earliest passages that this theme will be preeminent throughout the Gospel.

71. The separate head wrapping among the grave clothes may also be intended to evoke the high priest's "turban," which was worn "wrapped" around the head. Salvoni, "Proof," 72–76.

72. Hasitschka, *Befreiung*, 66–67.

73. Grelot, *Les Juifs*, 78.

lamb in favor of the unleavened bread interpretation, there is, as we have seen, a connection between the Passover lamb and the unleavened bread of Passover. John's Jesus may therefore be portrayed as Passover lamb and as unleavened bread/manna at the same time. The reference to the removal of leaven at the time of Jesus' crucifixion identifies Jesus with the bread of Passover and harkens back to the Bread of Life Discourse in chapter 6, so we see that that Discourse was a prolepsis of Jesus' crucifixion, in which he would offer his "flesh for the life of the world" (6:51).[74] According to Marianne M. Thompson, John's identification of Jesus as the "true bread from heaven" creates not supersession and replacement of a Jewish festival but a "continuation of the narrative" of God's saving work throughout the history of the covenant people. The "discontinuity," writes Thompson, is "brought about by the striking of the eschatological hour."[75] Passover has not been abrogated, superseded, or replaced but re-located in Jesus, just as the temple and priesthood have been re-located to his person.[76]

Guilding has noted that every Passover reference in the Fourth Gospel is pervaded by symbolism, teachings of Jesus, and/or oblique references that point to Jesus' suffering, death, and resurrection.[77] This is only one way in which the Passover theme informs the whole Gospel, and connects the Passover directly to Jesus' death and resurrection. Jesus' words in John 6 instruct believers to consume his flesh (bread) and blood (the wine of the Cana wedding representing the sacrificial libation accompanying the bread offering of the *tôdāh*), both components of the *tôdāh* and *tāmîd* offerings and, as such, both evocative of Passover, and both given in and through Jesus' sacrificial death on the cross to transmit life to the world, as his words in John 6:33 had promised.[78]

Hyssop

The piercing of Jesus' side parallels the manner of Jewish ritual slaughter for sacrificial animals, particularly where the Passover victim is concerned: *m. Tamid* 4.2 records that the Passover lamb's preparation involved piercing the animal carcass's heart and draining the blood; this is evocative of the

---

74. See Knöppler, *Sühne*, 245.
75. Thompson, "Reflections," 272.
76. Ibid., 269.
77. Guilding, *Jewish Worship*, 66.
78. Knöppler, *Sühne*, 245.

Johannine picture of Jesus' blood "being drained off by the Jewish method of ritual slaughter, and so made available for sacrificial sprinkling."[79] The blood pouring from Jesus' side onto the wood of the cross evokes the application of the Passover lamb's blood to the doorposts of the Israelite houses in Egypt; this becomes clearer in the light of the use of hyssop to lift the sponge of vinegar to Jesus' lips, as hyssop was used on the night of the first Passover to apply the lamb's blood to the Israelites' doors (Exod 12:22).[80]

Several scholars have noted that hyssop is a rather flimsy plant, well suited to a sprinkling function as in application of the Passover lamb's blood to the Israelite's doorposts and in purification and ordination rites, but not strong enough to support a sponge for lifting to a crucifixion victim.[81] However, as is so frequently the case in John, we are dealing here with theological, not literal (in this case, botanical) facts. Perceiving this, Brown suggests that John uses hyssop in relation to the sour (or "vinegary") wine served to Jesus in response to his words "I thirst" (John 19:29) in order to portray Jesus as the Passover lamb, since "the most famous reference to hyssop is in Exod 12:22."[82] Peter Wick goes even further by pointing out that the Fourth Evangelist's choice of hyssop is intended to show that all functions associated with hyssop from the Old Testament are performed by Jesus in his death: cleansing (Num 14:4), cult/sacrifice (Num 19:6), atonement for sin (Ps 51:9), and the liberation from death brought about by the Passover lamb (Exod 12:21).[83] Certainly, then, the Passover lamb is in view here; but considering the connection we have established between

---

79. Daly, *Christian Sacrifice*, 206; Lindars, *Gospel of John*, 590. Brown also draws attention to this availability for sprinkling, but while agreeing that this sacrificial meaning is present, he adds that this cannot account for the presence of water in this scene and concludes that the flow of water indicates the giving of the Spirit. Daly additionally refers to the arrangement of the Passover lamb in the shape of a cross, with "a cross-piece at shoulder height to keep the carcass from slipping on the spit"; however, he cites Samaritan tradition as well as Justin Martyr's *Dialogue with Trypho* rather than biblical or rabbinic evidence. Brown, *Death of the Messiah*, 2:1180

80. Derrett, *Victim*, 147, 149; Nielsen, "Lamb of God," 253. See also Heyman, *Power*, 137.

81. Brown, *Death of the Messiah*, 2:1075-76; Vawter, "According to John," 462. On the use of hyssop to apply the paschal lamb's blood to the Israelites' doorposts, see Moloney, *Gospel of John*, 508; Nielsen, "Lamb," 253.

82. Brown, *Death of the Messiah*, 2:1076-77; also Knöppler, *Sühne*, 238; Metzner, *Verständnis*, 155; Moloney, *Gospel of John*, 508; Vawter, "According to John," 462.

83. Wick, *Gottesdienste*, 329. For hyssop's atonement significance and connection to the Passover lamb, see also Knöppler, *Sühne*, 234.

the Passover lamb and the lamb of the twice-daily *tāmîd* offering, it is also likely that John intends a reference to the *tāmîd*. There is also a connection to the *tôdāh*, since the drink offered to Jesus is wine (albeit soured), one of the components of the *tôdāh* sacrifice. For Brown, Jesus' pronouncement "It is finished" (John 19:30a), immediately following upon his drinking the "vinegary" wine, both completes Jesus' commitment to accomplishing his mission from the Father and fulfills the Scripture.[84] The scripture Jesus fulfills here, however, is not a particular chapter and verse in a particular book, but all the scriptures that elucidate the Passover.[85]

Sprinkled blood also occurs in Exod 24:5–8, where Moses sprinkles the people with the blood of ὁλοκαυτώματα (Exod 24:5, LXX) as a ratification of the covenant relationship between God and the people Israel. Hyssop is not mentioned in this verse, but it is significant that the sprinkled blood of a sacrificial victim is also effective in ratifying a covenant. Therefore, Jesus' outpoured blood at the crucifixion indicates that a covenant is being put into effect, which would indicate the presence of a covenant people. This parallel to Exodus signifies that, just as the covenant in the Exodus wilderness was contracted with the people Israel, the death of Jesus in John also contracts a covenant with Israel. However, given the distinction in John between Ἰσραήλ and Ἰουδαῖοι (which we will discuss in greater detail in chapter 5 of this thesis), the Fourth Gospel defines "Israel" as the people that accepts Jesus as sacrifice and temple. The Ἰουδαῖοι, aligned with the temple institution in Jerusalem, do not fit this category. It is imperative to state that this serves the purpose of re-locating the place of worship in the absence of the Jerusalem temple after 70 CE. In John, Ἰσραήλ refers to the people with the Glory in its midst, just as Israel in the Exodus had the Glory in its midst in the wilderness tabernacle.

Since Jesus is the temple, then "Israel" is the people with the Jesus-temple in its midst.

Son of Man as Temple

The scope of this study does not allow for a full treatment of the very intricate "Son of Man" theme in John; however a brief discussion of this theme is in order here as the portrayal of Jesus as "Son of Man" bears directly on the sacrificial significance of Jesus' death in the Fourth Gospel.

84. Brown, *Death of the Messiah*, 2:1072, 1077; Moloney, *Text and Context*, 76.
85. Brown, *Death of the Messiah*, 2:1078.

It is highly probable that John 1:51 is a reference to Gen 28:10–19, which relates the dream of Jacob. In this vision, the patriarch sees angels going up to heaven and back down to earth on a "ladder" or "stairway" (v. 12, סֻלָּם). When Jacob wakes, he proclaims, "How awesome is this place! This is none other than the house of God (אִם־בֵּית אֱלֹהִים), and this is the gate of heaven" (Gen 28:17). Then he "anoints" the stone he had used as a pillow (with wine and water, according to the rabbinic texts referenced above), sets it up as an altar, and names the place Beth-El (בֵּית־אֵל)—"house of God." In John 1:51, Jesus says that "the angels of God (ascend and descend) on *the Son of Man*"—meaning that he, as Son of Man, is the stairway by which heaven descends to earth and earth rises to heaven.[86] By evoking the Jacob event, then, Jesus is claiming to be the gate of heaven, the way in which human beings access God and God comes to humanity.[87] This necessarily signifies that the gate is a meeting place for the two. Jacob had said that the place of his dream was *both* the gate of heaven *and* the house of God. Of course, for those of the Israelite faith prior to 70 CE, the house of God was none other than the Temple in Jerusalem. The Temple itself was the "gate" through which humanity communicated with God and vice versa. Therefore, when Jesus places himself as the way between heaven and earth, he is claiming to be the meeting-place of the two realms. Jesus assigns the title "Son of Man" to this identity-picture. Hence, for John, the "Son of Man" is the temple, where God and humanity are united. It is significant that the Temple Incident in John takes place soon after the first "Son of Man" saying (2:13–16), as if John's Jesus is bearing out in action what he has just stated in words: that he himself is the true temple.[88]

The Johannine Resurrection

In the resurrection scene, the Servant motif comes to a climax. As mentioned in the Discursus (chapter 2), the "lifting up" of Jesus, to which Jesus himself refers frequently throughout the Fourth Gospel, is in fact a single action: the "lifting up" on the cross and the "lifting up" in the sense of being

---

86. Kinzer, "Temple Christology," 447–48.

87. Ashton, *Understanding*, 250. See also Theobald, "Abraham," 159–63. Kinzer ("Temple Christology," 448) notes that some rabbinic tradition identified Beth-El with the later location of the Temple Mount.

88. For Jesus' association with the temple, see Brown, *According to John (i–xii)*, 90–91.

exalted or glorified in his resurrection (cf. Isa 52:13).[89] By evoking the Servant, the evangelist once again reinforces the concept that Jesus performs the interrelated functions of the Akedah, *tôdāh*, *tāmîd*, and Passover sacrifices. It will be remembered that some rabbinic texts depicted Isaac as sacrificed and then restored to life by God. According to *Pirqe R. El.* 31, Isaac was raised to life by the voice that stayed Abraham's hand after dying of terror while bound to the altar. *Tg.* 1 Chr 21:15, as discussed in the last chapter, states that Isaac's ashes lay on the altar but that Isaac was then raised back to life. The difference between Jesus and Isaac, for the Fourth Evangelist, is that Jesus is the *perfect* sacrifice—a characteristic also predicated of Isaac but which John rejects.[90] For John, Jesus is not simply Isaac *redivivus*; the intent rather is to show by the Isaac parallels that Jesus perfectly performs and fulfills the functions attributed to Isaac in some contemporary circles, to which the sources we have discussed to this point bear witness. In the next chapter, we will take up the idea that there would have been a perceived need to provide an alternative to Jerusalem temple sacrifice as it could be prone to errors that would render the sacrifices invalid. This too would have been a concern for the Fourth Gospel in the aftermath of the Jerusalem temple's destruction.

The two angels at Jesus' empty tomb have drawn much scholarly interest. Of course the Synoptics share a tradition of the presence of angels at the empty tomb; but there the angels typically make the announcement that Jesus has been raised. In this case, as Culpepper states, they "announce nothing"; so one must ask what purpose they serve.[91] An intriguing answer is offered by Robert Fortna, who sees in these angels the fulfillment of the promise in John 1:51: that Nathanael (representative of Israel) will see "the angels of God ascending and descending on the Son of Man,"[92] a clear allusion to Gen 28:10–22, the account of the "ladder"—or, more accurately, "stairway"—seen by Jacob in a dream at Bethel. Jesus has already been manifested as Son of Man on the cross, but it is only with the resurrection that the meaning of the crucifixion event is fully revealed. Now, the burial shelf where Jesus' corpse had lain forms an image of the "ladder" of the Genesis passage.

---

89. Nielsen, "Lamb of God," 245–49.
90. Rosenberg, "Suffering Servant," 387–88.
91. Culpepper, *Gospel and Letters*, 241.
92. Fortna, *Fourth Gospel*, 192. Ashton disagrees (*Understanding*, 482).

Also located on the shelf are the vacant grave clothes, which are not mentioned when Mary Magdalene peers into the tomb but only when Peter enters it later. As mentioned briefly above, John alone among the Gospels includes the detail of the separate head covering, which is lying "wrapped" and by itself. The statement that the grave "bands" or "strips" are made of *linen* (ὀθονίοις, John 19:40; 20:5–7) is reminiscent of the material of the high priest's vestment (Exod 28:5ff. βύσσος, LXX) as Jesus' χιτών had been at the crucifixion.[93] Taken together, the mention of linen and of a separate head wrapping may be a reference to the vestments of not just a priest but of the high priest, who alone wore a "turban" on his head in a manner of being "wrapped."[94]

John 19:41 clearly states that Jesus is entombed in a garden. When Mary Magdalene first encounters the risen Jesus, after the departure of Peter and the Beloved Disciple, she mistakes him for "the gardener" (20:15b). The allusions to Eden denote not only newness of creation but also the temple: through references to the primordial creation, we are brought back to John 1, to the λόγος who "pitched his tent" or "tabernacled" (ἐσκήνωσεν) among humankind, eliciting a link to the wilderness tabernacle of Exodus.[95] Hence, Jesus has been the temple in John through his life, beyond his death, and into his resurrected state, meaning that he will eternally be the temple. Jesus' resurrected body, never again susceptible to destruction (unlike the Jerusalem temple building), assures his eternal presence in the midst of believers.[96] Thus, he is the tabernacle in Israel's midst. This is *contra* the work of Mary Coloe, who has argued that Jesus is the temple only during

---

93. The difference in Greek terms between the NT text and the LXX is slight, with ὀθόνιον signifying simply "linen" and βύσσος signifying "fine linen." This does not indicate a distinction in meaning that would preclude an identification of Jesus' burial cloths with the vestments of the high priest. In the Synoptics (Matt 27:59; Mark 14:51–52; 15:46; Luke 23:53), Jesus' grave clothes are referred to as σινδών, specifically indicating a purpose of burial. Only in Luke is the term βύσσος employed, and then not in the burial account but in the parable of the "Rich Man and Lazarus" (Luke 16:19). Luke changes the term for Jesus' burial cloths from σινδών to ὀθόνια in 24:12, the only Synoptic parallel to John 20:5–7, in which Peter and "the other disciple" see the ὀθόνια in Jesus' tomb. It could be argued, therefore, that John is not specifically employing ὀθόνιον to identify Jesus as high priest, but may instead be working from a Lukan source. However, the Johannine addition of the head wrapping is significant, and as Salvoni suggests, may argue in favor of a high-priestly identification taken together with the term ὀθόνιον. Salvoni, "Resurrection Proof," 72–76.

94. Salvoni, "Resurrection Proof," 72–76.

95. Köstenberger, "Second Temple," 232.

96. Nielsen, "Lamb," 246.

his lifetime and that after his death the community becomes the temple.[97] Rather, the Gospel's audience is *Israel* with the temple of the risen Jesus in its midst, just as the ancient Israelites possessed the dwelling of God in their midst in the form of the wilderness Tabernacle.[98] As Thompson states regarding the prolepsis of Jesus' raised body in John 2:21, "the text does not say that if the Jerusalem temple is destroyed it will be replaced by *another* temple, but rather that if the temple of Jesus' body is destroyed, it will be raised up in three days."[99] In this way, "John presents Jesus as the indestructible eschatological temple."[100] Reinforcing the ongoing necessity for a material place of worship, Thompson adds, "The argument in John is not that Jesus' followers do not need a temple, but rather that in him they have a temple which cannot be destroyed."[101] It is still imperative that there be a place for sacrificial worship. We will discuss the issue of worship space in John in greater depth in the next chapter.

Temple as Eden

Several scholars have noted that the Jerusalem Temple's design was meant to evoke the Garden of Eden[102]—a microcosmic representation of the natural world, indeed of the entire universe, in its originally-created perfection, when man and woman walked in friendship with God and in harmony with all of creation. Indeed, the Eden account in Genesis has been interpreted as a view of "an archetypal sanctuary, that is a place where God dwells and where man should worship him."[103] Towards the end of the first century CE, the *Apoc. Ab.* makes an intriguing reference to the Jerusalem Temple. Observing the earth from a heavenly vantage point, the patriarch Abraham

---

97. See e.g., Coloe, "Dwelling," 244; Coloe, *God Dwells*; Coloe, *Household*; Coloe, "Raising"; Coloe, "Temple Imagery."

98. Thompson, "New Temple," 344, 346–48, 351.

99. Thompson, "Reflections on Worship," 267. Emphasis in original.

100. Ibid. See also Lee, "Spirit of Truth," 284–86; Kinzer, "Temple Christology," 455.

101. Thompson, "Reflections on Worship," 267.

102. Barker, *Gate*, ch. 2; Bloch-Smith, "King of Glory," 18, 24–25; Chalvon-Demersay, "Symbolisme," 168–69, 171–75; Fletcher-Louis, "Dissolution," 123–24; Himmelfarb, "Garden," 68; Hurowitz, "Exalted House," 80, 87–88; Levenson, "Temple," 282–85, 297–98; Stager, "Jerusalem," 38–47, 66; Wenham, "Sanctuary Symbolism," 19–25.

103. Wenham, "Sanctuary Symbolism," 19.

sees "the likeness of heaven and the things that were therein" (21:2).[104] The following passage, 21:3–22:1, describes the natural world, including "the garden of Eden and its fruits" (21:6). Philo assigns cosmic significance and symbolism to the vestments of the Jewish high priest in *Mos.* II.117–126, affirming the importance of Temple worship and the Jewish festival calendar in the order of creation. In this passage, Philo associates each part of the high priest's garb with some aspect of the natural world, including "the stones at the breast" of the priestly ephod, which, for Philo, signify the zodiac. By associating the high priest's garments with the created cosmos in this way, Philo makes a connection between cosmic order and priestly function in the Temple cult. In *1 En.* 14:8–25, Enoch travels to, and is given an extensive tour of, the heavenly temple, and there is a clear connection between the heavenly throne of God in 14:18–20 and the earthly throne of 25:3–5, a high mountain upon which God will eventually "visit the earth," execute judgment, and dwell forever.[105] The "mountain" (= Zion/the earthly Temple) will support the throne of God (the Holy of Holies in the restored Temple) and provide access to the tree of life (through proper observance of ritual and worship practices). Most significantly, "Like Ezekiel, the author of the Book of the Watchers transplants Eden to the Temple—in the eschatological future. At the eschaton, God's redemption of Israel will include the restoration of all creation, and the resulting new creation will be characterized by water, as in Ezek 47:1–12; Zech 14:8; Joel 3:18; Gen 2:10ff; and several passages in 2 Baruch."[106] In John's Passion narrative, the water that pours from Jesus' side when pierced by the lance evokes Ezekiel's vision of the restored temple, as mentioned above; but it is also indicative of the waters flowing from that temple, which themselves represent the primordial waters/river of Eden.[107] Hence, Jesus as temple is also Jesus as Eden, the "place" in which humanity encounters God, communicates with God, and is in full union with God. Against other possible ideas of a restored temple that may have circulated at the time of the Fourth Gospel's composition, John presents the "restored temple," a perfect embodiment of Eden, as the person of Jesus, the place of worship.

---

104. Rubinkiewicz, *Apocalypse of Abraham*.
105. Himmelfarb, "Garden," 69.
106. Um, *Temple Christology*, 63–64, 66–67.
107. See Kinzer, "Temple Christology," 449.

Summary and Conclusions

The fact that John's crucifixion scene is saturated with Passover imagery argues largely in favor of Jesus' being the Passover lamb whose voluntary, obedient suffering and death liberates his followers from sin and from sin's consequence, death, in precisely the same way that Isaac's voluntary self-offering brought about atonement and liberation from death for his descendants through the Passover and the Exodus.[108] Indeed, John's Passion narrative is entirely a cultic scene.[109] Each component of Jesus' arrest, trial, and death combine to paint a dramatic image of him as the Passover lamb.[110]

---

108. See Dennis, *Jesus' Death*, 355; Metzner, *Verständnis*, 147–48, 152, 156–58, 355.
109. Wick, *Gottesdienste*, 330.
110. Knöppler, *Sühne*, 248.

4

Relocation of Worship Space

From Institution to Person

THE CHIEF ARGUMENT OF this thesis is that the Fourth Gospel was composed in response to the aftermath of the Jerusalem temple's destruction, particularly as part of the religious disorientation of Jesus-believers, whether Jewish or Gentile, who could no longer worship at that temple nor, due to the exclusivity of the worship of the God of Israel, frequent Roman temples.[1] John presents Jesus as temple through Jesus' identity and function as sacrifice, in order to provide a place of worship for these believers, as this necessity for a locus of God's presence (the "Glory") and for a mechanism of atonement remained.[2] Hence, the Gospel was not composed as a polemic directed toward "Jews" by the new religion of "Christianity," but rather was created within the cultural-religious framework of an intra-Jewish debate that attempted to answer the question: *Where do we now worship?* This view of John throws into question the idea of a "Johannine (Christian) Community," since the Gospel would have been intended for a much wider audience as part of the worship question.[3] Rather than being a matter of ethnic categories (Jew vs. Gentile) or of Judaism vs. Christianity, John's polemic is a matter of intra-Jewish liturgical debate: In the absence of the Jerusalem temple, what is the correct way to conduct Jewish worship?

---

1. Köstenberger ("Second Temple," 235) notes that the Jerusalem temple's destruction "left worship of Jesus at least temporarily without operational alternative." While Ullucci agrees (*Animal Sacrifice*, 134–35), he concludes that this situation removed worship from sacrifice to text, rather than (as we argue) driving the Jesus-sect to find a new location for sacrifice.

2. Metzner, *Verständnis*, 135.

3. Köstenberger has argued convincingly in this line throughout his essay "Destruction of the Second Temple," although he still unfortunately categorizes the Gospel as being addressed to "Christians" (esp. 216, 220).

Josephus attributes the fall of Jerusalem and the temple to the "fratricidal hatred" of Jews amongst themselves, an interpretation of events not unlike the ancient prophetic critiques that had been leveled against the temple institution by Jeremiah and Ezekiel; only later would Church Fathers attribute these events in terms of the sinfulness of the Jewish people as a whole for committing "deicide."[4] This study, however, suggests that John takes a unique approach. The oblique reference to the temple's destruction in John 2:19–22 indicates that the Fourth Evangelist too was attempting to answer this problematic question, and the solution offers itself in a shift of worship from the destroyed temple not to a rebuilt temple, but to the person of Jesus.[5]

"Mobile Sanctity"[6]

Even before the writing of John, the sect that produced the Dead Sea Scrolls had created an alternative locus of worship by defining their own community as the temple, the true dwelling of the divine Presence, in light of their conviction that the Jerusalem temple was deficient. This shift of worship space occurred while the temple was still standing. A similar concept can be found in Paul's writings, with the difference that Paul does not seek to change the locus of worship from temple institution to Jesus-communities but to *expand* or "de-centralize" the temple's holiness to those communities, so that the communities became "satellite" temples.[7] Though Paul and the

---

4. See Hadas-Lebel, "La Prise," 159–60.

5. See Grelot, *Les Juifs*, 108–9; 175–78; Köstenberger, "Second Temple," 227–28. Though Grelot is correct in his basic claim that the "reorganization of Judaism" after 70 played a large role in the composition of the Fourth Gospel, he addresses the concept according to the "Johannine Community" trope in which the "Christians" of Jewish origin were expelled from the synagogues by the Judean religious authorities. He also claims that John's criticism is not directed toward the "Jews" of Jesus' own day, but those authoritative Ἰουδαῖοι who were at the time of the Gospel's composition responsible for expelling "Christians of Jewish origin" from the synagogues. Although Grelot is correct in his insight that the Jerusalem temple's destruction was essential to the purpose of the Fourth Gospel, and that the result was a relocation of worship from the Jerusalem temple to the person of Jesus, his argument still hinges on the "Christian Johannine Community" vs. "the Jews," rather than seeing this relocation as essentially Jewish, maintaining the Jewish concept of a location in which God's glory dwelt and which, thereby, was the appropriate location of sacrificial worship maintaining relationship with the God of Israel.

6. This term is borrowed from Boustan, "Dislocation."

7. Troost-Cramer, "De-centralizing."

Qumran sect differed in that the latter claimed to replace the Jerusalem temple while the former made no such claim, both in separate ways closely fit a concept of "mobile sanctity." Thus the idea of either removing or dispersing/expanding the holiness of the temple into other locations, thereby rendering those other locations fit and appropriate places of worship, was current even before the writing of the Fourth Gospel.[8]

In the late first century, the idea of "mobile sanctity" became even more pronounced, as the work of Ra'anan S. Boustan has shown.[9] The spatial aspect of worship remained in Judaism even after the Jerusalem temple no longer existed, and "Blood cult remained the dominant paradigm for religious ritual and piety throughout late antiquity, providing the ritual logic and symbolic idiom for the novel modes of ritual-liturgic action that came to characterize Judaism and Christianity."[10] The temple makes prominent appearances in post-70 New Testament canonical texts, such as the statement in Luke 24:53 that the apostles after Jesus' ascension "were continually in the temple," and throughout Acts that the temple was a prominent place for the preaching of the early kerygma.[11] While these portrayals may or may not be historically factual in every particular, they show that the temple remained prominent enough in the minds of early Jesus-believers to merit much attention in the Luke-Acts diptych.

The rabbis in the aftermath of the events of 70 CE did not, as is too frequently claimed, carry out an "agenda of supplanting the physical cult with an edifice of learned discourse and pious prayer. Rather, [the rabbinic] texts are marked by a palpable tension between appropriating the Temple cult to augment hermeneutically oriented rabbinic authority and prestige, on the one hand, and preserving sensual experience as a privileged site of religious meaning and authority, on the other."[12] The Mishnah, for example, proposes that "the study of the laws of sacrifice was tantamount to the actual performance of sacrifice in the Temple," demonstrating that performance of sacrifice, in some form, was still considered to be

---

8. Steven Fine (*Holy Place*) has shown that synagogues or προσευχαί were believed to possess the same level of holiness as the temple quite early, before or contemporary with Paul. See also Swarz, "Judaism," 314.

9. Boustan, "Dislocation," 135–46. See also Boustan, "Confounding," 265–87.

10. Stroumsa, *End of Sacrifice*; Boustan, "Dislocation," 138; Biale, "Blood," 45. The quote is from Boustan.

11. Acts 2:46; 3:1–3, 8; 5:20–21, 25; 21:26; 22:17.

12. Boustan, "Dislocation," 138.

essential.[13] The rabbinic evidence features descriptions and portrayals of the temple vessels in settings outside of the temple after those vessels had been taken in triumph by Rome, indicating that the reverence for these sacred utensils continued even after their displacement from the temple (which displacement rendered them unable to be actually used in worship praxis). Hence, their sanctity did not depend upon their location or even upon their ability to be employed in worship; they are spoken of in these sources as if they possess sanctity in their own right.[14] After the temple's destruction, there was a sense that its sacredness had become dislocated or "loosed" and *mobile*, no longer confined to a particular location but spatial nonetheless, as sanctity seemed to "travel with" the temple vessels. Cultic emphasis therefore remained, apparently unabated, at least for a time. Perhaps the continued existence of the temple vessels with their innate sanctity was what allowed the post-70 CE rabbis to characterize prayer, almsgiving, ethical living, and Torah study as possessing a sacrificial character: these actions would have been in some way sanctified by the fact that the temple vessels still existed somewhere in the world.

In addition to the continuing emphasis on sacrifice and cultic references in the rabbis, early martyrologies also provide evidence that sacrifice—specifically, blood sacrifice—continued to be the primary paradigm for describing worship and relation to God.[15] Laura Nasrallah has discussed at length the phenomenon of early Christians' identity being very much based on sacrifice, and that sacrifice served in the post-temple period to differentiate Christians from both Jews and Greco-Roman polytheists. The early Christian texts that Nasrallah discusses, chief among them the martyrologies of Polycarp and Ignatius of Antioch, depict Christians persecuted for essentially refusing to adopt Roman worship as sacrifices themselves.[16] Such texts posit that Jews and Romans alike had sacrifice all wrong, and make a point of the absence of animal sacrifice in the worship praxis of Jesus-believers, while emphasizing in sacrificial terms the passion and death of Christ as well as the (sacrificial) suffering of martyrs caused by their

---

13. Swarz, "Ritual Theory," 298.

14. Boustan ("Dislocation," 145) discusses the phenomenon of visiting the captured temple vessels on display in Rome, and rabbinic texts describing the viewing of these vessels by laypeople, as "almost akin to a theophany."

15. Boustan, "Confounding," 265. See also Ullucci, *Animal Sacrifice*, 82. For the relation of early Christian martyrologies to sacrificial ideology, see Nasrallah, "Embarrassment," 145.

16. Nasrallah, "Embarrassment," 151.

allegiance to him.[17] Sacrificial language permeates these ancient writings. Considering what we have discussed regarding the Fourth Gospel's passion narrative as an illustration of sacrifice and temple, the claim that the earliest Christians had no sacrifice and no altars is difficult to defend. John's Gospel clearly shows Jesus as sacrifice and dwelling of the divine Glory, and the cross as the altar where the perfect atonement sacrifice takes place.

John's Worship Shift as Anti-imperial Polemic

In his book *John and Empire*, Warren Carter argues extensively that John was written primarily as anti-Roman polemic, with the goal of juxtaposing the Kingdom of God against the Kingdom of Rome.[18] Carter does not place much emphasis on the temple, focusing instead on the economic realities of the Roman Empire and arguing that John presents Jesus and the Kingdom of God reversing the damage and death-dealing caused by Rome. Where Rome brings want, the Kingdom of God, represented and put into action by Jesus, brings abundance (exemplified by the Cana wedding, the feeding of the multitude, and Jesus' claims to be water and food).[19] Where Rome brings death, the Kingdom of God brings life (exemplified by the raising of Lazarus).[20] Temple and worship also form part of the picture; but Carter, working on the basis of the tradition that John was composed in Ephesus, argues that it was specifically the pagan temples of that city that the author of John places as a foil to the Jesus-community.[21] The Gospel's references to Jesus as temple (e.g., John 2:19a, 21) "suggest a strong disqualification of the temple of Artemis and of the Sebastoi as places of legitimate encounter with the divine for Jesus-believers, distancing Jesus-believers from them."[22] Carter's working premise that John was written in Ephesus may be argued

---

17. Ibid., 146–49.
18. See also Heyman, *Power*, 145.
19. Carter, *Empire*, 220–27.
20. Ibid., 271–72.

21. Carter (*Empire*, 257–64) agrees with Mary Coloe that the community is portrayed as temple. According to Carter, this identification makes sense in terms of John's overarching concern against Rome, and the evangelist portrays the Jesus-community as temple obeying Jesus' words against the idea of the entire empire as a temple honoring the emperor by obeying his commands.

22. Ibid., 262.

against; but even if the Gospel were written elsewhere Carter's essential point holds true, as temples to Roman deities were ubiquitous fixtures throughout the empire. No matter where John was written, Roman temples would have been prominent features of everyday life. The essence of Carter's argument, that John presents a temple that is an alternative to Roman worship, is correct. We must add, however, that the *Jerusalem* temple is also in view: even if John were composed in the Diaspora, the Jerusalem temple would still have been a major presence in the lives of Jesus-believers among those communities, as we have discussed.[23] With that temple gone, Jesus-believers throughout the Roman Empire were left with few options for where they could worship. There was the option of going the way of Jamnia; but it is possible that some, or many, Jesus-believers rejected this path precisely because they may have viewed the rabbis' identification of prayer, Torah study, and almsgiving as sacrifice as inadequate successors to the temple's sacrificial system. Hence, John rejects both Roman worship and the form that "mainline" Judaism was taking after 70 CE, proposing an alternative sacrifice/worship space in the crucified and resurrected Jesus.

John's relocation of worship space to the person of Jesus is neither unique nor surprising within this milieu. Indeed, if the phenomenon of sacralizing spaces beyond the temple enjoyed a healthy existence while the temple was present (as in Qumran and Paul), all the more would this become an absolute necessity in the temple's absence after 70 CE, when John was composed.[24] This religio-cultural situation gave rise to a widespread reassessment of worship, a "systematic discourse about ritual," which Michael D. Swarz identifies as "ancient ritual theory."[25]

Ancient Ritual Theory

Kathryn McClymond has shown that a major aspect of the post-temple climate consisted of the rabbinic school, particularly as expressed in the Mishnah, critiquing the former sacrificial system on the grounds that the rites performed in the temple were subject to error and that no sacrifice was guaranteed to be performed perfectly. In particular, the opportunity for error lay most in the blood manipulations, which if not done exactly according to specifications would render a sacrifice null and void and result

---

23. See Köstenberger, "Second Temple," 217–18.
24. Ibid., 222–23 (citing Davies).
25. Swarz, "Ritual Theory," esp. 295–97, 316.

in terrible spiritual/covenant consequences for the offending priest (and presumably for the people also, especially where the atonement sacrifices were concerned).[26] Such acknowledgment that temple ritual was prone to human mistakes, and that thereby the covenant relationship with God might be placed in peril, reveals a struggle to define the most right and true location for, and manner of, worship. This is highly relevant to understanding the portrayal of Jesus as sacrifice in the Fourth Gospel. Ultimately, John and the rabbis were dealing with exactly the same problem.

> Over the course of the extended rabbinic debates regarding ritual practice, the text unseats the priest as the central agent (by focusing on his errors and keeping his voice out of the conversation) and replaces him with the rabbi. The priest repeatedly fails to fulfill his role as ritual agent by failing to manipulate the blood successfully. He dis-authorizes himself. Ultimately, this ritual discourse reorients the reader. Over the course of a review of the Mishnaic material the reader is repositioned within a tannaitic system, rather than a cultic one, and the sacred of the Temple is replaced with the sacred of the rabbinic academy.[27]

McClymond's insight here regarding the Mishnah's critique of the priestly role is most significant. The Mishnah's concern was specifically with the ways in which the blood manipulations—the high priest's major role—could go wrong, and that accordingly no sacrifice could be guaranteed to be valid; therefore (according to this Mishnaic passage) the system was replaced by the rabbinic school (although, as we have seen above, the rabbinic school was still considered in sacrificial/worship space categories).[28] The Fourth Gospel argues on a similar basis; but instead of continuing the worship intent of the error-prone temple rites by re-locating them to intellectual pursuits, Torah study, and the rabbinic schools, the Gospel finds continuance of sacrificial worship in the person of Jesus, whose self-offering John presents as the only sacrifice that had been performed perfectly and who was the only priest who could possibly be free of error. If the issue was blood manipulation, as McClymond convincingly shows, then in the Fourth Gospel Jesus, as priest, manipulates the sacrificial blood—foreshadowed in the Cana wine and actualized when his own blood is poured

---

26. McClymond, "Spilled Blood," 237–42, 247.

27. Ibid., 247–48.

28. For the primacy of blood manipulations in the high priest's role, see also Swarz, "Ritual Theory," 302.

out upon the altar of the cross—perfectly and without even the possibility of error. The passion narrative, as discussed above in chapter 3, would therefore demonstrate that Jesus had succeeded where the temple priests had failed, and that Jesus also claims the authority of which the temple priesthood had divested itself through ignorance, political entanglements, economic gain, or a host of other factors that would disqualify them from liturgical service.[29] This is not unlike what the Qumran sect had done. In the debate about where to worship, the Fourth Gospel claims to provide in Jesus the only location in which sacrifice had been offered perfectly. The rabbinic academies transferred the locus of worship to Torah study; John shifted that locus from the temple to Jesus without changing the meaning of sacrificial worship, but only altering the way in which it is done.[30]

John's Jesus-Temple and Spatial Theory

In his book *Gathered Around Jesus*, Eric C. Stewart presents a case that the Gospel of Mark portrays Jesus as an alternative worship space. While it is not the task of this thesis to assess the merits of the argument as it pertains to Mark, Stewart's work is instructive for our purposes.

Spatial theory holds that space a.) does not possess intrinsic meaning but is *assigned* meaning as "the result of social and cultural activity"; and b.) reflects and enforces the power structures of the society that creates the space.[31] One example of the latter in the ancient Mediterranean would be the Jerusalem temple with its degrees of "graded holiness." The various courts, locating groups in proximity to the Holy of Holies according to their religion, nationality, or gender, illustrated not only the power of the divine Presence but also the status of the priests. Even within the priesthood, the spatial division of Holy Place from Holy of Holies and the criterion of entering the latter as the unique prerogative of the high priest is evidence of the assigning and use of space to define power. Power is at its peak within the Holy of Holies, and accordingly the high priest with access to it is in the highest power position; conversely, power decreases with distance from this structure, with the lowest-power groups and individuals located at the farthest court (the Court of the Gentiles).

---

29. See Derrett, *Victim*, 143; Lizorkin-Eyzenberg, *Jewish Gospel*, 17.
30. Ibid., 305–6, 316; Wick, *Gottesdienste*, 329, 332.
31. Ibid., 44, 51–55.

Stewart points out that these characteristics of space apply not only to human-built structures and institutions but also to geography. Geographical locales are subject to the same culturally-assigned meanings and power associations as are buildings, giving rise to "place-myths."[32] "Historical geography" therefore views geography too as a "socially-produced space," and examining geography in this light accordingly becomes a *social* science.[33] An example of this would be the traditional claims of Jerusalem and Mount Zion to be the place assigned directly by God to be the dwelling of the divine Presence.[34]

We may apply spatial theory to the Fourth Gospel in terms of a.) the Jerusalem temple and b.) the Gospel's Judea-Galilee rivalry. In re-locating the place of sacrifice to the person of Jesus, space and its accompanying power are shifted. Jesus is the worship space. Power is thereby stripped from the Jerusalem temple and, by association, from Judea itself. The new power space being Jesus, and the only geographical locales that accept him being Samaria and Galilee, power is accordingly re-located to those geographical spaces and, by extension, to those within their populations who worship at/in the Jesus-temple.

The situation in John is this:

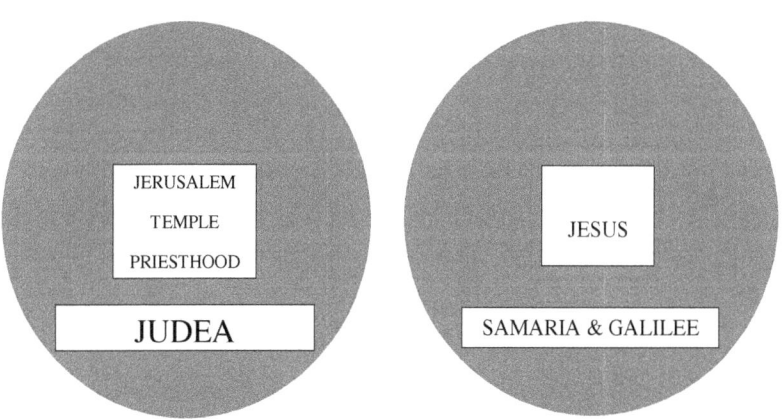

Figure 2

32. Ibid., 55–57.
33. Ibid., 38–39, 48.
34. As e.g., in Deut 12:5, 11, 13–14, 18, 21, 26; 14:23–25; 15:20; 16:2, 6; and Neh 1:9.

Each respective geographical space has its worship space within it and, indeed, derives its power claims from that worship space. In John, since the worship space is Jesus, power is removed from Jerusalem/Judea and situated in Samaria/Galilee, since the latter geographical region possesses Jesus, the true sacrifice and temple, as its worship space. John counters the ancient Judean understanding of God choosing Jerusalem/Mount Zion as divine habitation and worship space with Jesus as the alternative divine habitation and worship space.

Perhaps the most significant aspect of Stewart's work that can shed some light on the Judea-Israel rivalry in John is a discussion of zone theory. Where texts and maps work together to portray space in a way that suits the interests of the authors or cartographers, zone theory in the Greco-Roman world held that "one's place of origin played a significant role in determining one's character."[35] This is nowhere more evident in John than in Nathanael's comment "Can anything good come out of Nazareth?" (John 1:46). However, the idea that a person's place of origin determined his or her character appears throughout the remainder of the Fourth Gospel in the form of recurring debates regarding Jesus' place of origin. The Messiah is said to not come from Galilee while Bethlehem is brought up and rejected as Jesus' place of origin (7:41–42); the religious authorities claim that "no prophet is to arise from Galilee" (7:52) and inform the "man born blind" that they do not know where Jesus is from (9:29). Johannine irony is in evidence on those occasions when the crowds and/or authorities claim to know where Jesus is from, and that no one would know the Messiah's origins when he appears (7:27). However, Jesus' true origin—from heaven—has been made clear to the Gospel's audience in the first verses of the Prologue: the audience knows that Jesus has come down from heaven, from God. This knowledge renders absurd the debates regarding Jesus' geographical place of birth. If, in the world in which John was composed, a person's place of origin determined his or her character, then Jesus' character is determined by his origin from heaven—not from Bethlehem or from Galilee. In this light, Nathanael's comment "Can anything good come from Nazareth?" takes on something of the nature of a "thesis statement" for the Gospel, a major indication that the Gospel is going to challenge ideas of space. The issue is not an ironic statement of Jesus' origin in Nazareth, but of the Gospel's theme that he (ultimately) does not come from Nazareth at all. That is why Jesus answers Nathanael that the latter "will see the angels of

---

35. Stewart, *Gathered*, 95–96, 99–100.

God ascending and descending upon the Son of Man" (1:51): Jesus is telling Nathanael about his true place of origin.

The same approach can be taken in examining the Judea-Israel opposition in John. According to zone theory, people from Judea would have a specific character, and people from Galilee/Samaria would have a different, specific character.[36] The character applied to each in John is Judeans = hostile to Jesus, Galileans/Samaritans = friendly to Jesus.[37] We might expand this characterization to Judeans = those who worship at the Jerusalem temple; Galileans/Samarians = those who worship in the absence of the Jerusalem temple, at least a majority of the time. The characteristic of Judeans as those who worship at the Jerusalem temple is directly related to their characteristic as those who are hostile to Jesus: they are hostile to him precisely because of their connection to the Jerusalem temple. By the same logic, the Galileans/Samaritans are friendly toward Jesus precisely due to their characteristic as those who worship outside of the Jerusalem temple. In fact, the evangelist re-locates the latter's point of origin to heaven, sharing Jesus' own origin: they are those who are "born from above" (3:3, 7) and "born of the spirit" (3:6, 8); "God is spirit" (4:24), therefore the origin of those who accept Jesus as worship space is also from God. Those who do not accept Jesus as worship space are from Judea—Ἰουδαῖοι.

Hence, John reverses notions of spatial power and status: Whereas most adherents of the Israelite faith viewed the center of the inhabited world (οἰκουμένη[38]) as Jerusalem by virtue of the temple, John shifts the locus of power to the lower-status region of Galilee and the despised region of Samaria. In the conversation with the Samaritan woman in John 4, both concepts of cultic worship, Judean and Samaritan alike, become focused on the "kind and manner of worship revealed by" the presence of Jesus.[39] Whereas worship for both Judeans and Samaritans had formerly been "localized," in Jesus worship now becomes "personified"; in the same way that the person of Jesus takes over the functions of the Jerusalem temple and of the Gerizim

---

36. Though such distinctions are distasteful to modern sensibilities, zone theory deals with categories perceived by the ancients. I do not address zone theory here in order to make an argument for how we should view people-groups today, but to support my argument that such categorizations, being in view in the ancient Near East, would have informed the Johannine rivalry between Judea/Ἰουδαῖοι and Samaria/Galilee/Ἰσραήλ.

37. This is discussed in Meeks, "Galilee and Judea," although Meeks makes no reference specifically to "zone theory" in his discussion.

38. On Jerusalem as οἰκουμένη, see Stewart, *Gathered*, 62, 80, 104–6.

39. Kinzer, "Temple Christology," 448; Frühwald-König, *Tempel*, 138.

holy site, he also fulfills the functions of other holy locations throughout the Gospel (as seen in the healing at the Bethesda pool in John 5) and of the holy festivals (Tabernacles, Dedication, and most especially Passover).[40]

Here, we may also see how this spatial scheme applies to John's polemic against Rome. Greeks and Romans alike had based their claims to dominance on their geographical position in the οἰκουμένη.[41] Josephus, however, posits that the Israelite territories as a whole took centrality over Rome's claims to the centrality of the city of Rome; Judean territory even occupied a small part of that city in the presence of the temple vessels that were kept there after the temple's destruction in 70 CE: where the temple vessels were, there was Judean territory.[42] Hence, we understand that "Judean territory" is defined by where worship takes place, similar to our discussion of the Cana wedding above, in which it was claimed that the presence of jars and water for "Judean" purification rites effectively "brought" the Jerusalem temple into Galilee. The Fourth Gospel takes a similar approach in defining territory according to worship, but shifts the emphasis from geographic locale to a person: the locus of worship, and thereby of power, lies in the person of Jesus.

It was not uncommon in the Roman era to treat a person as a "geographic" center. The case in point for our study is the treatment of the Roman emperor, who was defined as the center of the empire.[43] In a very real way, the emperor *was* Rome, and brought Rome with him wherever he traveled; if the emperor visited a certain city, then Rome itself had come to that city. Occasionally, the same view was taken of teachers and philosophers, who would be a "center" that traveled throughout the οἰκουμένη to bring and gather wisdom, and to which people would come to "seek advice and favors" and/or to attach themselves to the teacher/philosopher's lifestyle.[44] "As holy men, philosophers represent[ed] fluid sacred space"; sometimes, these figures even "displaced the emperor as the symbolic center of the empire."[45] Josephus's locating "Judean territory" in Rome because of the

---

40. Frühwald-König, *Tempel*, 137; 172–73, 215.

41. Stewart, *Gathered*, 101, 106.

42. Ibid., 105. This is rather similar to the construct of a nation's embassy constituting that nation's "soil" even though the embassy is located within the territory of a foreign land.

43. Ibid., 171–77.

44. Ibid., 172–73.

45. Ibid., 172–73, 176.

temple vessels held there and the Roman view of the emperor as a "mobile Rome" show that for both Jews and Romans, sacred space/power space was flexible, not static. Therefore, we should not be surprised when the Fourth Gospel portrays Jesus as a "geographical" center, a locus of power. However, John's use of this phenomenon takes power away from Rome and the emperor equally as from Jerusalem and its religious authorities, claiming that Jesus, whose origin is from God/heaven, is the center. Essentially, John's Jesus is "mobile heaven."

The Gospels are no exception to the concept that texts also "create their own conceptions of space."[46] What the Gospels say about worship space, whether synagogue or temple, reflect their authors' attitudes toward, and meaning attributed to, those spaces. According to Stewart, what synagogues and temples were historically is of less import in understanding the Gospels than what any particular Gospel *says about* synagogues and temples. There were many anti-Jerusalem-temple movements, among them the Qumran community and the groups that built the temples at Elephantine and Leontopolis.[47] These sects arose specifically from a debate—and doubt—regarding the Jerusalem temple's legitimacy.[48] There was also a sense of "ongoing Exile," which took two main forms: 1.) The Babylonian Exile had never truly ended and the people were still in exile; or 2.) There had only been a partial return from the Exile.[49] The Qumran sect was of the latter belief, claiming that, since the temple was not legitimate, the Exile was ongoing and would only end with the eschaton, the Messianic age.[50] The Fourth Gospel claims that this age has arrived because of a spatial orientation to Jesus, emphasized in the Gospel's portrayal of Jesus as Passover lamb bringing about a new deliverance, as had been done in the Exodus.

---

46. Ibid., 137.
47. See Köstenberger, "Second Temple," 219.
48. Stewart, *Gathered*, 141.
49. Ibid., 168.
50. Ibid., 169.

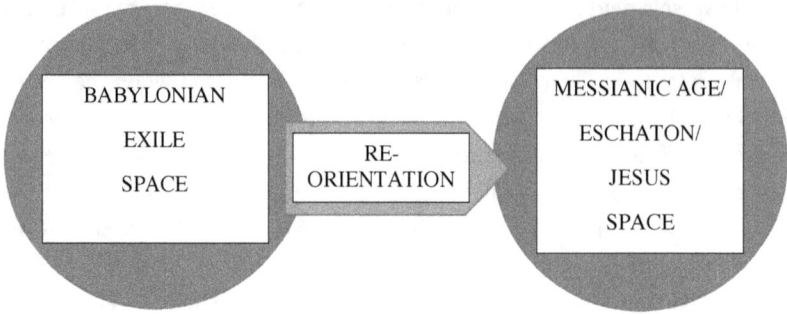

Figure 3

Given that John equates Jesus with Galilee/Samaria, we can safely propose that the Gospel places Judea and the Jerusalem temple on the left side of the diagram, defining Jerusalem and its temple, and by extension all of Judea, as (continuing) Exile space. Galilee/Samaria, by contrast, is the eschatological space in which the Messiah, Jesus, forms the new center, which is characterized by liberation.

These concepts of space apply not only to the material realm, but to metaphysical realms as well. According to Stewart, "Roman architecture and art sometimes mimicked the shape of the cosmos" as a microcosm.[51] The work of Margaret Barker has shown that the design of the Jerusalem temple functioned in much the same way.[52] We have seen in chapter 2 above that Philo had assigned cosmological significance to the Jerusalem temple as well as to the high priest. Jewish thought had anticipated a new cosmos at the eschaton.[53] In the eschatology presented by the Fourth Gospel, Jesus is the "new" center of this apocalyptic cosmos, the place where heaven and earth meet, a space to which the Synoptics refer as the "Kingdom of God."[54] The mention of Jesus' χιτών, recalling the high-priestly garment that mirrored the firmament, solidifies this identification and reinforces the crucifixion scene as the eschatological temple event.

It is the overt Passover imagery of Jesus' crucifixion that provides "direct proclamations of the change in kind of worship": in a post-70 CE context, John's Jesus has replaced the defunct temple institution and its

---

51. Ibid., 118.
52. Barker, *Gate*, chs. 4 and 5.
53. Stewart, *Gathered*, 122–25.
54. Ibid., 127; Wick, *Gottesdienste*, 329.

functions, and thereby represents that institution for the Johannine community.[55] Therefore, John does not claim the invalidity of temple worship; temple and sacrifice are still very much in view, and are given legitimacy in John by the clear portrayal of Jesus as place of sacrifice. We should accordingly not assign the invalidation of the Jerusalem temple institution to John but to the Roman government that brought it to an end, with the Gospel simply addressing the significance and aftermath of the event. Since the temple was already gone at the time of John's composition, there would have been no need for the Gospel to invalidate an institution that had already lost its purpose. Rather, John seeks to re-locate the worship center away from an already-defunct space to the space that is the person of the risen Jesus, present among believers as the Shekhinah was present in the midst of the Israelites in the Exodus.[56] Therefore, John does not abstract worship to a nebulous "spiritual" idea. Worship continues to be located in physical space; only instead of a building and an institution, the Fourth Gospel claims that this physical space is the risen body of Jesus (this is the plain sense of the text at 2:19, 21).

John 4:6–26: Worship Space in Jesus' Discourse with the Samaritan Woman

The crux of Jesus' dialogue with the Samaritan woman in John 4:6–26 is worship space. Should one worship on Mt. Gerizim, which in fact possessed a more ancient pedigree as nearby Shechem (4:5) had housed the Ark of the Covenant long before the Jerusalem temple had even been conceived; or on Mt. Zion in Jerusalem, the site chosen, according to tradition, by God himself?[57] The answer provided in this dialogue is that the person of Jesus is the appropriate worship space. This identification is highlighted by the absence of the temple on Mt. Gerizim, which lay in ruins at the time in which this scene takes place. The Gospel utilizes the absence of the Samaritans' worship space (in the scene, as a framework for Jesus' conversation with the Samaritan woman) as an illustration of the absence of the Judean worship space (still standing as the scene occurs but absent at the actual time of the Fourth Gospel's composition). This passage encapsulates John's central

---

55. Wick, *Gottesdienste*, 332.

56. Frühwald-König, *Tempel*, 221; Kinzer, "Temple Christology," 447; Koester, *Dwelling*, 105–6.

57. See Lindars, *Gospel of John*, 187–88.

theme of Jesus as worship space: by definition, the place where the divine Presence dwells and the space in which sacrifice is offered.

Stephen T. Um's work on temple Christology will helpful for "unpacking" the scene at Jacob's well. First, Um notes that the language in which Jesus describes the lifegiving water he offers is "remarkably parallel to the background themes of the new creation found in early Jewish traditions (both biblical and post-biblical)."[58] Once again we have the presence of water, evocative of Eden traditions and possibly of the Feast of Tabernacles, both of which, as we have seen, relate to temple worship. Um highlights the linguistic choices of the Gospel's author in denoting Jacob's well as a φρέαρ, "a well dug in order to retrieve a rich supply of water," but the source of Jesus' proffered water as a πηγή, "a source most frequently understood to be a fountain or a perennial spring supplying fresh water."[59] The latter term is the same as that in the LXX of Isa 35:6a–7; 49:10; Joel 4:18; *Jos. Asen.* 2:20; 1QH 16:16, all of which speak of the eschatological redemption/new creation in terms of water arising from a πηγή.[60] Hence, the "life-giving water" that Jesus offers is connected to temple and worship associations with water, and the scene at Jacob's well presents two options for worship location: Jerusalem or Mt. Gerizim. Jesus clarifies that neither of these places is the correct location of worship; rather, the reference to water in terms of the eschatological restored creation identifies him as the correct worship location.

"Spirit and Truth"

A potential difficulty in identifying Jesus as worship space in John arises in two individual verses: the famous verse at 4:23, "The hour is coming, and is now here, when the true worshipers will worship the Father in spirit and truth;" and "it is the spirit that gives life; the flesh is useless" in 6:63. We have addressed the latter passage above. Um interprets Jesus' prediction of worship "in Spirit and truth" (John 4:20–24) as "*a new worship empowered by the reality of eschatological life found in the True Temple of God.*"[61] This interpretation is helpful in addressing the problem of how "Spirit and truth" can refer to any temple at all: "Spirit and truth" seem to be free of any

58. Um, *Temple Christology*, 136.
59. Ibid., 138–39.
60. Ibid., 139.
61. Ibid., 173. Emphasis in original. See also Barrett, *According to St. John*, 237–38.

associations with the material realm, including a physical body. If Jesus is sacrifice and therefore is temple, how can the Gospel advocate worship "in spirit and truth" and claim that the material realm is "useless"?

The premise on which a traditional understanding of these passages is based lies in a dissociation of worship from physical ritual.[62] There is only a problem if we accept the idea that true, free, "spiritual" worship must be divorced from physical temple and material sacrifice—concepts which were not in view at the time of the Fourth Gospel's composition. Rather, "spirit and truth" in John 4:24 need not be *divorced from* temple and sacrifice but, considering the importance of a location for sacrificial worship in John as we have seen so far, may indicate a participation in the eschatological temple *with its sacrifice*, which is Jesus.[63] The discussion between Jesus and the Samaritan woman to this point has revolved around the proper location in which to worship: in Jerusalem or on Mount Gerizim? Jesus' reply, that one must worship "in Spirit and truth," indicates that the locus of worship is sitting right in front of the woman—it is the person of Jesus himself.[64] Köstenberger states well the dilemma of claiming that Jesus-as-temple removes worship from any location at all: after stating that "physical locations of worship are inadequate," he immediately claims that "Jesus now is the proper focus of worship."[65] The problem here is that John depicts Jesus' resurrected body as the temple. The argument removing "worship in spirit and truth" from a physical location must contend with the Gospel's claim of Jesus' raised body, which is certainly portrayed in John as a physical location. Additionally, as Dorothy Lee notes, "πνεῦμα in the Fourth Gospel generally refers to the Holy Spirit rather than an interior attitude of the worshipper;" hence, the πνεῦμα of John 4:23 may well look forward to the "spirit of truth," that is, the Spirit of God, to which Jesus refers more than

---

62. A similar phenomenon may be observed in the current distinction between "religion" and "faith" among evangelical and/or fundamentalist Christians of the present day, with *religion* describing "legalistic ritual" and *faith* an internal, intellectual "spiritual life."

63. See Lee, "Spirit," 279–83.

64. See Moloney, *Gospel of John*, 128: "What Jesus is about to announce as the new 'place' for true worship is already present because Jesus is present." However, as noted above, Moloney's interpretation renders this "place" as the dedication of the believer's life to the Father. This effectively takes the focus off of Jesus as the actual temple—that is, the locus of *sacrifice*—and removes worship to an abstract realm of spiritualization.

65. Köstenberger, "Second Temple," 228–29, 235–36. Confusingly, Köstenberger expresses agreement that Jesus' body is the temple by quoting Walker: "Jesus himself, in his own body, was a new 'Temple'" (Köstenberger, "Second Temple," 235).

once in the Farewell Discourse (14:17; 15:26; 16:13).⁶⁶ When Jesus tells the Samaritan woman that true worshipers must worship in "spirit and truth," it is likely that the "spirit *of* truth" is in view. There is another connection in this dialogue to the Farewell Discourse, in which Jesus claims to be "the truth" (14:6).⁶⁷ Given this connection, we have once again a reference to the person of Jesus as worship space: if worshipers are to worship in the Holy Spirit (the "spirit of truth"), as well as in truth, the meaning is that worship is to be done "in" Jesus himself.⁶⁸ The effect of this is that worship space, and the ritual that takes place within it, is not abrogated: it is only the Judean and Samaritan *geographical* places of worship that are inconsequential. There is no longer a separation of worship into geographical realms and both peoples, formerly estranged from one another, now have the possibility of coming together to worship in the Jesus-temple.⁶⁹ To emphasize this shift in location, geographical imagery is employed, particularly in Jesus' use of the term "way" or "path" to describe his own self (14:6).⁷⁰ This recalls the state of affairs that had existed in the earliest days of Israel, the age of the Judges and the later united monarchy under Saul, David, and Solomon. John's Jesus is the temple to which the nations will come to worship Israel's God at the time of Israel's redemption. Knöppler is correct to state that in John 4 "all cult places have lost their meaning, and thereby their purpose, since only Christ is the place established by God for worship ἐν πνεύματι καὶ ἀλεθεία."⁷¹ The Fourth Gospel displaces the eschatological temple from *any* geographical center and repositions it in Jesus, who is the post-70 CE τόπος, dwelling of the divine Glory.⁷² Indeed, it is precisely Jesus' words

---

66. Lee, "Spirit," 280–81. While Brown argues that "spirit and truth" here "has nothing to do with worshiping God in the inner recesses of one's own spirit; for the Spirit is the Spirit of God, not the spirit of man, as John 4:24 makes clear," he also claims that 4:23 "shifts from the place of worship (20–21) to the manner of worship" (Brown, *According to John (i–xii)*, 180–81). I am arguing that the shift with which this passage deals is precisely a shift of place, from geographical temples to the person of Jesus.

67. Lee, "Spirit," 280–81.

68. See Kinzer, "Temple Christology," 448.

69. Brown, *According to John (i–xii)*, 187–88.

70. Lee, "Spirit," 286.

71. Knöppler, *Sühne*, 248. Translation mine.

72. Brown, *According to John (i–xii)*, 34–35, 503–4; Brown, *According to John (xiii–xxi)*, 716, 751.

about where worship should be performed that persuade the Samaritan woman that he is "Messiah."[73]

If "God is spirit" (4:24), then to worship "in Spirit and truth" simply means to be in relationship with God: the relationship which was established in Eden, severed, then restored through the worship rites of the earthly temple. Since that temple was gone at the time of the writing of John, a new/different temple had to take its place, otherwise there would be no relationship between God and humanity. In this regard, the Fourth Gospel made a striking assertion: that this new temple, the facilitator of relationship between God and humanity, was not a reconstructed building and reconstituted, organized priesthood, but the person of Jesus. To worship "in Spirit" is to worship "in God," and there is no reason why this manner of worship need exclude temple and sacrifice. Indeed, in the Mediterranean world of the first century CE, temple and sacrifice were the *only* way in which one worshiped "in God," that is, in the relationship with God which only sacrificial worship could maintain. An abstract, strictly intellectual "spiritualization" of worship would have been alien to the first-century Mediterranean world, Jews and Romans alike. Interpretations of the Samaritan well scene that "internalize" worship and remove it to the realm of the mind alone, as if the Fourth Evangelist were abrogating sacred space, would seem to throw an anachronism of later Christian (specifically, Reformation) ideas against ritual space and practice onto the Gospel, which originated in a time when such an absence of ritual space and practice would have been unthinkable. The Fourth Gospel still advocates a worship place, which is naturally the place of sacrifice: The person of Jesus is the sacrifice and thereby the sacred space in which worship is "reoriented" and "relocate[d]."[74]

It is highly significant that Jesus' discussion with the Samaritan woman is bracketed in a chiastic structure between two events with temple overtones: Jesus' turning the water to wine at Cana (John 2:1–12), followed immediately by the temple incident (John 2:13–25) and the dialogue with Nicodemus (John 3:1–36) on one side, and the second miracle in Cana (John 4:46–54) on the other.[75] The temple incident itself, a critique of temple and cult not unlike those found in the canonical prophetic books, utilizes cultic language and famously, in 2:21, identifies the anticipated risen body

---

73. Frühwald-König, *Tempel*, 137.

74. Thompson, "Reflections," 269.

75. For this structure see Brown, *According to John (xiii–xxi)*, 194–95; Kinzer, "Temple Christology," 453.

of Jesus, who has been identified as Son of God in the Prologue, as the true place of worship.[76] According to this scheme, the scene with Nicodemus is in the center, with the temple incident immediately preceding and the scene with the Samaritan woman immediately following. Events at Cana in Galilee form the outermost brackets. Given this structural observation, we have in John 2–4 a lengthy and complex image of Jesus as the temple.

Summary and Conclusions

Ancient ritual theory and spatial theory are both helpful in understanding John's relocation of worship space from geographical locale to person. "Locating" honor in a person was known in the first century; and the concept of "mobile sanctity" also current at that time demonstrates that holiness was not viewed as limited to one geographical place, even in Judaism, which required a single temple. Other temples were constructed (Elephantine and Leontopolis) and synagogues were regarded as possessing holiness equal to the temple even before the temple's destruction.

The Fourth Gospel fits this paradigm by portraying Jesus as sacrifice. Since the place of sacrifice was the place of worship in the ancient Near East, to claim that Jesus is sacrifice is to claim that he is the place of worship. The "Jesus-as-temple" theme in John is entirely dependent upon re-locating the *sacrifice*. The very presence of the temple theme indicates that (*contra* Ullucci and others) John displays a strong interest in sacrifice: as we have discussed, temple cannot be separated from sacrifice.

At this point, the Bread of Life Discourse, the water and wine of Cana, the blood and water of the crucifixion, and the appellation of *lamb* to Jesus coalesce. As discussed in chapter 3 of this thesis, these elements' appearance in John, along with the sacrificial characteristics of the whole Passion narrative beginning as early as Jesus' arrest, correspond to the offerings of Passover, *tôdāh*, and *tāmîd*, and perform the functions of each of those sacrificial rites. Through this, John re-locates the place of worship from the (defunct) Jerusalem temple to the person of Jesus. Therefore, the Gospel does not abstract worship to the intellect or to a nebulous "spiritual" realm devoid of material elements: Jesus' risen body, sacrifice and temple, is an actual location in the midst of the Gospel's audience, just as the Exodus tabernacle had been in the midst of Israel in the wilderness.

---

76. Frühwald-König, *Tempel*, 105.

5

The Translation of Ἰουδαῖοι as "Judeans"

Fundamental to John's Theme of Jesus as Temple and Sacrifice

ONE OF THE MOST notoriously difficult matters in translating and interpreting the Fourth Gospel is the question of how the term Ἰουδαῖοι should be translated. Typically, this term is translated into English as "Jews," which at the very least is an anachronism that throws the separation of Judaism and Christianity as two distinct religions back into an era to which that distinction is not proper.[1] In the words of Paul Beauchamp, "The problem is not that of a Jewish people over against a Christian people: the first Christian people did not cease to be a Jewish people."[2] At the very worst, a universal translation of Ἰουδαῖοι as "Jews" has exacerbated if not outright caused extreme anti-Jewish ideologies that have historically led to atrocities against the Jewish people and continue to provide fodder for anti-Judaism to the present day.[3] While the scope of this thesis will not allow for an examination of this particular phenomenon, and while it is not the intention of this study to fully address the complex historical and socio-religious matters surrounding the use of the word *Jews* in English translations of the Fourth Gospel, it is hoped that the argument presented here will demonstrate that

---

1. "On any reading of the Gospel, the debate between Jesus and 'the Jews' of John's narrative takes place in the first century CE, not in the twentieth or twenty-first" (De-Boer, "Depiction," 142, 144–45).

2. Beauchamp, "Un Livre," 17. Translation mine.

3. DeBoer's observation that the Fourth Gospel does not advise its audience to hate the Ἰουδαῖοι, and that the word μισέω is found only in reference to "hating" one's life and to sentiments "directed to Jesus and his followers," is of no help, since the latter hatred is responsible for the Ἰουδαῖοι's persecution of Jesus and would naturally lead to contempt for that group. DeBoer, "Depiction," 143.

115

"Jews" is an unacceptable translation of Ἰουδαῖοι in John and should be abandoned in favor of the term *Judeans*. Far from being an arbitrary hermeneutical choice or an attempt to make the Fourth Gospel more palatable to today's audiences, this translation is warranted by, and essential to, the Fourth Gospel's theme of Jesus as sacrifice and temple.[4]

This chapter will argue that the Gospel's Ἰουδαῖοι are to be understood as the population and religious leadership of the geographical territory of Judea, which is the place of opposition to Jesus for the express reason that Judea is the location of the temple institution in Jerusalem. The Ἰουδαῖοι oppose Jesus; the Samaritans and Galileans, whose lands have traditionally been separated from the Jerusalem temple, embrace him.[5]

References in the Gospel to "fear of the Ἰουδαῖοι" would only make sense if these passages refer to non-Judeans fearing Judeans. After all, in John, as Malcolm Lowe states, "nobody ever feared to be openly Jesus' follower in Galilee" according to the Fourth Gospel.[6] This harkens back to the period of the divided kingdom of Israel and Judea during the monarchic period, a period to which the Fourth Evangelist appeals in order to make his case that Jesus is place of worship. The temple and sacrifice theme is determinative for how Ἰουδαῖοι should be translated.

Ἰουδαῖοι and Ἰσραήλ

The term Ἰουδαῖοι is consistently contrasted with the term Ἰσραήλ throughout John, with "Israel" found four times and the majority of interactions (seventy occurrences) involving the Ἰουδαῖοι.[7] I suggest that the reason for this distinction is that the Gospel's audience is the "Israel" to which the narrator refers. The members of this audience have Jesus as their temple in the

---

4. Judith Lieu has noted that anti-Jewish interpretive tradition does not necessarily indicate that anti-Jewishness is embedded in the NT texts themselves. Lieu, "Anti-Judaism," 104.

5. Martyn, *History and Theology*, 106–7, 156–57. While Martyn casts this geographical division as part of the "two-level drama" reflecting the experience of what he terms the "middle stage" of the "Johannine Community," the observation about Jesus being accepted in Samaria/Galilee and rejected in Judea is correct.

6. Lowe, "ΙΟΥΔΑΙΟΙ," 122.

7. Tomson, "'Jews,'" 192. See also Moloney, "'Jews,'" 16, 17. Charles L'Éplattenier numbers the occurrences of Ἰουδαῖοι at 66 and points out that the Synoptics use this term solely during the Passion narrative, whereas the term appears all throughout John. L'Éplattenier, "'Les Juifs,'" 127.

post-70 CE absence of the temple in Jerusalem. Brown is correct in observing that "Israel" denotes in John an elect group, which has Jesus; he is incorrect, however, to define this along "birth" and ethnic lines.[8] As discussed in chapter 4 above, regarding the meaning assigned to space, geographical considerations are significant: the geographical territory of the Johannine "Israelites," the regions of Samaria and Galilee that correspond to the ancient Northern Kingdom, does not host the temple institution and its rites; and, in fact, were historically opposed to the Jerusalem temple.[9] Additionally, the name "Israel" is that of the covenant people called out of Egypt who hosted the presence of God in the wilderness tabernacle. Ἰουδαῖοι, on the other hand, is the term assigned in John to those in whose territory the temple institution exists and whose exclusive focus on that institution causes a failure to recognize the Jesus-temple in their midst. This is on display most prominently in John 9, the account of the "Man Born Blind." The preceding chapter of this thesis argued that the reason for the healed man's persecution by the temple-affiliated authorities was due to his recognition of, and affiliation with, the Jesus-temple at the expense of the Jerusalem temple institution. It is important to note that the "man born blind" is of the same faith as the Ἰουδαῖοι; that is, this pericope does not represent a struggle of "Jews" against a new and different religion, "Christianity." The Gospel rather presents rival temples, Jerusalem and Jesus; and claims that of the two, Jesus is the true dwelling of God's Glory, the perfect sacrificial offering, and hence the true place of worship. This is directly in line with the traditional and ancient faith of Israel. John places the location of worship in Jesus by calling upon solidly *Jewish* categories. The meaning of temple and sacrifice is not changed; much less are they rendered obsolete and abrogated. Rather, as argued above in chapter 4, they retain their meaning while being re-located from institution (Jerusalem) to person (Jesus). In a supreme expression of Johannine irony, the Ἰουδαῖοι possess a temple building and institution but not an actual dwelling of the divine Presence (the "Glory," δόξα), reminiscent of Ezek 10–11 when the Glory departs the temple due to the iniquities of Jerusalem.[10] The scholarly arguments

8. Brown, *Community*, 48, 56.

9. Lizorkin-Eyzenberg, *Jewish Gospel*, 63–64.

10. Moloney (*Text and Context*, 20–39) argues that "Israel" in John refers to a group not defined by national, political, and ethnic identity but rather by ethnic Jews and Gentiles being brought together into a new community by Jesus' action on the cross. At the same time, Moloney unfortunately maintains that the overall negative connotation of Ἰουδαῖοι "has *nothing* to do with national, political, or religious affiliation. It has

that have claimed throughout the years that John's characterization of the Ἰουδαῖοι indicates a historical break away from Judaism and toward Gentile Christianity are well-known (and unfortunately, numerous) and need not be reiterated here; some of the most influential were reviewed in the introduction chapter of this thesis. At this point, it must be said that one of the reasons for the problematic nature of such arguments is that they seem not to take into consideration the ancient prophetic tradition of temple criticism on view in the prophetic writings of the canonical scriptures. Jeremiah and Ezekiel are the prime examples of this; Amos and Micah also show criticism of a corrupt priesthood and dissipated worship practices. Jesus' stand placing himself against the Jerusalem temple in John 2 is not that much different than Jeremiah's scathing speech against the temple in Jer 7:1–7; yet Jeremiah apparently never ceased to be Jewish. The critiques leveled by the prophets were *intra-faith* debates;[11] and the Fourth Gospel stands entirely in line with this tradition.

As seen in chapter 4 above, the Fourth Gospel does not claim that worship must be space-less, but changes the space from institutional building to person. Hence, the Gospel does not criticize Jewish worship but *re-locates* it, and the demonization is not of Jews as an ethnic group or of Judaism as a religion, but of anyone who does not worship in the location that the evangelist/narrator identifies and advocates. The latter group does not exclusively comprise Ἰουδαῖοι but includes polytheist Romans, as we have also seen. Those who maintain continuation with the Jerusalem

---

everything to do with the definitive rejection of Jesus as the revelation of God." Hence, we are back once again to Ἰουδαῖοι/"Jews" used as a symbol of turning away from God and of an obstinate, blind refusal to do God's will. Moloney states clearly that the Ἰουδαῖοι formed a group of ethnic Jews while the "Johannine Christians" were comprised of both ethnic Jews and Gentiles. What divided them was "belief in" Jesus as God's revelation. Therefore, the religious affiliation cannot be avoided. Moloney is, I think, well-intentioned in attempting to "rescue" John from charges of ethnic anti-Semitism; but the problem of Jews being used as a symbol of wrong-headed religion remains.

A similar view is found in DeBoer, who makes the tenuous claim that John does not depict the Ἰουδαῖοι themselves as evil—only their behavior in getting Jesus arrested and killed. DeBoer, "Depiction," 147. We might well ask how legitimate is a literary separation between identity and action. Brown sees in John "anti-temple views" that come from the influence of a group within the "Johannine Community," whose anti-temple ideas were reinforced by the Samaritans they converted. Brown, *Community*, 22–23, 35, 38–39, 49. Rather than John being "anti-temple," however, the present study argues that it is anti-*Judean*. Since the Gospel portrays Jesus as the temple, it cannot be anti-temple *per se*.

11. Lieu, "Anti-Judaism," 105–7.

temple authorities, the Ἰουδαῖοι, are guilty equally with polytheist Gentiles of not seeing/recognizing the dwelling place of the divine Presence, as is made clear by the association of the temple authorities with the Roman civil power, a political relationship exemplified within the passion narrative when the Ἰουδαῖοι assert their allegiance to Caesar (John 19:15). As the prophets had said of the leaders of their own day, these are exactly the people who should recognize and honor God's dwelling.[12] The Fourth Gospel's animosity toward the group labeled Ἰουδαῖοι is entirely a matter of where to worship.

Many attempts to identify a best translation take an intertextual approach, examining the usage of Ἰουδαῖοι in extra-biblical texts contemporary with John. Peter J. Tomson's work has shown that Philo, Josephus, rabbinic texts, the Qumran writings, apocryphal and pseudepigraphical texts, the Palestinian Talmud, and even contemporary coins and inscriptions universally employ the term "Israel" as a general rule when referring to the whole covenant people, but switches to "Jews" when depicting speech situations involving interactions with Gentiles.[13] Hence, when Jews are speaking of and among themselves, they use the self-descriptor "Israel"; when they speak of themselves among Gentiles or within a Gentile social or literary context, they use Ἰουδαῖοι. Hence, the two terms were a way of employing "in-group/out-group" speech, a method that began during the Babylonian Exile and post-exilic period, when inhabitants of the former Kingdom of Judah became separated from their geographical place of origin yet maintained their identity.[14] The synoptic usage of "Jew" and "Israel" as synonymous terms used in various speech settings generally fits this pattern.[15] Where John is concerned, this usage would account for Nicodemus' being called "teacher of Israel" and "leader of the Ἰουδαῖοι" in the same passage (John 3:1, 10).[16] Tomson reads this as an indication of narrative provenance: the Fourth Gospel was Jewish in origin but redacted within a non-Jewish setting and intended to be read by a non-Jewish audience; thereby, the shifts between Ἰουδαῖοι and "Israel"

---

12. See e.g., Grelot, *Les Juifs*, 189.

13. Tomson, "'Jews,'" 181–82; also Tomson, "Names," 120–40.

14. Tomson, "Names," 124–25.

15. Tomson, "'Jews,'" 190–91. Tomson highlights this by drawing attention to Pilate and other Romans referring to Jesus as "King of the Ἰουδαῖοι" while the chief priests employ the phrase "King of Israel."

16. Ibid., 192.

have no other significance than being leftovers from sources that the evangelist and/or later redactors allowed to stand in later editions of the text.[17] Tomson subscribes to the theory, found also in Martyn and in Brown, that John was composed in stages according to the situation of the "Johannine Community" at any given time in the development of its Christology.[18] Tomson posits that the Gospel's initial stage of formation was within an "inner-Jewish" setting and accordingly used the term "Israel" throughout; but a later stage in the Gospel's development, characterized by conflict and separation between "the synagogue" and the "Johannine (Christian) community" as the latter moved increasingly into a Gentile setting, is responsible for the presence of the term Ἰουδαῖοι and for the hostility associated with that term in the Gospel.[19]

If we accept Tomson's argument, we must conclude that John does *not* employ "Israel" as a term denoting an "elect" group. Since Tomson's argument recognizes no essential difference in group identity between "Israelite" and "Judean," the appellation Ἰουδαῖοι would be ultimately *interchangeable* with "Israelites" and therefore must appropriately be translated as "Jews" in a strict sense of religious affiliation. Tomson's view (in line with the view of several others) depends much upon traditional/historical and wider contemporary usage of the two terms, as well as on the "Johannine Community" theory.

An alternative approach is to argue that Ἰουδαῖοι should be translated as "religious authorities," or similarly, in the majority of occurrences if not

---

17. Ibid., 192, 194–95, 198. According to Tomson, the preservation and "patchwork editing of received material" accounts for the apparent contradictions in the use of the term Ἰουδαῖοι, e.g., Jesus being identified as Ἰουδαῖος and claiming that "salvation is from the Ἰουδαῖοι" (4:22), while at the same time the Ἰουδαῖοι are "from the devil" (John 8:31) and seek to kill him.

18. Tomson, "'Jews,'" 195, 197; see also Brown, *Community*, 22–24. Martyn, *History and Theology*, 147–67. Similarly, C. K. Barrett (*John and Judaism*, 59ff.; 69–71) proposed that the "anti-Jewish" or less Jewish elements found in the Gospel as it now stands are due to later, post-*birkat* reinterpretations of an originally Hellenistic Jewish form, and Brown envisions a "high-Christology" group in the Gospel's middle formation stages. For challenges to the theory of *birkat* influence in John, see e.g., Bernier, *Aposynagōgos*, esp. 27–76; Köstenberger, "Second Temple," esp. 214, 217, 218; Langer, *Cursing*, esp. ch. 1; Lieu, "Anti-Judaism," 108–9.

19. Tomson, "'Jews,'" 195–97. This is also suggested by DeBoer's view in "Depiction," 152. For the concept of stages in the development of John, see Brown, *Community*, 22–24; Grelot, *Les Juifs*, 92–100; Martyn, *History and Theology*, 154–57; Moloney, "'The Jews,'" 18.

in every occurrence in John.[20] Charles L'Éplattenier, while acknowledging that ᾽Ιουδαῖοι can be translated in a multitude of ways, argues that it must signify the religious authorities of Jerusalem from John 5 onwards, as this part of the Gospel marks the beginning of "the theme of a reciprocal trial of the Jews and of Jesus, on a primary point well-attested in the Synoptics: they reproach Jesus for violating the Sabbath."[21] In John 7, the charge against Jesus that he has "made himself equal to God" leads to mutual accusations in this "two-way trial": Jesus accuses the ᾽Ιουδαῖοι of trying to kill him, the ᾽Ιουδαῖοι respond that he has "a demon," Jesus levels the infamous accusation that they themselves have the devil as their father.[22] In this trial motif, the ᾽Ιουδαῖοι are clearly the religious authorities; however this application does not apply in every instance. In John 11:54, where Jesus stops "walking openly" among "the ᾽Ιουδαῖοι" and remains in Ephraim instead, it would make no sense to translate ᾽Ιουδαῖοι as "Jews" in the strictly religious sense, as Jesus would be expressing reluctance to be seen in public among "Jews" and then go directly to a locale in which there were yet more religious "Jews"; for this reason, the meaning of ᾽Ιουδαῖοι here must be "Judeans."[23] The same applies in 11:7–8, where Jesus' determination to return to ᾽Ιουδαία is met with resistance by his disciples, who protest that the ᾽Ιουδαῖοι had recently tried to stone him.[24] In the context of John 11:54, Jesus is not concerned to avoid "Judean leaders" specifically; he avoids Judea altogether, indicating that it is the whole of Judea (and, by association, its population) that poses difficulty for him. Therefore, ᾽Ιουδαῖοι here should be translated not as authorities specifically but as "Judeans" generally—the residents of the geographical territory of Judea.[25] While it could be argued that since this passage comes at the end of the Lazarus episode, in which

---

20. Brown (*Community*, 40–43) claims that the authorities designated by the term ᾽Ιουδαῖοι represent the authorities within the "Johannine Community's" own *sitz im leben* who were responsible for expelling the "Johannine Christians" from their synagogue. Hence, for Brown, ᾽Ιουδαῖοι refers both to "the authorities" and to "hostile inhabitants of the synagogues in the Johannine community's own time." Under this proposal, even if ᾽Ιουδαῖοι indicates "religious authorities," the term cannot be distinguished from Jews and Judaism in general. See also Charlesworth, "Exclusivism," 256–57; Grelot, *Les Juifs*, 92–96.

21. L'Éplattenier, "'Les Juifs,'" 127–28. Translation mine.

22. Ibid., 128–29.

23. Lowe, "ΙΟΥΔΑΙΟΙ," 120.

24. Ibid.

25. In agreement with Grelot, *Les Juifs*, 15–17, 40–41; Lowe, "ΙΟΥΔΑΙΟΙ."

we find many Ἰουδαῖοι "believing in" Jesus, it is also evident that even these Ἰουδαῖοι are getting Jesus into serious trouble by broadcasting Lazarus' restoration to life, which has the result of spurring the temple authorities (also referred to as Ἰουδαῖοι) to increase their efforts to destroy Jesus. At this point, Grelot is correct to state that "The motive is no longer religious, but political: it concerns sparing relations between the 'nation' with the Romans who dominate it."[26] This is on display in the account of the "Man Born Blind" (John 9) as well as in Jesus' trial before Pilate. Even the most devout supporter of Jesus who truly accepts him is dangerous if that supporter is located in Judea, allowing such support to (even if inadvertently) put Jesus in danger by proximity to the temple authorities.

As is the case with John's parallels with Akedah traditions and connections to other sacrificial practices, we must examine the whole context of the Gospel itself in order to determine the way in which *John* employs the terms Ἰουδαῖοι and Ἰσραήλ/Ἰσραηλίτης.[27] I do not intend to dispute that the term Ἰουδαῖοι was used in many historical and contemporary texts and contexts to refer to the covenant people when addressing Gentiles and the term Ἰσραήλ when addressing the "in-group"; I am disputing that this is *the Fourth Gospel's* usage. There can be no question that in the vast majority of occurrences in the Gospel, the latter term applies to those who treat Jesus with hostility and the former to those who embrace him.

The two scholars that most clearly represent the opposing arguments in this debate are Adele Reinhartz and Malcolm Lowe, whose work crystallizes the debate and to which we must accordingly give a good deal of consideration.

Adele Reinhartz

Reinhartz presents a case that the Fourth Gospel's use of Ἰουδαῖοι should be translated as *Jews*, in every instance and without being enclosed in scare quotes. She refers to the work of several scholars who argue that the Gospel's Ἰουδαῖοι do not represent actual Jews but Jews "as symbol or

---

26. Grelot, *Les Juifs*, 41. Translation mine.

27. Judith Lieu discusses the vital importance of reading Ἰουδαῖοι with an eye to the first-century audience and context of multitudinous Jewish groups and sects, rather than presuming that twenty-first-century understandings of the term "Jews" would have informed the Gospel itself. Lieu, "Anti-Judaism," 110–12. See also Lizorkin-Eyzenberg, *Jewish Gospel*, 200.

metaphor" for the Gospel's running theme of darkness, the world hostile to God and to his agent, Jesus (and she is correct that many scholars have made this unfortunate argument, as can be seen in the work of Brown, Moloney, and Barrett in particular).[28] Reinhartz argues that John's "anti-Jewish elements are inherent in the texts themselves and not attributable solely to the interpretive tradition."[29] The characters referred to as Ἰουδαῖοι are on the wrong side of the two Johannine "poles" of light and darkness, belief and unbelief, salvation and destruction. Considering John 6:49, 58 as an example, the unbelieving Ἰουδαῖοι, trapped in the darkness of opposition to God, "are destined to die in their sin. This is a destiny they share with their ancestors, who ate manna and died, in contrast to believers, who eat the bread of life that is Jesus himself and live forever."[30] By extension, Reinhartz argues, this idea carries forward through the millennia so that present-day Jews share the same fate. While Reinhartz is correct in the claim that the "interpretive tradition" has indeed gone along these lines, I wish to challenge her assertion that such interpretations are warranted by an anti-Judaism inherent in the Fourth Gospel itself, by arguing that such a tradition does *not* present an accurate interpretation of the Fourth Gospel's overall presentation of the Ἰουδαῖοι.[31]

Reinhartz acknowledges that the meaning of Ἰουδαῖοι is not monolithic throughout the Gospel, but depends upon context. Ἰουδαῖοι should be translated as "Jewish religious authorities" or "leaders of the Jewish people" in passages such as 9:22, 19:38, and 20:19, in all of which the people, clearly of the Israelite faith, are afraid of the Ἰουδαῖοι. In these cases, it would be nonsensical for "the Jews" to be afraid of "the Jews"; therefore Ἰουδαῖοι refers in such passages to a specific group, namely the temple authorities whose possess a power that can rightly instill fear in the populace.[32] A geographic meaning is justified in passages such as John 11, which situates Bethany, the

---

28. Reinhartz, "'Jews' and Jews," 215. For "the Jews" as representative of the "world" that "loves darkness," see Brown, *Community*, 23, 63–69. Moloney's views are similar, as we have seen above.

29. Reinhartz, "'Jews' and Jews," 214. See also Ruether, "Theological Anti-Semitism," 192.

30. Reinhartz, "'Jews' and Jews," 216.

31. We will return to this discussion later in this chapter, in Section 5.2 "Individual Passages."

32. Reinhartz, "'Jews' and Jews," 217–18. Kysar ("Anti-Semitism," 118) argues, agreeing with von Wahlde, that Ἰουδαῖοι should be translated as "authorities" or "leaders" in every instance. Kysar follows the "Johannine community" theory in this assessment.

setting for Lazarus' resurrection, in Judea.³³ However, citing Shaye Cohen's work, Reinhartz states that

> Before the mid-to late second century BCE, to be sure, Ἰουδαῖος was primarily an ethnic-geographic term, properly translated "Judaean"; but by the second half of the second century BCE, the term was applied also to people who were not ethnic or geographic Judeans but who affiliated either religiously by coming to believe in the God of the Judaeans or politically by joining the Judaean state as allies or citizens ... by the time the Fourth Gospel was written ... the term was used to denote both an ethnic-geographic and a religious identity, and ... even the former was not limited to Jews who lived in Judaea or who were born of Judaean parents.³⁴

The Fourth Gospel, therefore, can and does use the term Ἰουδαῖοι in contexts that indicate "ethnic-geographic, political, and religious elements."³⁵ Accordingly, continuing to follow Reinhartz and Cohen, John's "feasts of the Ἰουδαῖοι" "are not defined by their geographical location but by the identity of their celebrants"; and the Gospel describes rituals and practices of the Ἰουδαῖοι whose observance is not limited to Judea but extends also to Galilee and to Diaspora settings.³⁶ (A prime example of this would be the Cana wedding, at which, as discussed above, "Judean" rites carry into Galilee.) The titulus atop Jesus' cross reads "King of the Ἰουδαῖοι" even though Jesus is from Nazareth in Galilee; here again, therefore, Ἰουδαῖοι cannot be limited to referring to people who live in Judea.³⁷ Hence, the translations "Jews" and "Jewish," with a strongly religious connotation, are most appropriate in these cases. "This is particularly the case," writes Reinhartz, "if we view the Gospel as having been written in

---

33. Reinhartz, "'Jews' and Jews," 218.
34. Ibid., 218–19. See also Tomson, "Names," 125.
35. Reinhartz, "'Jews' and Jews," 219.
36. Ibid. Ashton explains "feasts of the Ἰουδαῖοι" in John as having much the same sense as modern-day colloquial references to cultural festivals: "When in England people refer to a religious custom of Poles or Pakistanis they are implying that the custom in question originated in Poland or Pakistan. In fact, one could often substitute 'as is done in Poland' or 'as the custom is in Pakistan' without changing the sense.... And at least in the context of a wedding-feast in Galilee it would certainly seem odd to speak of *Judean* rites of purification. But this oddity derives from the limitation of the English word and does not affect the Greek" (Ashton, "Identity and Function," 45–46).
37. Reinhartz, "'Jews' and Jews," 220.

the Diaspora, where . . . the term was most commonly used for the Jewish nation as a whole."[38]

Reinhartz acknowledges that it is odd for John to use Ἰουδαῖος for Jesus but not for his disciples or for others who are well-disposed toward him, and mentions particularly in this regard Jesus' identification of Nathanael as a "true Ἰσραηλίτης" rather than a "true Ἰουδαῖος," likely for the purpose of separating believers from the group called Ἰουδαῖοι.[39] I agree that Ἰσραήλ and Ἰουδαῖοι designate separate groups, the former an elect group and the latter an "out-group"; however I differ from Reinhartz in the significance of that separation. Reinhartz essentially accepts the "Johannine Community" hypothesis. While questioning Martyn's famous "two-level reading," Reinhartz nonetheless retains the basic concept that the Fourth Gospel reflects a hard historical distinction between Judaism and a "Johannine church."[40] "In following Jesus," she claims, "Jews relinquish the ethnic and national categories that hitherto marked their lives . . . from the Johannine perspective, those Jews who become believers cease being Jews . . . in becoming a follower of Jesus, one passed . . . from one religious/ethnic group to another."[41]

While many of Reinhartz's points cannot be disputed, such as the historical reality that the term Ἰουδαῖοι was used and understood in a wide range of cultural, ethnic, religious, and political meanings, we must ask whether *the Fourth Gospel* employs the term according to this usage.[42] It does not necessarily follow that the Fourth Evangelist was required to use terms in ways identical to ways in which those terms were used elsewhere. The Evangelist was certainly free to adapt terms to suit his own purposes and to utilize terms in a way that brought his message home to the intended audience. The overall context of the whole Gospel must determine the

---

38. Ibid.

39. Ibid., 221. See also Martyn, *History and Theology*, 157.

40. Reinhartz, "'Jews' and Jews," 224. See also Reinhartz, "Grammar of Hate," 419–20, 426. While Reinhartz agrees that a historical hostile communal situation between "Jews" and "Christians" is to blame for the anti-"Jewish" polemic of John, she rejects the idea that expulsion from synagogues was ever a part of this experience.

41. Reinhartz, "'Jews' and Jews," 224–25. See also Barrett, *John and Judaism*, 70–71; DeBoer, "Depiction," 156; Martyn, *History and Theology*, 46–66, 154–57. DeBoer, however, does not predicate this of John but argues that the Gospel puts this into the mouths of the Ἰουδαῖοι themselves. Therefore, it is the Ἰουδαῖοι who force a separation between "Jews" and "Christians"; Reinhartz is arguing the opposite.

42. See Lowe, "ΙΟΥΔΑΙΟΙ," 117.

translation of Ἰουδαῖοι; and indeed that context is the Gospel's worship locus theme. Where Reinhartz asserts that Ἰσραήλ and Ἰουδαῖοι essentially come down to ethnic categories in John, even when they are used in geographic contexts or to designate temple-affiliated authorities, I suggest that the Johannine usage of these respective terms is in every instance surrounded by the dispute regarding place of worship. Since this dispute would have been an intra-Jewish one in the post-70 CE years, the Fourth Gospel, I contend, does not posit a separation of identity between "Jews" and "Christians," but between those of the Jewish faith who have Jesus as place of worship and those of the Jewish faith who do not. Essentially, throughout John the insistence is on the correct way to worship *according to Jewish categories*, which continued to focus on sacrificial categories as we have seen. John's assertion that the Jesus-temple group, whom the Gospel designates as "Israel," is the group practicing sacrificial Jewish worship correctly is no less Jewish than the assertions of the Qumran community that they were the only group practicing correct Jewish worship. In a very similar way that the Qumranites claimed that the Jerusalem temple was corrupt while always identifying as Jews, the Gospel of John claims that Jesus is the sacrifice and temple entirely in line with Jewish worship tradition and praxis.

Malcolm Lowe

Lowe represents the aspect of the Ἰουδαῖοι debate opposite to that represented by Reinhartz. Lowe is in agreement with Reinhartz on some points, including the historical use of Ἰουδαῖοι as a self-identifier for Diaspora Jews.[43] Lowe posits a much later time frame for the end of the term Ἰουδαία as a reference to a geographical area, placing the usage as an *exclusively* religious affiliation in the late second century CE.[44] He also reminds us that Josephus uses Ἰουδαῖοι in a variety of senses, including to indicate residents of the geographical territory of Ἰουδαία, indicating that the geographical sense was contemporary with the NT.[45] Moreover, Lowe reminds us, Dio Cassius employed Ἰουδαῖοι to indicate the geographical "as the basic sense" of the term, long after the period in which Reinhartz argues that the strictly geographic sense of Ἰουδαῖοι had faded.[46] Lowe acknowledges

---

43. Ibid., 104.
44. Ibid., 130.
45. See also Tomson, "Names," 123–24.
46. Lowe, "IOYΔAIOI," 105.

with Reinhartz that Ἰουδαῖοι could indicate both geographic affiliation as well as religious, since "in the ancient Mediterranean world almost every people had its own national religion, so that to be a member of that religion was in a sense to have that nationality."[47] Hence, a person who lived in Alexandria could justifiably call himself a Ἰουδαῖος if he followed the religion whose cultic center was the temple in Jerusalem.[48] As discussed above, the Jerusalem temple was significant to the identity of Diaspora communities, which engaged in prayer and practices similar or identical to those of their religious counterparts in Palestine and paid the temple tax in order to have a share in the temple rites and their benefits. However, with all this it must be said that the orientation of all these practices was toward the geographical location of Judea/Jerusalem; Diaspora residents called themselves Ἰουδαῖοι precisely because they identified as members of the religion centered by virtue of the temple in the geographical territory of Judea.[49] Certainly, Gentiles considered "Judaism" to be "primarily the religion of [geographical] Judea."[50] Usage of Ἰουδαῖοι within Palestine typically distinguished residents of Judea from residents of other areas or provinces of the region, such as Galilee, Samaria, Idumea, etc.[51]

Based on Synoptic usage (particularly that of Matthew), Lowe claims that the term Ἰσραήλ in John may refer to the whole of Palestine and not simply to Samaria/Galilee, the first-century CE correspondents to the ancient Northern Kingdom of Israel. Lowe's chief support for this usage rests on Jesus' triumphal entry (John 12:12), in which he is welcomed (presumably by Judeans) as "King of Israel"; and on Jesus' identification of Nicodemus as "a teacher of Israel" even though the latter is clearly a resident of Judea. Ἰσραήλ in the latter passage would encompass Judea as well.[52] In the first case, as Lowe admits, the crowd has come to Jerusalem/Judea to observe Passover. Lowe interprets this to mean that these people, presumably inhabitants of Judea, "subscribed to the wider sense of Israel."[53] Lowe notes that, unlike the Synoptics, John does not depict a generalized "crowd" demanding Jesus' death before Pilate, but only the temple-affiliated

---

47. Ibid., 107. See also Grelot, *Les Juifs*, 19; Tomson, "Names," 124–26.
48. See also Tomson, "Names," 124.
49. See Lowe, "ΙΟΥΔΑΙΟΙ," 109.
50. Ibid., 108.
51. Ibid., 130.
52. Ibid., 110–11.
53. Ibid.

authorities (this continues, and brings to a climax, the trial motif begun in chapter five).⁵⁴ The reference to Zech 9:9 ("Fear not, daughter of Zion, behold your king") in Jesus' triumphal entry would indicate, according to Lowe, that John includes Jerusalem within "Israel." However, as the crowd is composed not only of Judean residents but also of pilgrims from the Diaspora, their hailing of Jesus as their king would fit the Gospel's use of Ἰσραήλ for those who accept Jesus, as we have already argued.

As for the "feasts of the Ἰουδαῖοι," the phrase ἑορτὴ τῶν has parallels in the LXX, even though an equivalent of "Passover of the Ἰουδαῖοι" does not.⁵⁵ Lowe additionally notes that both of these phrases in John "occur only in reference to feasts requiring a pilgrimage to Judea" or "when something is needed to explain why people are suddenly faced with a journey to Judea."⁵⁶ An example is John 7:2–3, where Jesus' brothers tell him to go to "Judea" for ἑορτὴ τῶν Ἰουδαίων. Hence, the meaning is "a feast of the Judeans" or, considering a possible Semitic genitive, "a Judean feast."⁵⁷

A difficulty arises when Ἰουδαῖοι turn up in Capernaum in John 6. Where ἑορτὴ τῶν Ἰουδαίων occurs in this chapter (verse 4), no pilgrimage to Judea is mentioned; Lowe explains this as a later interpolation, as the phrase does not appear in certain early manuscript traditions.⁵⁸ Lowe also, however, allows the possibility that the descendants of Judean settlers in Galilee as a result of the Hasmonean conquest of the area would still have been referred to as Ἰουδαῖοι in the first century CE.⁵⁹ This would support the present thesis' contention that the Fourth Gospel's division between Ἰουδαία and Ἰσραήλ is based upon the ancient rivalry between the northern and southern kingdoms, which in turn illuminates John's temple theme: Judea and the Judeans boasted the Jerusalem temple; John identifies those ironically without the temple institution but with the legitimate sacrifice and temple as "Israel." With famous irony, however, the evangelist makes the lack of the temple institution the requirement for proper worship: only those who do not affiliate with the Jerusalem temple institution are able

---

54. Grelot, *Les Juifs*, 78–79; L'Éplattenier, "'Les Juifs,'" 129.

55. Lowe, "ΙΟΥΔΑΙΟΙ," 116.

56. Ibid.

57. Ibid., 117.

58. Ibid. Charlesworth ("Exclusivism," 254–56, 277) also argues in favor of increasing "anti-Jewish" polemic as the Fourth Gospel was edited over time, to reflect the developing *siz im leben* of the "Johannine Community."

59. Lowe, "ΙΟΥΛΑΙΟΙ," 121n65.

to worship God properly, that is, in and through the person of Jesus. The Jerusalem temple proves to be an *obstacle* to worship. This is the essence of the hostility between Jesus and the Ἰουδαῖοι in every instance of conflict throughout the Gospel.[60]

Lowe additionally points out that passages in which Ἰουδαῖοι occurs "in a Judean context" and accordingly must be translated as "Judeans" are thirty-six in number, while Ἰουδαῖοι occurring "in a Galilean context" number only two.[61] In each case, there are two distinct groups: 1.) Ἰουδαῖοι and 2.) people who accept Jesus, the latter of whom are overwhelmingly Galilean or Samaritan. While Reinhartz would attribute this to "Christians" pitted against "Jews," this is not justified by the Gospel's usage.

Individual Passages

The first instance we encounter of Judean opposition to Jesus is in John 1:31, when John the Baptist claims that he "came baptizing so that [Jesus] might be made known to Israel" (1:31)—not, by implication, that he might be made known to Judea.[62] In 1:19-28, the term Ἰουδαῖοι refers specifically to the religious authorities affiliated with the Jerusalem temple, as does the use of the term in 2:13.[63] The statement in 1:11 that the Word "came to what was his own, and his own people did not receive him" harkens back to Wisdom traditions in which the divine Wisdom searched for a dwelling on earth and came to rest in Israel (*Sir.* 24:7).[64] Barrett understands "his own" to refer to

---

60. Judith Lieu ("Anti-Judaism," 109; also "Temple and Synagogue," 51-69) has observed that the temple is "the focus of action and conflict" in John. See also Lizorkin-Eyzenberg, *Jewish Gospel*, 127.

61. Lowe, "ΙΟΥΔΑΙΟΙ," 122.

62. Brown and Barrett have respectively observed that the term Ἰσραήλ, though only used four times in John, always possesses a positive significance, as opposed to the negative usage of Ἰουδαῖοι throughout. Barrett, *According to St. John*, 177; Brown, *According to John (i-xii)*, 56; Brown, *Community*, 57-58. See also Kinzer, "Temple Christology," 450-51.

63. Barrett, *According to St. John*, 172, 177-78; DeBoer, "Depiction," 148; Grelot, *Les Juifs*, 29; Lindars, *Gospel of John*, 102; Lizorkin-Eyzenberg, *Jewish Gospel*, 31-34; Lowe, "ΙΟΥΔΑΙΟΙ," 123-24.

64. Barrett, *According to St. John*, 163; Koester, *Dwelling of God*, 24-25, 109-10; Lindars, *Gospel of John*, 90. Koester (*Dwelling*, 109-10) notes other literature predating the Fourth Gospel that predicates characteristics of the divine Wisdom that we see in the Johannine attributes of the λόγος, e.g., *Prv* 8; *Wis* 9:2; *Sir* 1:1; 15:7; *Bar* 4:1; 3:12, 37; *1 En* 42:2.

Israel; others argue that Jesus' "own" is Judea.⁶⁵ Barrett, however, also offers the intriguing alternative that "it would be possible to speak of a coming of the Logos in a Platonic sense to the created world, which was his natural counterpart, or in the Stoic sense to rational men."⁶⁶ As we have seen, Philo made connections between the high priest and the λόγος; since Jesus is clearly portrayed as high priest in John as discussed above, the idea that the λόγος appears to the created world as priest to "his own" creation, not only to one part of it, makes a great deal of sense for the Fourth Gospel.

Next, Nathanael calls Jesus "the king of Israel" (1:47-49) in an immediate context of temple imagery, the reference to the vision of Jacob's stairway in 1:50-51 as discussed in chapter 2 above. This proclamation, which Jesus tacitly acknowledges as accurate (1:50, "you believe because I told you that I saw you" etc.), will later be contrasted with the ironic proclamation that Jesus is "King of the Ἰουδαῖοι" in the titulus ordered by Pilate at the crucifixion (19:20-22), vehemently protested by the temple authorities in a certain rejection of Jesus as the King of Judea (cf. 19:15, "we have no king but Caesar").⁶⁷ Jesus' response that Nathanael is "a true Israelite" in 1:47 prefigures the dichotomy between Israel and Judea that will follow throughout the Gospel.⁶⁸ When Nathaniel calls Jesus the "king of Israel" (John 1:49), he is not expressing a Davidic hope but showing himself to be one of the elect who accepts Jesus as the temple—a member of "Israel" (ἀληθῶς Ἰσραηλίτης, 1:47) which has the temple and the Glory in its midst. There is no evidence of Davidic messianic expectations anywhere in John. The closest we find is at John 7:42, where in a debate about Jesus' origin the

---

65. Barrett, *According to St. John*, 163; Lizorkin-Eyzenberg, *Jewish Gospel*, 15; Meeks, "Galilee and Judea," 165.

66. Barrett, *According to St. John*, 163. See also Lizorkin-Eyzenberg, *Jewish Gospel*, 27-28.

67. See Grelot, *Les Juifs*, 158. The NRSV has "the emperor" for "Caesar."

68. Lindars' statement that Nathanael's confession indicates that he "is a man of pure Jewish stock, in spite of the fact that he is apparently resident in Galilee" confuses the Judea/Israel distinction that pervades the Fourth Gospel. Lindars, *Gospel of John*, 118. Barrett carries forward his argument that "Israel" is placed over against Ἰουδαῖοι only in the sense that the Ἰουδαῖοι, as "Jews," are false Jews as opposed to the true Jews, identified as "Israelites." Barrett, *According to St. John*, 184-85. Similarly, Martyn argues that "true Israelite" designates someone who is not even Jewish any longer. Martyn, *History and Theology*, 157. See also Meeks, who claims that "'the Jews' symbolize the natural people of God, who, however, reject God's messenger, 'the Galileans' symbolize those who are estranged from the natural people of God, but become truly God's people [i.e., "Israel"] because they receive God's messenger" ("Galilee and Judea," 165).

"crowd" (ἐκ τοῦ ὄχλου) suggests that the Messiah is to come from Bethlehem. However, there is no evidence that this is a Johannine endorsement of Davidic messiahship for Jesus, and there is equally no evidence that the term "Israel" as it is used in John has any Davidic connotation. When the crowds at Jesus' entry into Jerusalem hail him as "king of Israel," they are not operating on concepts of "king" from Samuel-Kings-Chronicles but from the Torah (especially, for example, Leviticus 23). Unlike the accounts in Mark and Matthew, the crowd in John does not hail Jesus as "son of David."[69] John has no interest in a Davidic expectation. The fig tree too is significant, as a traditional symbol of Israel. Nathanael's confession that Jesus is "king of Israel" confirms John the Baptist's mission to make Jesus "known to Israel": Jesus is indeed made "known to Israel" in being made known to a "true Israelite," represented by Nathanael.[70]

As discussed in chapter 2 above, the changing of water into wine at Cana in John 2:6 shows Jesus as the one who performs the function of priest who will offer sacrifice; this occurs in *Galilee*, not in the sanctioned locus of sacrifice in Judea. By Jesus' performance of this cultic action, the water for priestly ablutions and for washing sacrificial victims becomes present beyond the Jerusalem temple; hence the place of worship is dis-located, or rather re-located.

During the dialogue between Jesus and Nicodemus in 3:1–15, Nicodemus is called "a ruler of the Judeans" in 3:1, but Jesus identifies him as a teacher of *Israel* in 3:10, even though apparently Jesus was still in Jerusalem as he had been at John 2:23. Grelot suggests that this apparent difference is actually due to *Judeans* being the Hebrew term and *Israel* being the Aramaic; the personal name "Nicodemus" being Greek in origin, all three terms taken together reflect Nicodemus's identity as a leader within a cosmopolitan setting.[71] According to this view, there is no difference between "Judean" and "Israel," and Nicodemus represents the failure of Israel

---

69. Mark 11:10; Matt 21:9.

70. Moloney, "'The Jews,'" 21; Moloney, *Text and Context*, 26. As mentioned above, Moloney does not separate Ἰσραήλ as a group separate from Ἰουδαῖοι, in an attempt to break down ethnic categories by arguing that "Israel" includes both ethnic and non-ethnic Jews while Ἰουδαῖοι means those who reject Jesus (and thereby God). One of the problems here is that Ἰουδαῖοι cannot include the polytheist Romans who reject Jesus; another is that Moloney's categories end up translating Ἰουδαῖοι as "Jews" and we are thereby back at the exact root of the problem as to how Ἰουδαῖοι should be translated.

71. Grelot, *Les Juifs*, 29.

to understand the Gospel message.⁷² Barrett argues that the designation of Nicodemus as a "teacher of Israel" marks him as a teacher of the people of God, again as opposed to the Ἰουδαῖοι; however, this is with Barrett's understanding of "Jew" and "Israelite" as specifically religious terms, where "Israelite" is synonymous with "Christian," distinct from "Jew," as if the two were separate faiths already at the time the Fourth Gospel was written.⁷³ The Gospel associates Nicodemus with the Jerusalem temple leadership (Ἰουδαῖοι) while at the same time qualifying him as an "Israelite" due to his seeking out of Jesus.⁷⁴ Nicodemus thus appears to be straddling a line between affiliation with the Jerusalem temple institution and an awareness that Jesus is the temple. Nicodemus is already on this road by his insight that God is "with" Jesus (3:2c), and that Jesus is a significant "teacher" (3:2b).⁷⁵ His involvement in Jesus' burial reinforces his qualification as an "Israelite": when he assists in giving Jesus a proper burial, he is assisting in the sacrifice that is Jesus' death. The "we" to whom Nicodemus refers in 3:2b likely refers to "Israel"—those who had "believed in" Jesus as a result of the signs he had done up to this point, rather than to the religious authorities to whose number Nicodemus also belongs.⁷⁶

As we have seen, John 4 is an extended contrast between Judea and Samaria defined by worship locus; we may include Galilee with Samaria as being separate from Judea.⁷⁷ When Jesus is accused of being possessed by a demon and of being a Samaritan in 8:48-49, it is only the first charge that he refutes; he does not address the accusation of being a Samaritan. We see here at the very least a sympathy with Samaria akin to that demonstrated

---

72. Ibid., 30.

73. Barrett, *According to St. John*, 211. Brown argues that the Fourth Evangelist uses Ἰσραήλ to refer to the inclusion of the Gentiles in the people of God, so that Ἰουδαῖοι is essentially an exclusive, narrowly ethnic term while "Israel" indicates an inclusive, multi-ethnic group based on a shared internal religious belief in Jesus. Brown, *According to John (i–xii)*, 442–43. While I agree that the Fourth Gospel's use of "Israel" indicates acceptance of Jesus, I am also arguing that the categories Ἰουδαῖοι and Ἰσραήλ bear directly on the Gospel's identification of the temple and the geography-based rivalry surrounding that institution.

74. *Contra* Lindars, who interprets Nicodemus's lack of belief as evidence of "the failure of the old Law" (Lindars, *Gospel of John*, 154).

75. Barrett, *According to St. John*, 205.

76. Ibid.

77. Lindars argues that religiously Galilee "sided with Judea against the Samaritans." *Gospel of John*, 180.

towards Galilee.[78] Although some have seen here an indication of Samarian provenance for the Gospel, Jesus' neglect to correct the accusation of being a Samaritan may simply reflect John's inclusion of Samaria with Galilee as a single entity that, in embracing Jesus, identifies as *Israel* with the divine Glory in its midst, in contrast to Judea which has a temple that lacks the Glory, not unlike the situation in Ezek 10:18ff. and 11:23, when God's Glory leaves the temple, in fact *leaves Judea altogether*, and takes up residence among the exiles in Babylon. This is also reminiscent of Wisdom's search for a place in which to abide and settling finally in Israel, as mentioned above. (This theme will occur again in John 8:38, when Jesus is said to be in the Father's *presence*, implying that he is the divine Glory.) Since the Gospel uses "Israel" in reference to those who accept Jesus as the correct locus of worship, the perfect temple, the place where perfect sacrifice was offered, Jesus' conversation with the woman at the well centers on this very identification; and since the woman arrives at a certain level of acceptance of Jesus as temple, she is part of Israel.

The reason why Jesus is "greater than Jacob" (John 4:12) is because Jesus is the temple, the sacrifice offered in the temple, and the priest who offers the sacrifice. He is the means of worship and thereby the means of access to God, which is of course greater than the patriarchs through whom the worship came to Israel.

Although "the gift of God" which Jesus identifies as himself is typically interpreted as the "living water" of which he speaks in John 4:10, I suggest that it actually means access to God's grace through proper worship.[79] The Torah and the worship cultus had been God's gift to Israel; both are now present in the person of Jesus.[80] Jesus is therefore offering the Samaritan woman (and, in fact, all Samaritans, as becomes clear toward the end of the pericope when the woman's neighbors come to accept Jesus) the gift of the correct worship location.

The most significant feature of this scene, however, is Jesus' assertion that "salvation is from the Ἰουδαῖοι" (John 4:22). As Frühwald-König states, the Gospel interprets the cultic tradition "under the paradigm of Christology . . . by this new interpretation, it is not a question of a break

---

78. For possible Samaritan provenance and/or influence, see, among other works, Brown, *Community*, 22, 36–40, 44, 48, 56, 77; Lindars, *Gospel of John*, 36–37, 331–32; Lowe, "ΙΟΥΛΑΙΟΙ," 110.

79. For the "gift" as the "living water," see e.g. Lindars, *Gospel of John*, 181–82.

80. See Moloney, *Text and Context*, 178–81.

with tradition, but rather of its continuation or fulfillment."[81] Salvation is connected to temple worship; Jesus' identification by the Samaritan woman as a Ἰουδαῖος is ironic in that Jesus performs the Judean temple institution's purpose and functions. Jesus can be called Ἰουδαῖος, and can say that "salvation is from the Ἰουδαῖοι," as a way of evoking temple worship. "Salvation is from the Ἰουδαῖοι" because the Ἰουδαῖοι have been the custodians of the worship place and rites ordained by God; now that those rites and that place are gone (at the time of the Gospel's composition), they are to be found in the person of Jesus.[82]

John 5 and 9 form a diptych.[83] Both scenes take place in Jerusalem; the specific location of both healings being near the temple is significant. Chapter 5 features a long-paralyzed man—presumably a Judean—who does not hesitate to turn Jesus in to the Ἰουδαῖοι for performing a healing on a Sabbath. Here, Ἰουδαῖοι may be understood as religious authorities, specifically those associated with the leadership of the temple: the temple is close by, and the Ἰουδαῖοι clearly have some measure of authority to demand that the healed man give them the information they seek. The latter is also a Ἰουδαῖος.[84] In chapter 9, the story of the man born blind crystallizes the temple dispute: Jesus' first encounter with this man, as with the paralytic in chapter five, is just outside of the temple area (8:59–9:1). The blind man too is a Ἰουδαῖος, who is persecuted by his fellow Ἰουδαῖοι because the man born blind finds and accepts the rival temple.[85] After the healing, when Jesus finds the now-healed man *within* the temple area, he informs him that he is seeing the Son of Man (9:35–37): that is, he is encountering the divine Glory (as Jesus was identified in 1:14, 50–51), which dwells in the temple. The word employed for the blind man's persecutors is "Pharisees" in verses 13, 15, 16, and 40, but Ἰουδαῖοι in verses 18 and 22.[86] Leaving aside the issue of whether these different monikers reflect two different authors or redactors, we might again define Ἰουδαῖοι as temple authorities; but "Pharisees" certainly implies a degree of authority as well. Both terms

---

81. Frühwald-König, *Tempel*, 137. Translation mine.

82. For the Johannine unification of southern and northern worship in Jesus, see Lizorkin-Eyzenberg, *Jewish Gospel*, 16, 18, 77, 117, 192, 231, 267.

83. E.g., Barrett, *According to St. John*, 255.

84. For Ἰουδαῖοι as temple authorities in this verse, see Brown, *According to John (i–xii)*, 208; Lindars, *Gospel of John*, 216.

85. See Wick, *Gottesdienste*, 329.

86. Brown, *According to John (i–xii)*, 373.

are connected with the infamous ἀποσυναγῶγος. In fact, as Grelot points out, the Ἰουδαῖοι in chapter 9 are the same Ἰουδαῖοι, official temple authorities with interrogatory functions, with whom Jesus spars in some of the most severely hostile passages in the Gospel: 7:14-18, 23-30, 33-36 and probably also in 8:22-59.[87] Space does not allow for a detailed discussion of Martyn's *birkat ha-minim* theory, according to which the Fourth Evangelist was directly referring to a formal excommunication of Jesus-believers from their home synagogues around the year 80 CE and that the final form of the Gospel was shaped by a series of "traumas" inflicted upon the community whose experiences are recorded or suggested in it.[88] The only thing that is abundantly clear in this passage is that the Jerusalem religious authorities display hostility toward the healed man consistent with Judean hostility throughout the rest of the Gospel. Since the blind man is a Ἰουδαῖος, and Jesus' words to the Ἰουδαῖοι in 9:41 ("Now that you say 'We see,' your sin remains") are an unequivocal condemnation of the Ἰουδαῖοι's refusal to "see" his true identity, it is obvious that the blind man is an example of one who started out as a blind Ἰουδαῖος and, like Nathanael, only became "a true Israelite" when he recognized Jesus' true identity (worship locus) and was no longer numbered among the Jerusalem temple-affiliated Ἰουδαῖοι as a result. It must be noted that this is not a distinction between "Christianity" and "Judaism," but between "Judea" and "Israel."

DeBoer's claim that the Ἰουδαῖοι's self-description as "disciples of Moses" (9:28) sets them *against* the disciples of Jesus is problematic, since in the very next passage Jesus states that if the Ἰουδαῖοι believed Moses they would accept him (Jesus) because Moses wrote about Jesus, as DeBoer himself acknowledges.[89] However, DeBoer presses the point by arguing

---

87. Grelot, *Les Juifs*, 77.

88. Brown, *According to John (i–xii)*, 374, 379–80; Martyn, *History and Theology*, 59–65, 70, 146, 152. See also Barrett, *John and Judaism*, 59ff.

89. DeBoer, "Depiction," 152–53, 154. Brown too (*According to John (i–xii)*, 379–80) thinks that this scene pits the "disciples of Moses," who stand for "the Jews at the end of the first century who have once and for all rejected the claims of Jesus of Nazareth and who regard his followers as heretics," against the "disciples of Jesus," who represent "the voice of the Christian apologists who think of the Jews as malevolently blinding themselves to the obvious truth implied in Jesus' miracles." Similarly, Martyn portrays an "either Moses or Jesus" choice, with Nicodemus as the prime example of a "Jamnia Loyalist" who is trying, through his dialogue with Jesus, to "gain midrashic data" that will eliminate an either/or decision. Martyn argues along similar lines in his discussion of "children of Abraham" in John 8. Martyn, *History and Theology*, 101–4, 108–23. However, as I argue, the Gospel's point is that a good disciple of Moses is also a disciple

that the Jews—in a *strictly religious* sense of the term Ἰουδαῖοι—"have forced a choice where none needed to be made"; hence the Fourth Evangelist "has been forced to agree that discipleship to Jesus is indeed incompatible with discipleship to Moses when, and only when, the latter adopts as a basic premise the rejection of Jesus as the Messiah."[90] This explanation, however, runs into difficulty. The meaning of Jesus' words is that true disciples of Moses accept Jesus; therefore, Jesus' own disciples are the true disciples of Moses. So it cannot be the case that there are two divided camps, disciples of Moses on one side ("Jews") and disciples of Jesus on the other ("Christians"). Rather, the plain sense of the text is that the disciples of Jesus accept Jesus precisely because they are disciples of Moses. Here, then, is another indication that John reflects not a "Christian" group but a group that is convinced that its way of being Israel is the only correct way. Although DeBoer argues that the religious meaning of "disciples of Moses" precludes Ἰουδαῖοι from being translated as "Judean" in this passage, it is precisely the point that Jesus' disciples are Moses' true disciples that allows us to translate "Judean" here.

John 8 is a watershed for the Judea-Galilee rivalry. In 8:12–20, Jesus announces in the temple area that he and the Father are one, another indication that Jesus is the divine Glory. As Knöppler notes, there are "suggestions of Old Testament atonement theology" in John 8, especially in 8:21–24, verses that suggest that there is no atonement outside of the presence of Christ.[91] This concept makes great sense since Jesus is the temple, where dwelt the Presence of God, and which was the only place where atonement could be effected precisely because of that Presence. This is reinforced in 8:38 when Jesus claims to be "in" the Father's Presence. This is also one of the famous "'I am' sayings," which themselves indicate an identification of Jesus as the divine Glory.

When Jesus refers to "this world" in 8:23, intriguing possibilities arise for the identity of "this world." A solid majority of scholars interpret "this

---

of Jesus. John does not present the hard choice Martyn claims. Brown too sees John's "chief priests" as representatives of Jamnia Judaism (Brown, *Community*, 22, 66). The present study agrees that John presents a divergent path from Jamnia in the aftermath of the Jerusalem temple's fall; but that this is another way of being Jewish, not the unique religion of "Christianity."

90. DeBoer, "Depiction," 154.

91. Knöppler, *Sühne*, 248. See also Frühwald-König: "the value and the claim of the temple as the place of God's revelation are only maintained in connection with the person of the Son of God" (Frühwald-König *Tempel*, 104). Translation mine.

world" as the material/physical world, and/or the world that is opposed to Jesus and rejects him—that is, "the Jews" represent this hostile world.[92] I wish to challenge this consensus by suggesting that the phrase "this world," particularly as it is used in this passage, carries a hint of temple cosmology. Jesus is presumably still in the temple area when he speaks these words, therefore he may not be referring to the "world" in a general sense but to the temple as a "world." This would bring to the fore traditions of temple cosmology and refer forward to Jesus' conversation with Pilate in 18:36 that his "kingdom does not belong to this world." Rather, Jesus' kingdom belongs to the "world" *represented* by the Jerusalem temple—that is, to the *heavenly* temple to which the earthly was meant to correspond. Jesus is not a *model* or *imitation* of the heavenly temple, but the "real thing." Jesus accordingly tells the religious authorities in 9:40–41 that their sin remains because they claim "we see." This means that they think they see the Glory when they look upon the temple building and its rites, when in fact the Glory is standing right in front of them and they cannot see it.

Jesus' notorious charge in 8:44 that the Ἰουδαῖοι have the devil as their father must be addressed. Jesus speaks these harsh words during the Feast of Tabernacles, which as we have seen plays a major role in John's identification of Jesus as worship space. DeBoer's claim that this passage is one in which Ἰουδαῖοι must mean the Jerusalem authorities is surely correct, even though his affirmation that it is the behavior of the Ἰουδαῖοι that is diabolical, and not they themselves, is problematic.[93] DeBoer's argument rests largely on the idea that the use of Ἰουδαῖοι in John reflects the existence of "Johannine Jewish Christians" on one side and "the Jews" on the other, a view of the "Johannine Community" put forward by Martyn, Brown, and others.[94] Once again, it cannot be stated often enough or strongly enough that the Fourth Gospel does not represent the emergence of a Christian "Johannine church," but rather the existence of a group within Judaism that was convinced, much as the Qumran community had been, that they were the only ones who were accurately following the faith of Israel.[95] Of course, if the Ἰουδαῖοι oppose Jesus, the dwelling of the divine Glory, they "have the

---

92. E.g. Barrett, *According to St. John*, 341, 346–49; Grelot, *Les Juifs*, 91, 190–91; Kysar, "Anti-Semitism," 118; Lieu, "Anti-Judaism," 112–13; Lindars, *Gospel of John*, 320; Martyn, *History and Theology*, 3; Moloney, *Text and Context*, 40.

93. DeBoer, "Depiction," 148.

94. Ibid., 149.

95. Lieu, "Anti-Judaism," 106.

devil as their father." The Gospel never levels the same charge against Galileans or Samaritans, who are typically affiliated with "Israel." Judith Lieu has noted that much scholarship has argued that the "vituperative polemic" found in primary sources roughly contemporary with the Fourth Gospel was typical of the socio-religious context, and formed in a pre-Holocaust age; therefore the "anti-Semitism" heard by post-Holocaust ears was not in view when John was written.[96]

At the Feast of the Dedication in 10:22–33, the temple theme is prominent again, as the purpose of this festival was to commemorate the restoration of ritual purity and proper worship after the temple had been defiled by the accretion of Greek influences in the Maccabean era.[97] Here, the Ἰουδαῖοι threaten to stone Jesus to death. In 10:34, Jesus refers to "your law" and then quotes Ps 82:6. What is meant by "your law"? Brown insists that the phrase always "has a hostile connotation," based on his argument that the Gospel was written "against a background of Jewish-Christian hostility."[98] Similarly, Jacques Dutheil sees the Johannine references to "the festivals of the Jews" (citing John 5:1; 6:4; 7:2) and the explanations of Hebrew/Aramaic words and phrases as an indication that Judaism and Christianity were already completely distanced from each other as two distinct faiths: "Little by little; but in the Gospels, one is already there: the Christians become strangers to the Jews, whence come the expressions revealed as much in the Synoptics as in John . . . "[99] C. K. Barrett claims that, once again, the evangelist's self-awareness as a Christian is expressed by a supplanting of Judaism; in this case, Gospel's author "wished to press home upon the Jews the fact that the truth of the Christian position was substantiated by their own historical documents"—hence, "your law."[100] This is not unlike Brown's suggestion that "your law" may function rhetorically in a sense of "the law that you yourselves accept."[101] The pronoun is absent in Ps 45, Sinaiticus, Bezae, and other manuscript traditions; however there may be

---

96. Ibid., 103–4.

97. See Kinzer, "Temple Christology," 449.

98. Brown, *According to John (i–xii)*, 312, 341, 403. Brown's reliance on the *Dialogue with Trypho* as evidence that "your law" was used also in John as polemic introduces an anachronism into the Gospel. Unlike the case with the rabbinic writings under discussion continuing earlier traditions, I have found no evidence that such a usage of "your law" was current prior to the *Dialogue*. See also Grelot, *Les Juifs*, 98–100.

99. Dutheil, "Procés," 207. Translation mine. See also Grelot, *Les Juifs*, 89–92.

100. Barrett, *According to St. John*, 384.

101. Brown, *According to John (i–xii)*, 341, 403.

justification for its presence.¹⁰² As Samaritans did not include the Psalms among their recognized scriptures, but only recognized the Five Books of Moses as God's word, could Jesus be speaking to his Judean audience from a Samaritan—that is, a northern—viewpoint? After this confrontation, Jesus travels to Transjordan (10:40) because the disciples of John the Baptist are there and will certainly welcome Jesus.¹⁰³

In John 10, the term Ἰουδαῖοι is used throughout to designate the religious authorities. Grelot suggests that the term "Pharisees," used in John 7, is absent here because John may be re-locating to this point the Synoptics' final trial scene before the "council of elders of the peoples, chief priests, and scribes."¹⁰⁴ For John, this group, hostile to Jesus and constantly seeking his death, are the Ἰουδαῖοι. This makes sense in the context of Jesus placing himself as "the good shepherd" over against the false shepherds or "wolves" who devour Israel, identified as Israel's own leaders. This, like the temple incident, stands very much in the prophetic tradition, especially as we read in Jeremiah and Ezekiel.

In 12:41, the reference to the prophet Isaiah's vision of "his glory" may refer to the Glory of God or to the glory of Jesus. That it refers to the Glory of God, God's divine Presence, is most likely, given that the Glory was attributed to God in 1:14. Therefore, the Fourth Gospel claims that when Isaiah experienced his vision of the heavenly temple (Isa 6) he saw Jesus, who is God's Presence/Glory.¹⁰⁵ Barrett (artificially) separates the "glory of God," which Isaiah saw, from the "glory of Christ" that is referred to in John 12:41.¹⁰⁶

Finally, in 19:12, 15b the Judean religious authorities proclaim their allegiance to Caesar as their only king. This is a reverse of the faithfulness Judah proclaimed to the house of David in 1 Kgs 12:20b; but as discussed above, John is not interested in portraying Jesus as the heir of David.¹⁰⁷ Whereas in 1 Kgs 12:16–20 the people of the ten northern tribes broke away from David's grandson and Solomon's heir Rehoboam, the situation

---

102. א*, D, Θ, Old Latin, and Sinaitic Syriac also lack "your," reading only "in [the] law." Lindars, *Gospel of John*, 373; also Barrett, *According to St. John*, 384; Grelot, *Les Juifs*, 91.

103. See Brown, *According to John (i–xii)*, 414; Lindars, *Gospel of John*, 377.

104. Grelot, *Les Juifs*, 77.

105. See Brown, *According to John (i–xii)*, 486–87; Kinzer, "Temple Christology," 453–54, 457; Lindars, *Gospel of John*, 439.

106. Barrett, *According to St. John*, 432; Kinzer, "Temple Christology," 457.

107. See Meeks, "Galilee and Judea," 159.

is now reversed: the north (Samaria-Galilee) remains faithful to God by accepting the Glory present in Jesus, while the south (Judea) breaks away from the kingship of God (made clear in John 19:15) to choose a ruler, the Roman emperor, who is essentially usurping a power that has not come from God. It is the Judean religious authorities, aligned with the Jerusalem temple institution, who reject Jesus as king by pledging allegiance to Caesar only. This, as many scholars have noted, harkens back to 1 Sam 8:7, where God explains to the judge/prophet Samuel that the people, in asking for a human king, have rejected God as their king.[108] Lowe also brings out an important point regarding the appellations βασιλεὺς τῶν Ἰουδαίων/βασιλεὺς Ἰσραήλ in the Fourth Gospel: the former is used only by Romans, the latter only by the Ἰουδαῖοι themselves, "whether in praise or in scorn."[109] Lowe dismisses explanations of "in-group/out-group" usage in favor of claiming that "the Messiah was supposed to be king of all Israel and not merely of Judea."[110] As for the titulus on the cross, the Synoptics along with John have Pilate himself commanding the wording βασιλεὺς τῶν Ἰουδαίων. Not only does this reinforce Lowe's point that only the Romans use this phrase; but it contributes to the theme of misunderstanding in John. No one in the Gospel really knows who Jesus is or what his origin is; Pilate, failing to see the truth (18:38), calls Jesus the king of the Ἰουδαῖοι—perhaps to spite the Judean rulers and religious authorities who had just sworn allegiance to Caesar in 19:15. Lowe also suggests that Pilate may have seen Jesus as a Ἰουδαῖος because the charge of rebellion had been brought by Judean authorities; this would make sense in the historical context of Judea at Passover as a hotbed of political unrest.[111] Pilate would have used the phrase βασιλεὺς τῶν Ἰουδαίων on the public charge as a warning to other potential rebels who might consider starting trouble in his procurate.

Barrett goes so far as to claim that this rejection in John indicates that the entirety of Israel has "abdicated its own unique position under the immediate sovereignty of God," giving way to the church (as discussed above). While Barrett claims that Ἰουδαῖοι typically refers to the Jerusalem religious authorities, affiliated with the institutional and geographical

---

108. See Barrett, *According to St. John*, 546; Lindars, *Gospel of John*, 572 (though Lindars incorrectly attributes the Johannine rejection to "the Jews" as a whole, when it is clear that the only people present at Jesus' condemnation are the temple leadership).

109. Lowe, "ΙΟΥΔΑΙΟΙ," 118. See also Tomson, "Jews," 180–83, 191–203.

110. Lowe, "ΙΟΥΔΑΙΟΙ," 119.

111. Ibid., 118–19.

center of hostility toward, and rejection of, Jesus, he also argues (similarly to Moloney) that the negative manner in which those authorities and Jerusalem are portrayed points to the end of Judaism's legitimacy as a religion, the "supplanting" of Judaism by Christianity.[112] Hence, in no case does it "seem that John means 'the Judeans' (as distinct from the Galileans)."[113] For Barrett, John makes a decisive separation of Christianity from Judaism; following the "persecuted Johannine Christian community" paradigm, they are two distinct religions by the time the Gospel is written.[114] Barrett cites the trial scene as evidence of this dichotomy.[115] Similarly, Brown argues that the "Jewish" rejection of Jesus in John 19:15 indicates that the Jewish people have broken "the covenant whereby God or his Messiah was Israel's king" and therefore signifies that, in the context of an envisioned first-century "Christians vs. Jews" conflict, the "Jews" as a whole have "renounced their status as God's people."[116] That this is a specifically (and geographically) *Judean* rejection, however, is clear from the fact that the group rejecting Jesus (and hence God) as king in John is made up solely of temple-affiliated authorities. Throughout this passage, it is *Judeans*, those affiliated with the temple located in the geographical territory of Judea, who reject Jesus' authority and demand his execution. Jesus' death is really the destruction of a rival temple that threatens the authorities' own locus of status, economic power, and political stability. Ἰουδαῖοι must be translated accordingly as "Judeans." It cannot be understood to refer to the whole of the people Israel; much less generally applied to ethnic Jews of either the first century or of later times.[117]

---

112. Robert Kysar claims that "the message of Jesus is everywhere presented as superior to the *religion* of the Jews;" the same goes for the superiority of Jesus' "message" over the temple: "The conclusion is inescapable that the text of the narrative nurtures a negative mentality toward Jews and Judaism" (Kysar, "Anti-Semitism," 113–27, 117). Emphasis mine. See also Ruether, "Theological Anti-Semitism," 192.

113. Barrett, *According to St. John*, 171–72.

114. See also Barrett, *John and Judaism*, 59ff; Brown, *Community*, 22–24, 66–69; Moloney, *Text and Context*, 39–42.

115. Barrett, *John and Judaism*, 71.

116. Barrett, *According to St. John*, 546; Brown, *According to John (xiii–xxi)*, 894–95. Adele Reinhartz similarly argues that the Fourth Gospel portrays the Jewish people as being "expelled" from God's covenant, shown especially in John 8:31–59, where the Ἰουδαῖοι claim covenant membership by virtue of their descent from Abraham only to have Jesus respond that they are descended rather from "the devil" and thereby outside of the covenant. Reinhartz, "Grammar of Hate," 422–24.

117. Lizorkin-Eyzenberg ultimately suggests that Ἰουδαῖοι should stand un-translated

Jesus' Origins

There is some question regarding who is defined as Jesus' "own" or "own country/people" in John 1:11. Is it Judea or Galilee? As Wayne Meeks reminds us, Jesus' arising from Galilee is precisely the point of contention in 1:46 ("Can anything good come from Nazareth?") and 7:40–52 ("The Messiah will not come from Galilee, will he?" "No prophet arises from Galilee"). Jesus' "own" nation or people can be considered to be Judea only in the sense that Jesus is the divine Glory and God had chosen Jerusalem as the place where the divine Glory should reside. Since God had willed that the Glory be housed in Jerusalem, Judea can in this sense be said to be Jesus' "own." This is the meaning of 1:44: the place where the Glory was chosen to dwell, and the people among whom the Glory dwelt, ironically did not recognize (and accordingly receive) the Glory. Others—those from Samaria and Galilee, where according to Judean tradition God had *not* chosen a permanent dwelling-place—did. This also resolves the apparent difficulty at 4:43–44, where Jesus departs Judea and heads for Galilee because "a prophet has no honor in his native place."[118] For Brown, as the subsequent Galilean reception of Jesus displays a rather "shallow" faith ("Unless you people see signs and wonders, you will not believe," 4:48), the evangelist's point is to show that the Galileans in fact "believe in" Jesus no better than the Judeans.[119] Hence, Jesus is accepted neither in his physical domicile (Galilee/Nazareth) nor in his "spiritual" home (Judea/Jerusalem). This could be supported by 6:26, in which Jesus chastises the Galilean crowd for pursuing him in the hope that he might provide another meal, akin to the loaves and fish he had multiplied in 6:11–13 (and which had impelled the same crowd to try to make Jesus king "by force," 6:15). However, considering the overall context of the Gospel and its overwhelmingly positive portrayal of Galilee/Samaria, the welcome in 4:45 cannot in any way be considered as a rejection. The Galileans do not reject Jesus. Their acceptance of him may be wrong-headed, because it is based on a misunderstanding of the meaning of Jesus' miraculous deeds (4:45); they may have the wrong idea in desiring to make him king; but they still accept him and, as we have observed, provide safe haven from the hostil-

---

in John. Lizorkin-Eyzenberg, *Jewish Gospel*, 14–15.

118. For a discussion of this difficulty, see Meeks, "Galilee and Judea," 163–65.

119. Brown, *According to John (i–xii)*, 187. The NRSV has only "you"; the translation here follows the NABRE, which by adding "people" sustains the plural of the Greek.

ity of the Ἰουδαῖοι. Jesus' "native place" in which he is not accepted must therefore be Judea; but it is so in a strictly symbolic or theological sense. The Glory had to leave Jerusalem because it was not accepted there. This is not much different than what we find in Ezek 9:3; 10:4, 18–19; 11:22–23, when the Glory departs the Jerusalem temple and moves eastward to dwell among the exiles (where the prophet observes it in Ezek 3:23). In John, the movement is northward instead of eastward, but the concept is identical. Meeks is correct in observing that Judea and Galilee function symbolically (or better, theologically) in John; he is not correct in his assignment of those symbols to "Jews" and "Gentile Christians." Judea in the Fourth Gospel represents the temple institution, not ethnic Jews; Galilee and Samaria represent the recognition of Jesus as the Glory and the temple (along with the temple's necessary sacrifice), not ethnic Gentiles.

Summary and Conclusions

It is imperative for the understanding of John's usage of the term Ἰουδαῖοι to realize that this term is entirely dependent upon the Gospel's theme of Jesus as sacrifice and temple. The Gospel was written to address worship questions for an "intra-Israelite" audience.[120] As Lowe writes, "John's Gospel is not anti-*Jewish* (but at most anti-*Judean*)."[121] Grelot takes an even stronger position by stating "No book of the New Testament is more profoundly Jewish than the Gospel of John. It is so, because Jesus himself was, and the others."[122] Indeed, John Ashton likens the Ἰουδαῖοι hostility in John to "a family row," which is quite close to the mark.[123] I would add to Grelot's words that Jesus is Jewish in John as the temple was Jewish, and as sacrificial worship was practiced within first-century Judaism. John attempts to *preserve* Jewish worship—not to abrogate it—in the absence of the Jerusalem temple. Ἰουδαῖοι is overwhelmingly predicated of the geographical area in which hostility toward Jesus is centered and of those

---

120. Lizorkin-Eyzenberg also states, accurately in my view: "Had the author imagined ... that, just a few centuries later, it would be primarily non-Israelites who would read and interpret his magnificent Gospel, being removed culturally and socio-religiously from its original setting, he might have been much more careful with the use of his terminology" (Lizorkin-Eyzenberg, *Jewish Gospel*, 18).

121. Lowe, "ΙΟΥΔΑΙΟΙ," 130n88. Emphasis in original.

122. Grelot, *Les Juifs*, 187. Translation mine.

123. Ashton, *Understanding*, 151.

hostile characters, Jesus' enemies, who hail from that region, in which the temple institution is located. Ἰσραήλ and Ἰσραηλίτης, on the other hand, are employed in reference to those characters receptive to Jesus, and by extension to the geographical location of safety for him. Far from portraying a conflict between two different religions, as a litany of scholars have argued, John portrays instead an "intra-Jewish" conflict, a struggle to identify the right place and manner of worship as the person of Jesus. The Fourth Gospel is a record of a movement that was convinced it was "doing the Israelite faith right," not unlike other contemporary sects of first-century Judaism. In the words of Brian D. Johnson,

> [John] presents Jesus as the true fulfillment or the correct interpretation of [Jewish] symbols. Jesus is the one who properly wears the Jewish titles, who takes the place of the temple as the place of worship, and as the one dwelling with his disciples . . . Jesus is that which gives Judaism meaning . . . [the evangelist] has interwoven several elements of Judaism and has presented Jesus as the answer to them all.[124]

I cannot agree with Charlesworth that John "violates much biblical theology" in its supposed "exclusivism," nor that "anti-Jewish" polemic belongs to a later stage of development that contradicts the essential heart of the Gospel's original inclusiveness and is therefore "not the word of God for our time."[125] The Gospel as it has been received, not as it may have been in a hypothetical primitive form, must be considered. While Charlesworth states that a Qumranesque "exclusivism" is not characteristic of John's original intent, I propose exactly the contrary: the Fourth Gospel fits precisely a first-century socio-religious context in which various groups or sects within Judaism were severally claiming to be the sole proprietors of the "right way" to express their identity as the covenant people Israel. The Qumran community was one; the audience for whom the Fourth Gospel was intended was another. The error that Brown, Martyn, Barrett, Moloney, and others commit is in presuming that a "high Christology" must signify that the Gospel evolved in stages, each one featuring a group that rose to numerical and accordingly theological prominence in the "Johannine (Christian) Community" and influenced the Gospel's redaction, until the community comprised a Gentile majority who brought with them a view of Christ as a divine being.

124. Johnson, "Salvation," 97–99.
125. Charlesworth, "Exclusivism," 276.

Jesus' harsh words to the Ἰουδαῖοι in John 5, 7, and 8 are directly in line with the reproaches aimed at Israel's "shepherds" by the prophets.[126] The temple incident in John 2 is likewise "in the best prophetic tradition," yet in John any critique of temple and cult is grounded in theological/Christological concerns and ideas: the whole purpose of temple- and cult-criticism in the Fourth Gospel is to show Jesus as the true dwelling-place of God's presence, an alternative, indeed a rival, to the temple in Jerusalem (a redundant institution at the time of John's composition).[127] The entirety of the dispute between Jesus and the Ἰουδαῖοι, beginning with the temple incident and continuing through the most vitriolic arguments of chapters 5, 7, and 8, are entirely based upon temple and cult and are meant not to demonize ethnic Jews but to show Jesus as the true place of God's presence, of God's revelation, of sacrifice, and thereby of worship.[128] Ironically, the disputes end when, in their zeal to preserve their temple institution, the Ἰουδαῖοι attempt to destroy the true dwelling of God's Glory—the person of Jesus—and by this drastic misunderstanding of worship space they make possible the eternal temple—Jesus' risen body—and make inevitable the destruction of their temple institution by Rome.[129]

---

126. L'Éplattenier, "'Les Juifs,'" 131.

127. Frühwald-König, *Tempel*, 104, 137.

128. Ibid., 104–5, 220. Frühwald-König, however, does not appear to distinguish between the ethnic, theological, and geographical character of Ἰουδαῖοι.

129. Ibid., 221–22.

6

Conclusion

Summary of Findings and Contributions of This Study

THIS THESIS HAS ENDEAVORED to demonstrate that the Gospel of John bases its temple Christology on the presentation of Jesus as sacrifice. Specifically, Jesus in John performs all of the functions of the Passover lamb, the *tāmîd*, and the *tôdāh* offerings. However, rather than depicting the end of Judaism, this scheme ensures the *continuation* of Jewish worship. The Gospel did not present this picture while the Jerusalem temple still stood. Had that been the situation, a case could be made for the Gospel standing against Judaism and claiming that Judaism was a religion that needed to be replaced. Such is not the case, however. John was written after the Jerusalem temple was destroyed, and the Gospel's picture of Jesus as the locus of worship makes sense as part of an intra-Jewish discussion about where to worship in the post-70 CE absence of the temple institution. John presents an alternative to both Roman temples and to the contemporary development of rabbinic Judaism: the temple is now found not among Roman gods or Torah study, but in the person of the risen Jesus. The Gospel achieves this by drawing upon Akedah traditions that linked the functions of Passover, *tāmîd*, and *tôdāh* with the self-offering of Isaac, which had ensured that his descendants would be delivered from death and from sin. Since all sacrificial worship was identified with the Akedah in traditions that attributed the location of the Jerusalem temple to that event, any Akedah associations in John also paint Jesus as the place of worship.

We have seen that this does not abstract worship to the intellectual realm. Since the body of Jesus is a physical location, John does not claim that worship must be removed from physical space. The Gospel merely re-locates the worship space, identifying the person of Jesus with the region of Samaria/Galilee and removing worship space from the region of Judea/Jerusalem. Samaria/Galilee, representing Israel with the Glory/divine Presence in its midst, is referred to as Ἰσραήλ while the ironically templeless Judea and its leaders are referred to as Ἰουδαῖοι.

There are four chief contributions of this thesis to scholarship on the Fourth Gospel:

1. The presence of Isaac typology in John deserves revisiting.

2. In connection with number one above, the sacrificial elements in the Fourth Gospel should be reconsidered, as their presence suggests that, contrary to much received tradition, John does not propose an end to Judaism or to sacrificial worship. The identification of Jesus as sacrifice in John does not equate to supersession. Jesus does not replace Jewish worship, but embodies it. While Daniel C. Ullucci is correct in claiming that the early Christian movement did not participate in *animal* sacrifice (at least, they no longer did so after the destruction of the Jerusalem temple), he is incorrect to claim that Christians abandoned sacrifice altogether.[1] This opens a door for a view of John that challenges some readings that claim that the Gospel has no interest in ritual, and that question the eucharistic tenor of John.

3. The issue of the translation of Ἰουδαῖοι should be reexamined specifically in the light of the Fourth Gospel's theme of worship location. The translation of Ἰουδαῖοι into English as "Jews" is difficult to defend, since the Gospel employs this term specifically in the connection of the worship-space debate and decidedly not in a replacement/supersession scheme. Ideally, translators and Christian faith communities would be willing to take up this reexamination. Also, according to this view, new possibilities arise for Jewish-Christian dialogue and a more accurate popular understanding of John's portrayal of the group titled Ἰουδαῖοι.

4. Given the likelihood that John was composed as a direct result of the destruction of the Jerusalem temple, for the purpose of contributing to the discussion of continuing Jewish identity and appropriate worship place and praxis, the consensus date of the Gospel's composition might be challenged. A conversation about worship such as we find

---

1. Ullucci, *Animal Sacrifice*, esp. 4, 134–35, ch. 4.

in John would likely not have occurred decades after the temple's destruction, but closer to the time of the event that prompted the Johannine view. With this, John's high Christology need not be attributed to a late composition date. The Christological implications of Jesus as sacrifice and worship space, the dwelling of God's Presence, would not be out of place in the post-temple setting. This would be supported by the lofty ideas of Logos and high priest (and of Logos *as* high priest) expressed in the writings of Philo that we have examined. In the Johannine portrayal of Jesus as Logos, high priest, and sacrifice, there is nothing that demands a late date, as such ideas were current even before 70 CE.

Our examination also contributes to the recent challenges to the "Johannine Community" hypothesis advanced by Martyn, Brown, and others as we have discussed. While the "Johannine Community" hypothesis is based on a *temporal* paradigm, the proposal of the present study is oriented toward a *spatial* paradigm.[2] Rather than providing a record of an insular group, increasingly persecuted over time for its gradual development of a "high Christology," the Fourth Gospel may be viewed as a record of one response to an event of massive consequence that forced a radical shift in Jewish worship and identity. Rather than a slow evolution, the Gospel of John, this study proposes, emerged in a sudden flash with the necessity of finding a new expression and mode of worship. Rather than go the route of Jamnia, John proposed an alternative path, ready-made in the already-existing traditions surrounding the passion, death, and resurrection of Jesus.

---

2. Many thanks to my advisor, Dr. Robert A. Hill, for this insight.

Bibliography

Ajer, Peter Claver. "The Death of Jesus and the Politics of Place in the Gospel of John." PhD diss., Graduate Theological Union, 2014.

Akpunonu, P. D. *The Vine, Israel, and the Church*. New York: Lang, 2004.

Aland, Barbara, Kurt Aland, Johannes Karavidopoulos, Carlo M. Martini, Bruce M. Metzger, eds. *The Greek New Testament*. 4th ed. Stuttgart: Deutsche Bibelgesellschaft (United Bible Societies), 1998.

Allegro, John M., ed. *Qumran Cave 4: I (4q158–4q186)*. Vol. 5, *Discoveries in the Judaean Desert of Jordan*. Oxford: Clarendon, 1968.

Ashton, John. "The Identity and Function of the ΊΟΥΔΑΙΟΙ in the Fourth Gospel." *Novum Testamentum* 27.1 (1985) 40–75.

———. *Studying John: Approaches to the Fourth Gospel*. New York: Oxford University Press, Clarendon, 1994.

———. *Symbolism in the Fourth Gospel: Meaning, Mystery, Community*. Minneapolis: Fortress, 1995.

———. *Understanding the Fourth Gospel*. New York: Oxford University Press, 2007.

Attridge, H. W. "Temple, Tabernacle, Time, and Space in John and Hebrews." *Early Christianity* 1.2 (2010) 261–74.

Augenstein, J. "Jesus und das Gesetz Im Johannesevangelium." *Kirche und Israel* 14.2 (1999) 161–79.

Azar, M. "The Scriptural King." *St. Vladimir's Theological Quarterly* 50.3 (2006) 255–75.

Barker, Margaret. *The Gate of Heaven: The History and Symbolism of the Temple in Jerusalem*. Reprint, Sheffield, UK: Sheffield Phoenix, 2008 (1991).

Baron, L. "Interpreting the Shema: Liturgy and Identity in the Fourth Gospel." *Annali di storia dell' esegesi* 27.2 (2010) 53–60.

Barrett, C. K. *The Gospel According to St. John: An Introduction with Commentary and Notes on the Greek Text*. 2nd ed. Philadelphia: Westminster John Knox, 1978.

———. *The Gospel of John and Judaism*. Translated by D. M. Smith. Philadelphia: Fortress, 1975.

Barus, Armand. "John 2:12–25: A Narrative Reading." In *New Currents Through John*, edited by Francisco Lozada, Jr. and Tom Thatcher, 123–40. Atlanta: Society of Biblical Literature, 2006.

Bauckham, Richard. *The Testimony of the Beloved Disciple*. Grand Rapids: Baker Academic, 2007.

BIBLIOGRAPHY

Beauchamp, Paul. "Un Livre et Deux Communautés." In *Procés de Jésus, Procés des Juifs?*, edited by Alain Marchadour, 15–27. Paris: Cerf, 1998.

Beckmann, K. "Funktion und Gestalt des Judas Iskarioth Im Johannesevangelium." *Berliner Theologische Zeitschrift* 11.2 (1994) 181–200.

Bennema, C. "The Identity and Composition of Oi Ioudaioi in the Gospel of John." *Tyndale Bulletin* 60.2 (2009) 239–63.

Bernier, Jonathan. *Aposynagōgos and the Historical Jesus in John: Rethinking the Historicity of the Johannine Expulsion Passages*. Boston: Brill, 2013.

Biale, David. "Blood and the Covenant: The Jewish and Christian Careers of a Biblical Verse." In *Blood and Belief: The Circulation of a Symbol between Jews and Christians*, 44–80. Los Angeles: University of California Press, 2007.

Bloch-Smith, Elizabeth. "'Who Is the King of Glory?' Solomon's Temple and Its Symbolism." In *Scripture and Other Artifacts: Essays on the Bible and Archaeology*, edited by Michael D. Coogan, Cheryl J. Exum, and Lawrence E. Stager, 18–31. Louisville, KY: Westminster John Knox, 1994.

Borgen, Peder. *Bread from Heaven*. Leiden: Brill, 1965.

———. *Philo, John and Paul: New Perspectives on Judaism and Early Christianity*. Atlanta: Scholars, 1987.

Boughton, L. C. "The Priestly Perspective of the Johannine Trial Narratives." *Revue Biblique* 110.4 (2003) 517–51.

Boustan, Ra'anan S. "Confounding Blood: Jewish Narratives of Sacrifice and Violence in Late Antiquity." In *Ancient Mediterranean Sacrifice*, edited by Jennifer Wright Knust and Zsuzsanna Várhelyi, 265–87. New York: Oxford University Press, 2011.

———. "The Dislocation of the Temple Vessels: Mobile Sanctity and Rabbinic Rhetorics of Space." In *Jewish Studies at the Crossroads of Anthropology and History*, edited by Ra'anan Boustan, Oren Kozansky, and Marina Rustow, 135–46. Philadelphia: University of Pennsylvania Press, 2011.

Bowker, John. *Jesus and the Pharisees*. Cambridge: Cambridge University Press, 1973.

Bowman, John. *Fourth Gospel and the Jews: A Study in R. Akiba, Esther and the Gospel of John*. Pittsburgh: Pickwick, 1975.

Broer, I. "Die Juden Im Urteil Der Autoren Des Neuen Testaments: Anmerkungen Zum Problem Historischer Gerechtigkeit Im Angesicht Einer Verheerenden Wirkungsgeschichte." *Theologie und Glaube* 82.1 (1992) 2–33.

Brown, Raymond E. *The Community of the Beloved Disciple*. Toronto: Paulist, 1979.

———. *The Death of the Messiah*. Anchor Bible Reference Library. 2 vols. New York: Doubleday, 1993.

———. *The Gospel According to John (i–xii)*. Anchor Bible Series 29. Garden City, NY: Doubleday, 1966.

———. *The Gospel According to John (xiii–xxi)*. Anchor Bible Series 29A. Garden City, NY: Doubleday, 1970.

Buch-Hansen, Gitte. *It Is the Spirit that Gives Life: A Stoic Understanding of Pneuma in John's Gospel*. Beihefte zur Zeitschrift für die neutestamentliche Wissenschaft und die Kunde der älteren Kirche. Berlin: Walter de Gruyter, 2010.

Bultmann, Rudolf. *The Gospel of John: A Commentary*. Philadelphia: Westminster, 1971.

Byron, B. F. "Bethany Across the Jordan or Simply: Across the Jordan." *Australian Biblical Review* 46 (1998) 36–54.

Callaway, Mary C. "A Hammer that Breaks Rock in Pieces: Prophetic Critique in the Hebrew Bible." In *Anti-Semitism and Early Christianity: Polemic and Faith*, edited by Craig A. Evans and Donald A. Hagner, 21–38. Minneapolis: Fortress, 1993.

Caragounis, C. C. "Vine, Vineyard, Israel, and Jesus." *Svensk Exegetisk Årsbok* 65 (2000) 201–14.

Carter, Warren. *John and Empire: Initial Explorations*. New York: T. & T. Clark, 2008.

Ceresko, Anthony R. "The Rhetorical Strategy of the Fourth Servant Song (Isaiah 52:13—53:12): Poetry and the Exodus-New Exodus." *Catholic Biblical Quarterly* 56 (1994) 42–55.

Chalvon-Demersay, Guy. "Le Symbolisme Du Temple Et Le Nouveau Temple." *Recherches de Sciences Réligieuses* 82.2 (1994) 168–69, 171–75.

Chamberlain, John V. "Anti-Semitism and the Gospel in the New Testament." *Saint Luke's Journal of Theology* 23.3 (1980) 190–200.

Charlesworth, James H. "The Gospel of John: Exclusivism Caused by a Social Setting Different from That of Jesus." In *Anti-Judaism and the Fourth Gospel*, edited by Reimund Bieringer, Didier Pollefeyt, and Frederique Vandecasteele-Vanneuville, 247–78. Louisville, KY: Westminster John Knox, 2001.

———, ed. *The Dead Sea Scrolls: Hebrew, Aramaic, and Greek Texts with English Translations: Rule of the Community and Related Documents*. Vol. 1. Tübingen: J. C. B. Mohr (Paul Siebeck), 1994.

———, ed. *Jews and Christians: Exploring the Past, Present, and Future*. New York: Crossroad, 1990.

———, ed. *The Old Testament Pseudepigrapha*. Vol. 2, *Expansions of the "Old Testament" and Legends, Wisdom and Philosophical Literature, Prayers, Psalms, and Odes, Fragments of Lost Judeo-Hellenistic Works*, edited by J. H. Charlesworth, 35–142. Garden City, NY: Doubleday, 1985.

Chatelion Counet, Patrick. "No Anti-Judaism in the Fourth Gospel: A Deconstruction of Readings of John 8." In *One Text, a Thousand Methods: Studies in Memory of Sjef Van Tilborg*, edited by Patrick Chatelion Counet and Ulrich Berges, 197–225. Boston: Brill, 2005.

Chennattu, R. M. *Johannine Discipleship as a Covenant Relationship*. Peabody, MA: Hendrickson, 2006.

Chilton, Bruce D. "Jesus and the Question of Anti-Semitism." In *Anti–Semitism and Early Christianity*, edited by Craig A. Evans, 39–52. Minneapolis: Fortress, 1993.

Collins, Raymond F. "Speaking of the Jews: 'Jews' in the Discourse Material of the Fourth Gospel." In *Anti-Judaism and the Fourth Gospel*, edited by Reimund Bieringer, Didier Pollefeyt, and Frederique Vandecasteele-Vanneuville, 158–75. Louisville: Westminster John Knox, 2001.

Coloe, Mary L. *Dwelling in the Household of God: Johannine Ecclesiology and Spirituality*. Collegeville, MN: Liturgical, 2007.

———. "The Dwelling of God Among Us: The Symbolic Function of the Temple in the Fourth Gospel." *Pacifica* 12.2 (1999) 244.

———. *God Dwells with Us: Temple Symbolism in the Fourth Gospel*. Collegeville, MN: Liturgical, 2001.

———. "Raising the Johannine Temple (John 19:19–37)." *Australian Biblical Review* 48 (2000) 47–58.

———. "Temple Imagery in John." *Interpretation* 63.4 (2009) 368–81.

Cromhout, M. "In Pursuit of the Millennium: Judeans and Their Land." *Acta Theologica* 27.1 (2007) 22–45.

Culpepper, R. Alan. "Anti-Judaism in the Fourth Gospel as a Theological Problem for Christian Interpreters." In *Anti-Judaism and the Fourth Gospel*, edited by Reimund Bieringer, Didier Pollefeyt, and Frederique Vandecasteele-Vanneuville, 61–82. Louisville: Westminster John Knox, 2001.

———. *The Gospel and Letters of John*. Edited by Charles B. Cousar. Interpreting Biblical Texts. Nashville: Abingdon, 1998.

Daise, M. A. "Ritual Transference and Johannine Identity." *Annali di storia dell' esegesi* 27.2 (2010) 45–51.

Daly, R. J. *Christian Sacrifice: The Judeo-Christian Background Before Origen*. Studies in Christian Antiquity 18. Washington, DC: Catholic University of America Press, 1978.

———. *Origins of the Christian Doctrine of Sacrifice*. Philadelphia: Fortress, 1978.

Darr, John A. "Mimetic Desire, the Gospels, and Early Christianity: A Response to René Girard." *Biblical Interpretation* 1.3 (1993) 357–67.

DeBoer, M. "The Depiction of 'the Jews' in John's Gospel: Matters of Behavior and Identity." In *Anti-Judaism and the Fourth Gospel*, edited by R. Bieringer, Didier Pollefeyt, and Frederique Vandecasteele-Vanneuville, 141–57. Louisville, KY: Westminster John Knox, 2001.

Dennis, J. A. *Jesus' Death and the Gathering of True Israel: The Johannine Appropriation of Restoration Theology in the Light of John 11.47–52*. Tübingen: Mohr Siebeck, 2006.

———. "Restoration in John 11,47–52: Reading the Key Motifs in Their Jewish Context." *Ephemerides Theologicae Lovanienses* 81.1 (2005) 57–86.

Derrett, J. D. M. *The Victim: The Johannine Passion Narrative Revisited*. Shipston-on-Stour, UK: P. I. Drinkwater, 1993.

Diefenbach, M. *Der Konflikt Jesu Mit Den 'Juden': Ein Versuch Zur Losung Der Johanneischen Antijudaismus-Diskussion Mit Hilfe Des Antiken Handlungsverstandnisses*. Neutestamentliche Abhandlungen, Neue Folge. Münster: Aschendorff, 2002.

Dietzfelbinger, Christian. "Sühnetod im Johannesevangelium?" In *Evangelium, Schriftauslegung, Kirche: Festschrift für Peter Stuhlmacher zum 65. Geburtstag*. Edited by Jostein Ådna, Scott J. Hafemann, Otfried Hofius, and Gerlinde Feine, 65–76. Göttingen: Vandenhoeck & Ruprecht, 1997.

Dodd, C. H. *Historical Tradition in the Fourth Gospel*. New York: Cambridge University Press, 1963.

———. *The Interpretation of the Fourth Gospel*. Cambridge, UK: Cambridge University Press, 1960.

Donaldson, Terence L. "The New Testament and Anti-Semitism: Three Important Books." *Theological Students Fellowship Bulletin* 4.4 (1981) 12–14.

Dowell, Thomas M. "Jews and Christians in Conflict: Why the Fourth Gospel Changed the Synoptic Tradition." *Louvain Studies* 15 (1990) 19–37.

Draper, J. A. "Temple, Tabernacle and Mystical Experience in John." *Neotestamentica* 31.2 (1997) 263–88.

Dunderberg, I., C. Tuckett, and K. Syreeni, eds. *Fair Play: Diversity and Conflicts in Early Christianity: Essays in Honour of Heikki Raisanen*. Supplements to Novum Testamentum. Boston: Brill, 2002.

Dunn, James D. G. "The Question of Anti-Semitism in the New Testament and Writings of the Period." In *Jews and Christians*, edited by J. D. G. Dunn, 177–211. Tubingen: Mohr Siebeck, 1992.
Dunstan, G. J. O. "The Clothing of the Passion: Symbolism in the Passion Narrative of St. John." *Search* 22.1 (1999) 26–33.
duRand, J. A. "Does O Ochlos Refer to the 'Am Ha'ares in John 7:49?" *Ekklesiasticos Pharos* 77.1 (1995) 32–38.
Dutheil, Jacques. "Procés de Jésus, Procés des Juifs." In *Procés de Jésus, Procés des Juifs?*, edited by Alain Marchadour, 203–10. Paris: Cerf, 1998.
Edwards, Ruth B. "John and the Jews." *Expository Times* 113.7 (2002) 233–35.
Eisenbaum, Pamela. *Paul Was Not a Christian*. New York: HarperOne, 2009.
Evans, Craig A. "Faith and Polemic: The New Testament and First-Century Judaism." In *Anti-Semitism and Early Christianity*, edited by Craig A. Evans, 1–17. Minneapolis: Fortress, 1993.
———. "Feeding the Five Thousand and the Eucharist." In *John, Jesus, and History*, Vol. 2, *Aspects of Historicity in the Fourth Gospel*, edited by Paul N. Anderson, Felix Just, and Tom Thatcher, 131–38. Atlanta: Society of Biblical Literature, 2009.
Feldman, Louis H., trans. *Judean Antiquities 1–4*. Boston: Brill Academic, 2004.
Fine, Steven. *This Holy Place*. South Bend, IN: University of Notre Dame Press, 1998.
Fiorenza, Elisabeth Schüssler, ed. *Aspects of Religious Propaganda in Judaism and Early Christianity*. Center for the Study of Judaism and Christianity in Antiquity. Notre Dame, IN: University of Notre Dame, 1976.
Fitzmyer, Joseph A. "The Sacrifice of Isaac in Qumran Literature." *Jewish Studies Blog by Dr. Eli: Official Forum of Israel Institute of Biblical Studies*, December 16, 2012.
Fletcher-Louis, Crispin H. T. "Jesus, the Temple and the Dissolution of Heaven and Earth." In *Apocalyptic in History and Tradition*, edited by Christopher Rowland and John Barton, 117–41. Journal for the Study of the Pseudepigrapha Supplement Series. New York: Sheffield Academic, 2002.
Focant, C. "Du Temple à la Maison: L'éspace Du Culte En Esprit St En Vérité." *Revue Theologique de Louvain* 37.3 (2006) 342–60.
Fortna, Robert. *The Fourth Gospel and Its Predecessor*. Philadelphia: Fortress, 1988.
Freedman, H., and Maurice Simon, trans. *The Midrash Rabbah*. Vol. 1, *Genesis*. New York: Soncino, 1983.
———. *The Midrash Rabbah*. Vol. 2, *Exodus Leviticus*. New York: Soncino, 1983.
Freyne, S. *Galilee, Jesus and the Gospels: Literary Approaches and Historical Investigations*. Philadelphia: Fortress, 1988.
Frühwald-König, J. *Tempel Und Kult: Ein Beitrag Zur Christologie Des Johannesevangeliums*. Biblische Untersuchungen. Regensburg: Pustet, 1998.
Fuglseth, K. S. *Johannine Sectarianism in Perspective: A Sociological, Historical, and Comparative Analysis of Temple and Social Relationships in the Gospel of John, Philo, and Qumran*. Supplements to Novum Testamentum. Boston: Brill, 2005.
Fuller, Reginald H. "Jews in the Fourth Gospel." *Dialog* 16.1 (1977) 31–37.
Gese, Hartmut. "The Origin of the Lord's Supper." In *Essays on Biblical Theology*. Minneapolis: Fortress, 1981.
Geyser, A. S. "Israel in the Fourth Gospel." *Neotestamentica* 20 (1986) 13–20.
Ginsberg, H. L. "Oldest Interpretation of the Suffering Servant." *Vetus Testamentum* 63.3 (2013) 25–28.

Girard, René. "Is There Anti-Semitism in the Gospels?" *Biblical Interpretation* 1.3 (1993) 339–52.

Grappe, C. "Jean 1,14(–1) dans son Contexte et à La Lumiere de la Littérature Intertestamentaire." *Revue d'Histoire et de Philosophie Religieuses* 80.1 (2000) 153–69.

Grelot, P. *Les Juifs Dans L'évangile Selon Jean: Enquête Historique Et Réflexion Théologique.* Cahiers De La Revue Biblique. Paris: Gabalda, 1995.

Grigsby, Bruce H. "The Cross as an Expiatory Sacrifice in John." *Journal for the Study of the New Testament* 15 (1982) 51–80.

Gruen, Erich S. *Diaspora: Jews Amidst Greeks and Romans.* Cambridge: Harvard University Press, 2002.

Guilding, Aileen. *The Fourth Gospel in Jewish Worship.* Oxford: Clarendon, 1960.

Hadas-Lebel, Mireille. "La Prise de Jérusalem selon Flavius Josèphe: L'évenement et son interprétation juive, romaine et chrétienne." In *Procés de Jésus, Procés des Juifs?* edited by Alain Marchadour, 155–64. Paris: Cerf, 1998.

Hammer, Reuven, trans. *The Classic Midrash: Tannaitic Commentaries on the Bible.* New York: Paulist, 1995.

———. *Sifre: A Tannaitic Commentary on the Book of Deuteronomy.* New Haven: Yale University, 1986.

Hasitschka, Martin. *Befreiung von Sünde nach dem Johannesevangelium.* Wien: Tyrolia, 1989.

———. "Sozialgeschichtliche Anmerkungen Zum Johannesevangelium." *Protokolie zur Bibel* 1.1 (1992) 59–67.

Hawkin, David J., and Tom Robinson, eds. *Self-Definition and Self-Discovery in Early Christianity: A Study in Changing Horizons.* Lewiston, NY: Edwin Mellen, 1990.

Heil, John Paul. "Jesus as the Unique High Priest in the Gospel of John." *Catholic Biblical Quarterly* 57 (1995) 729–45.

Heyman, George. *The Power of Sacrifice: Roman and Christian Discourses in Conflict.* Washington, DC: Catholic University of America Press, 2007.

Himmelfarb, Martha. "The Temple and the Garden of Eden in Ezekiel, the Book of the Watchers, and the Wisdom of Ben Sira." In *Sacred Places and Profane Spaces: Essays in the Geographics of Judaism, Christianity, and Islam,* edited by Jamie Scott and Paul Simpson-Housley, 63–78. Contributions to the Study of Religion. Westport, CT: Greenwood, 1991.

Hogeterp, Albert L. A. "Paul's Judaism Reconsidered: The Issue of Cultic Imagery in the Corinthian Correspondence." *Ephemerides Theologicae Louvaniensis* 81.1 (2005) 87–108.

Hoppe, L. J. "Cana of Galilee: The Two Candidates." *Bible Today* 48, no. 3 (2010): 161–67.

Horst, Pieter W. van der. "The Birkat Ha-Minim in Recent Research." *Expository Times* 105.12 (1994) 363–68.

Hoskins, Paul M. "Deliverance from Death by the True Passover Lamb." *Journal of the Evangelical Theological Society* 52.2 (2009) 285–99.

———. *Jesus as the Fulfillment of the Temple in the Gospel of John.* Paternoster Biblical Monographs. Milton Keynes, UK: Paternoster, 2006.

Huizenga, Leroy Andrew. "The Aqedah at the End of the First Century of the Common Era: *Liber Antiquitatum Biblicarum,* 4 *Maccabees,* Josephus' *Antiquities,* 1 *Clement.*" *Journal for the Study of the Pseudepigrapha* 2.2 (2010) 105–33.

———. "The Battle for Isaac: Exploring the Composition and Function of the *Aqedah* in the Book of *Jubilees.*" *Journal for the Study of the Pseudepigrapha* 13.1 (2002) 33–59.

Hurowitz, Victor Avigdor. "Yhwh's Exalted House—Aspects of the Design and Symbolism of Solomon's Temple." In *Temple and Worship in Biblical Israel*, edited by John Day, 63–110. Library of Hebrew Bible/Old Testament Studies. New York: T. & T. Clark, 2005.

Hurtado, L. W. "Pre-70 C.E. Jewish Opposition to Christ-Devotion." *Journal of Theological Studies* 50.1 (1999) 35–58.

Hutchison, J. C. "The Vine in John 15 and Old Testament Imagery in the 'I Am' Statements." *Bibliotheca Sacra* 168.669 (2011) 63–80.

Jakovljević, Radivoj. "The Sense of Ebed Yahweh's Suffering." *Communio Viatorum* 30.1 (1987) 59–62.

Janzen, J. G. "How Can a Man Be Born When He Is Old?: Jacob/Israel in Genesis and the Gospel of John." *Encounter* 65.4 (2004) 323–43.

Johnson, Brian D. "Salvation Is From the Jews: Judaism in the Gospel of John." In *New Currents Through John*, edited by Francisco Lozada, Jr. and Tom Thatcher, 83–99. Atlanta: Society of Biblical Literature, 2006.

Josephus, Flavius. *Josephus: The Jewish War Books V–VII*. Translated by H. St. J. Thackeray. Loeb Classical Library 210. Cambridge, MA: Harvard University, 1997.

Kanagaraj, J. J. "Jesus the King, Merkabah Mysticism and the Gospel of John." *Tyndale Bulletin* 47.2 (1996) 349–66.

Karrer, M. "Auslegung im Horen auf Israel: Klaus Wengsts Kommentar zum Johannesevangelium." *Evangelische Theologie* 65.1 (2005) 73–78.

Kaufman, Philip S. "Anti-Semitism in the New Testament: The Witness of the Beloved Disciple." *Worship* 63 (1989) 386–401.

Kelber, Werner H. "Roman Imperialism and Early Christian Scribality." In *Postcolonial Biblical Reader*, edited by R. S. Sugirtharajah, 96–111. Malden, MA: Oxford University Press, 2006.

Kerr, A. R. *The Temple of Jesus' Body: The Temple Theme in the Gospel of John*. JSNT Supplement Series. New York: Sheffield Academic, 2002.

Kierspel, Lars. *The Jews and the World in the Fourth Gospel: Parallelism, Function & Context*. Tübingen: Mohr Siebeck, 2006.

Kim, S. S. "The Christological and Eschatological Significance of Jesus' Passover Signs in John 6." *Bibliotheca Sacra* 164.655 (2007) 307–22.

Kinzer, Mark S. "Temple Christology in the Gospel of John." In *Society of Biblical Literature Seminar Papers* 37.1, 447–64. Atlanta: Scholars, 1998.

Klawans, Jonathan. "Interpreting the Last Supper." *New Testament Studies* 48.1 (2002) 1–17.

Klein, Ralph W. "Anti-Semitism as Christian Legacy: The Origin and Nature of Our Estrangement from the Jews." *Currents in Theology and Mission* 11.5 (1984) 285–301.

Klenicki, L. "Anti-Judaism: A Core Problem of Christian Theology." *LWF Documentation* 48 (2003) 41–68.

Kloppenborg, John S., and John W. Marshall, eds. *Apocalypticism, Anti-Semitism and the Historical Jesus: Subtexts in Criticism*. London: T. & T. Clark International, 2005.

Knöppler, Frédéric. *Sühne im Neuen Testament*. Neukirchen-Vluyn: Neukirchner, 2001.

Koester, Craig R. *The Dwelling of God: The Tabernacle in the Old Testament, Intertestamental Jewish Literature, and the New Testament*, CBQ Monograph Series. Washington, DC: Catholic Biblical Association, 1989.

———. "Jesus as the Way to the Father in Johannine Theology (John 14,6)." In *Theology & Christology in the Fourth Gospel: Essays by the Members of the SNTS Johannine*

Writings Seminar, Leuven, edited by Gilbert van Belle, J. G. van der Watt, and P. J. Maritz, 117–33. Leuven: Leuven University Press, 2005.

———. "Messianic Exegesis and the Call of Nathanael (John 1.45-51)." *Journal for the Study of the New Testament* 39 (1990) 23–34.

Köstenberger, Andreas J. "The Destruction of the Second Temple and the Composition of the Fourth Gospel." *Trinity Journal* 26 (2005) 205–42.

———. "Jesus the Good Shepherd Who Will Also Bring Other Sheep (John 10:16): The Old Testament Background of a Familiar Metaphor." *Bulletin for Biblical Research* 12.1 (2002) 67–96.

———. *A Theology of John's Gospel and Letters, Biblical Theology of the New Testament*. Grand Rapids: Zondervan, 2009.

Kraus, Matthew A. "New Jewish Directions in the Study of the Fourth Gospel." In *New Currents Through John*, edited by Francisco Lozada Jr. and Tom Thatcher, 141–66. Atlanta: Society of Biblical Literature, 2006.

Kysar, Robert. "Anti-Semitism and the Gospel of John." In *Anti-Semitism and Early Christianity*, edited by Craig A. Evans and Donald A. Hagner, 13–127. Minneapolis: Fortress, 1993.

———. "Community and Gospel: Vectors in Fourth Gospel Criticism." *Interpretation* 31.4 (1977) 355–66.

———. "The Whence and Whither of the Johannine Community." In *Life in Abundance*, edited by John R. Donahue, 65–81. Collegeville: Liturgical, 2005.

Labahn, M., K. Scholtissek, and A. Strotmann, eds. *Israel Und Seine Heilstraditionen Im Johannesevangelium. Festgabe Fur Johannes Beutler Sj Zum 70: Geburstag*. Paderborn: Schöningh, 2004.

Langer, Ruth. *Cursing the Christians? A History of the Birkat HaMinim*. New York: Oxford University, 2012.

Laporte, Jean. *Eucharistia in Philo*. Studies in Bible and Early Christianity. New York: Edwin Mellen, 1982.

———. "Philonic Models of Eucharistia in the Eucharist of Origen." *Laval théologique et Philosophique* 39.2 (1997) 83–100.

Lauterbach, Jacob Z., trans. *Mekhilta de-Rabbi Ishmael*. JPS Classic Reissues. Philadelphia: Jewish Publication Society, 2010.

Lee, Dorothy. "In the Spirit of Truth: Worship and Prayer in the Gospel of John and the Early Fathers." *Vigiliae Christianae* 58.3 (2004) 277–83.

Leibig, Janis E. "John and 'the Jews': Theological Antisemitism in the Fourth Gospel." *Journal of Ecumenical Studies* 20.2 (1983) 209–34.

L'Éplattenier, Charles. "Les Juifs Dans le Quatrième Évangile." In *Procés de Jésus, Procés des Juifs?* edited by Alain Marchadour, 127–31. Paris: Cerf, 1998.

Levenson, J. D. "The Temple and the World." *The Journal of Religion* 64.3 (1984) 282–85, 297–98.

———. "Is There a Counterpart in the Hebrew Bible to New Testament Antisemitism?" *Journal of Ecumenical Studies* 22.2 (1985) 242–60.

Lierman, J., ed. *Challenging Perspectives on the Gospel of John*. Wissenschaftliche Untersuchungen Zum Neuen Testament. 2 Reihe. Tübingen: Mohr Siebeck, 2006.

Lieu, Judith. "Anti-Judaism in the Fourth Gospel: Explanation & Hermeneutics." In *Anti-Judaism and the Fourth Gospel*, edited by Reimund Bieringer, Didier Pollefeyt, and Frederique Vandecasteele-Vanneuville, 101–17. Louisville, KY: Westminster John Knox, 2001.

---. "Anti-Judaism, the Jews, and the Worlds of the Fourth Gospel." In *Gospel of John and Christian Theology*, edited by Richard Bauckham and Carl Mosser, 168–82. Grand Rapids: Eerdmans, 2008.

---. "Temple and Synagogue in John." *New Testament Studies* 45.1 (1999) 51–69.

Lightfoot, R. H. "Unsolved New Testament Problems, Pt. 3: The Cleansing of the Temple in St. John's Gospel." *Expository Times* 60.3 (1948) 64–68.

Lindars, Barnabas. *Gospel of John*. London: Oliphants, 1972.

Lindsay, Dennis R. "*Todah* and Eucharist: The Celebration of the Lord's Supper as a 'Thank Offering' in the Early Church." *Restoration Quarterly* 39.2 (1997) 83–100.

Lingad, C. G. *The Problems of Jewish Christians in the Johannine Community*. Tesi Gregoriana, Serie Teologia. Rome: Editrice Pontifica Universita Gregoriana, 2001.

Lioy, D. *Axis of Glory: A Biblical and Theological Analysis of the Temple Motif in Scripture*. Studies in Biblical Literature. New York: Lang, 2010.

Lizorkin-Eyzenberg, Eliyahu. *The Jewish Gospel of John: Discovering Jesus, King of All Israel*. CreateSpace Independent Publishing Platform, 2015.

Locher, C. "Die Johannes-Christen Und 'Die Juden.'" *Orientierung* 48.20 (1984) 223–26.

Lowe, Malcolm. "Who Were the 'ΙΟΥΔΑΙΟΙ?" *Novum Testamentum* 18.2 (1976) 101–30.

Malina, B. J., and R. L. Rohrbaugh. *Social-Science Commentary on the Gospel of John*. Minneapolis, MN: Fortress, 1998.

Manns, Frédéric. "The Binding of Isaac in Jewish Liturgy." In *The Sacrifice of Isaac in the Three Monotheistic Religions*, edited by F. Manns, 59–67. Jerusalem: Franciscan, 1995.

---. *L'Évangile De Jean Et La Sagesse*. Studium Biblicum Franciscanum. Jerusalem: Franciscan, 2003.

---. "La Galilée Dans Le Quatrième Évangile." *Antonianum* 72.3 (1997) 351–64.

---. "The Targum of Genesis 22." In *The Sacrifice of Isaac in the Three Monotheistic Religions*, edited by F. Manns, 69–80. Jerusalem: Franciscan, 1995.

Martyn, J. Louis. *History and Theology in the Fourth Gospel*. Louisville: Westminster John Knox, 2003.

McCaffrey, J. *The House with Many Rooms: The Temple Theme of Jn 14, 2–3*. Analecta Biblica. Rome: Pontifico Istituto Biblico, 1988.

McClymond, Kathryn. *Beyond Sacred Violence: A Comparative Study of Sacrifice*. Baltimore: Johns Hopkins University, 2008.

---. "Don't Cry Over Spilled Blood." In *Ancient Mediterranean Sacrifice*, edited by Jennifer Wright Knust and Zsuzsanna Várhelyi, 235–50. New York: Oxford University, 2011.

McGowan, Andrew. "How December 25 Became Christmas." *Biblical Research* 18.6 (2002) 46–48, 57–58.

McNamara, Martin, trans. *Targum Neofiti I: Genesis*. The Aramaic Bible vol. 1A. Collegeville, MN: Liturgical, 1992.

Meeks, Wayne A. "Galilee and Judea in the Fourth Gospel." *Journal of Biblical Literature* 85.2 (1966) 159–69.

---. *The Prophet-King: Moses Tradition and the Johannine Christology*. Leiden: E. J. Brill, 1967.

Mendels, D. *The Land of Israel as a Political Concept in Hasmonean Literature: Recourse to History in Second-Century B.C. Claims to the Holy Land*. Texte Und Studien Zum Antiken Judentum. Tübingen: Mohr Siebeck, 1987.

Metzner, Rainer. *Das Verständnis der Sünde im Johannesevangelium.* Tübingen: Mohr Siebeck, 2000.

Moloney, Francis J. *The Gospel of John.* Sacra Pagina, vol. 4. Edited by Daniel J. Harrington. Collegeville, MN: Liturgical, 2005.

———. *The Gospel of John: Text and Context.* Boston: Brill, 2005.

———. "'The Jews' in the Fourth Gospel: Another Perspective." *Pacifica* 15.1 (2002) 16–36.

Motyer, Stephen. "The Fourth Gospel and the Salvation of Israel: An Appeal for a New Start." In *Anti-Judaism and the Fourth Gospel*, edited by Reimund Bieringer, Didier Pollefeyt, and Frederique Vandecasteele-Vanneuville, 83–100. Louisville: Westminster John Knox, 2001.

———. "Is John's Gospel Anti-Semitic?" *Themelios* 23.2 (1998) 1–4.

———. *Your Father the Devil? A New Approach to John and "the Jews."* Paternoster Biblical and Theological Monographs. Carlisle, UK: Paternoster, 1997.

Murphy, Erika. "Devouring the Human: Digestion of a Corporeal Soteriology." In *Divinanimality: Animal Theory, Creaturely Theology*, edited by Stephen D. Moore, 51–62. New York: Fordham University, 2014.

Murray, G. "Jesus and the Feasts of the Jews." *Downside Review* 109.376 (1991) 217–25.

Nasrallah, Laura. "The Embarrassment of Blood: Early Christians and Others on Sacrifice, War, and Rational Worship." In *Ancient Mediterranean Sacrifice*, edited by Jennifer Wright Knust and Zsuzsanna Várhelyi, 142–66. New York: Oxford University, 2011.

Nelson, W. David, trans. *Mekhilta de-Rabbi Shimon Bar Yoḥai.* JPS Classic Reissues. Philadelphia: Jewish Publication Society, 2006.

Neubrand, M. "Das Johannesevangelium Und 'Die Juden': Antijudaismus Im Vierten Evangelium?" *Theologie und Glaube* 99.2 (2009) 205–17.

Neusner, J., ed. *"To See Ourselves as Other See Us": Christians, Jews, "Others" in Late Antiquity.* Chico, CA: Scholars, 1985.

Neyrey, J. H. "Jesus the Judge: Forensic Process in John 8, 21–59." *Biblica* 68.4 (1987): 509–42.

———. "Spaced Out: 'Territoriality' in the Fourth Gospel." *Harvard Theological Studies* 58.2 (2002) 632–63.

———. "Spaces and Places, Whence and Whither, Homes and Rooms: 'Territoriality' in the Fourth Gospel." *Biblical Theological Bulletin* 32.2 (2002) 60–74.

Nickelsburg, George W. "Reading the Hebrew Scriptures in the First Century: Christian Interpretations in their Jewish Context." *Word & World* 3.3 (1983) 238–50.

Nielsen, Jesper T. "The Lamb of God: The Cognitive Structure of a Johananine Metaphor." In *Imagery in the Gospel of John: Terms, Forms, Themes, and Theology of Johannine Figurative Language*, edited by Jorg Frey, J. G. Van der Watt, and Ruben Zimmerman, 217–56. Tübingen: Mohr Siebeck, 2006.

Notley, Steven R. "The Roots of Christian Anti-Semitism: Anti-Jewish Tendencies in the Synoptic Gospels." In *The Mountain of the Lord: Israel and the Churches*, edited by Beryl Norman, 49–72. London: Council of Christians and Jews, 1996.

Ostenstad, G. H. *Patterns of Redemption in the Fourth Gospel: An Experiment in Structural Analysis.* Studies in the Bible and Early Christianity. Lewiston, NY: Mellen, 1998.

Painter, John. "Church and Israel in the Gospel of John: A Response." *New Testament Studies* 25.1 (1978) 103–12.

———. "John 9 and the Interpretation of the Fourth Gospel." *Journal for the Study of the New Testament* 28 (1986) 31–61.

———. "Sacrifice and Atonement in the Gospel of John." In *Israel und seine Heilstraditionen im Johannesevangelium*, edited by Michael Labahn, Klaus Scholtissek, and Angelika Strotmann, 287–313. Ferdinand Schöningh, Zürich, 2004.

Pancaro, Severino. *The Law in the Fourth Gospel*. Leiden: Brill, 1975.

Pate, C. M. *Communities of the Last Days: The Dead Sea Scrolls, the New Testament & the Story of Israel*. Downers Grove, IL: InterVarsity, 2000.

Pawilkowski, J. "A Faith without Shadows: Liberating Christian Faith from Anti-Semitism." *Theology Digest* 43.3 (1996) 203–17.

Pazdan, M. M. "Nicodemus and the Samaritan Woman: Contrasting Models of Discipleship." *Biblical Theology Bulletin* 17.4 (1987) 145–48.

Perkins, Pheme. "Crisis in Jerusalem? Narrative Criticism in New Testament Studies." *Theological Studies* 50.2 (1989) 296.

———. "If Jerusalem Stood: The Destruction of Jerusalem and Christian Anti-Judaism." *Biblical Interpretation* 8.1 (2000) 194–204. Brill Online Books and Journals.

Petropoulou, Maria-Zoe. *Animal Sacrifice in Ancient Greek Religion, Judaism, and Christianity, 100 BC–AD 200*. Oxford: Oxford University Press, 2008.

Philo of Alexandria. *Allegorical Interpretation*. Vol. 1, *Philo*. Translated by F. H. Colson and G. H. Whitaker. Loeb Classical Library 226. Cambridge: Harvard University Press, 1929.

———. *Moses*. Vol. 6, *Philo*. Translated by F. H. Colson. Loeb Classical Library 289. Cambridge: Harvard University Press, 1935.

———. *On Abraham*. Translated by F.H. Colson. Loeb Classical Library 289 Philo Vol. VI. Cambridge, MA: Harvard University, 1935.

———. *On the Contemplative Life*. Vol. 9, *Philo*. Translated by F. H. Colson. Loeb Classical Library 363. Cambridge: Harvard University Press, 1941.

———. *On Dreams*. Vol. 5, *Philo*. Translated by F. H. Colson and G. H. Whitaker. Loeb Classical Library 275. Cambridge: Harvard University Press, 1934.

———. *On the Sacrifices of Abel and Cain*. Vol. 2, *Philo*. Translated by F. H. Colson and G. H. Whitaker. Loeb Classical Library 227. Cambridge: Harvard University Press, 1929.

———. *On the Special Laws*. Vols. 7 and 8, *Philo*. Translated by F. H. Colson. Loeb Classical Library 341. Cambridge: Harvard University Press, 1937, 1939.

———. *Questions and Answers on Exodus*. Philo Supplement 2. Translated by Ralph Marcus. Loeb Classical Library 401. Cambridge: Harvard University Press, 1953.

———. *Questions and Answers on Genesis*. Philo Supplement 1. Translated by Ralph Marcus. Loeb Classical Library 380. Cambridge: Harvard University Press, 1953.

———. *Who is the Heir of Divine Things?* Vol. 4, *Philo*. Translated by F. H. Colson and G. H. Whitaker. Loeb Classical Library 261. Cambridge: Harvard University Press, 1932.

Pippin, T. "'For Fear of the Jews': Lying and Truth-Telling in Translating the Gospel of John." *Semeia* 76 (1996) 81–97.

Poirier, John C. "Purity Beyond the Temple in the Second Temple Era." *Journal of Biblical Literature* 122.2 (2003) 247–65.

Porsch, F. "'Ihr Habt Den Teufel Zum Vater' (Joh 8,44): Antijudaismus Im Johannesevangelium?" *Bibel und Kirche* 44.2 (1989) 50–57.

Prosic, Tamara. *The Development and Symbolism of Passover until 70 CE*. London: T. & T. Clark, 2004.

Pryor, J. W. "Jesus and Israel in the Fourth Gospel—John 1:11." *Novum Testamentum* 32.3 (1990) 201–18.

———. *John: Evangelist of the Covenant People: The Narrative & Themes of the Fourth Gospel.* Downers Grove, IL: InterVarsity, 1992.

Quaegebur, J. *Ritual and Sacrifice in the Ancient Near East: Proceedings of the International Conference Organized by the Katholieke Universiteit Leuven from the 17th to the 20th of April 1991.* Leuven: Uitgeverij Peeters en Departement Oriëntalistiek, 1993.

Quarles, Charles L. "The New Perspective and Means of Atonement in Jewish Literature of the Second Temple Period." *Criswell Theological Review* 2 (2005) 39–56.

Quasten, Johannes. *The Catholic University of America Studies in Christian Antiquity.* Washington, DC: The Catholic University of America Press, 1978.

Rae, Murray. "Texts in Context: Scripture and the Divine Economy." *Journal of Theological Interpretation* 1.1 (2007) 23–45.

Reinhartz, Adele. *Befriending the Beloved Disciple: A Jewish Reading of the Gospel of John.* New York: Continuum, 2001.

———. "The Gospel of John: Introduction and Annotations." In *The Jewish Annotated New Testament*, edited by Amy-Jill Levine and Marc Zvi Brettler, 152–57. New York: Oxford University Press, 2011.

———. "The Grammar of Hate in the Gospel of John." In *Israel und seine Heilstraditionen im Johannesevangelium*, edited by Michael Labahn, Klaus Scholtissek, and Angelika Strotmann, 416–27. Zürich: Ferdinand Schöningh, 2004.

———. "'Jews' and Jews in the Fourth Gospel." In *Anti-Judaism and the Fourth Gospel*, edited by Reimund Bieringer, Didier Pollefeyt, and Frederique Vandecasteele-Vanneuville, 213–27. Louisville, KY: Westminster John Knox, 2001.

———. "The Johannine Community and Its Jewish Neighbors: A Reappraisal." In *What Is John? Vol. 2, Literary and Social Readings of the Fourth Gospel.* Edited by Fernando Segovia, 111–38. Atlanta: Scholars, 1998.

———. "Judaism in the Gospel of John." *Interpretation* 63.4 (2009) 382–93.

———. "A Nice Jewish Girl Reads the Gospel of John." *Semeia* 77 (1997) 177–93.

Richey, Lance Byron. "'Truly This Is the Savior of the World': Christ and Caesar in the Gospel of John." PhD diss., Marquette University, 2004.

Riesner, R. *Bethanien Jenseits Des Jordan: Topographie Und Theologie Im Johannesevangelium.* Basel: Brunnen, 2002.

———. "Bethany Beyond Jordan (John 1:28): Topography, Theology and History in the Fourth Gospel." *Tyndale Bulletin* 38 (1987) 29–63.

Ringe, Sharon H. "The Gospel for an Uprooted People: Perspectives on the Fourth Gospel." In *Strangers in a Strange Land: A Festschrift in Honor of Bruce C. Birch Upon His Retirement as Academic Dean of Wesley Theological Seminary*, edited by Lucy Lind Hogan, D. William Faupel, and David F. McAllister, 129–35. Lexington, KY: Emeth, 2009.

Roetzel, C. J. "Sacrifice in Romans 12–15." *Word & World* 6.4 (1986) 410–19.

Rosenberg, Roy A. "Jesus, Isaac, and the Suffering Servant." *Journal of Biblical Literature* 84.4 (1965) 381–88.

Rubinkiewicz, R., trans. *Apocalypse of Abraham.* In *The Old Testament Pseudepigrapha*, edited by James H. Charlesworth. Apocalyptic Literature & Testaments. New York: Doubleday, 1983.

Ruether, Rosemary Radford. "Theological Anti-Semitism in the New Testament." *Christian Century* 85.7 (1968) 191–96.

Salvoni, Fausto. "The So-Called Resurrection Proof (John 20:7)." *Restoration Quarterly* 22 (1979) 72–76.

Sanders, E. P., ed. *Jewish and Christian Self-Definition*. Vol. 2, *Aspects of Judaism in the Greco-Roman Period*. Philadelphia: Fortress, 1981.

Sandmel, Samuel. *Anti-Semitism in the New Testament*. Philadelphia: Fortress, 1978.

Schenke, L. "Die Literarische Entstehungsgeschichte von Joh 1,19–51." *Biblische Notizen* 46 (1989) 24–57.

Schneiders, S. M. "The Raising of the New Temple: John 20.19–23 and Johannine Ecclesiology." *New Testament Studies* 52.3 (2006) 337–55.

Schoni, M. "The Mother at the Foot of the Cross: The Key to the Understanding of St. John's Account of the Death of Jesus." *Near East School of Theology Theological Review* 17.2 (1996) 71–95.

Schroder, J. M. *Das Eschatologische Israel Im Johannesevangelium: Eine Untersuchung Der Johanneischen Israel-Konzeption in Joh 2-4 Und Joh 6*. Neutestamentliche Entwurfe Zur Theologie. Tübingen: Francke, 2003.

Schwank, B. "Jakobstraum (Gen 28,12) und Christologische Erfullung (Joh 1,51)." *Erbe und Auftrag* 81.5 (2005) 386–97.

Selong, Gabriel. "Cleansing of the Temple in Jn. 2:13–22: With a Reconsideration of the Dependence of the Fourth Gospel Upon the Synoptics." *Ephemerides Theologicae Lovanienses* 48.1 (1972) 212–13.

Sherwin, M. S. "Jesus as the Garden Dweller." *Homiletic and Pastoral Review* 108.7 (2008) 50–53.

Sidebottom, Ernest Malcolm. *The Christ of the Fourth Gospel: In the Light of 1st Century Thought*. London: SPCK, 1961.

Sloane, Andrew. "Justice and the Atonement in the Book of Isaiah." *Trinity Journal* 34.1 (2013) 3–16.

Smiga, George M. *Pain and Polemic: Anti-Judaism in the Gospels*. New York: Paulist, 1992.

Smit, P.-B. "Cana-to-Cana or Galilee-to-Galilee: A Note on the Structure of the Gospel of John." *Zeitschrift für die Neutestamentliche Wissenschaft* 98.1 (2007) 143–49.

Smith, D. Moody. *Johannine Christianity: Essays on Its Setting, Sources, and Theology*. Columbia: University of South Carolina Press, 1984.

Stager, Lawrence E. "Jerusalem as Eden." *Biblical Archaeology Review* 26.3 (2000) 38–47, 66.

Stegemann, E., ed. *Messias-Vorstellungen Bei Juden und Christen*. Stuttgart: Kohlhammer, 1993.

Stewart, Eric C. *Gathered Around Jesus: An Alternative Spatial Practice in the Gospel of Mark*. Eugene, OR: Cascade, 2009.

Stroumsa, Guy G. *The End of Sacrifice: Religious Transformations in Late Antiquity*. Translated by Susan Emanuel. Chicago: University of Chicago Press, 2009.

Swarz, Michael D. "Judaism and the Idea of Ancient Ritual Theory." In *Jewish Studies at the Crossroads of Anthropology and History*, edited by Ra'anan S. Boustan, Oren Kosansky, and Marina Rustow, 294–317. Philadelphia: University of Pennsylvania, 2011.

Tan, Yak-Hwee. "The Johannine Community: Caught in 'Two Worlds.'" In *New Currents Through John*, edited by Francisco Lozada, Jr. and Tom Thatcher, 167–79. Atlanta: Society of Biblical Literature, 2006.

Theobald, Michael. "Abraham-(Isaak-) Jakob, Israels Väter im Johannesevangelium." In *Israel und Seine Heilstraditionen in Johannesevangelium: Festgabe für Johannes*

Beutler SJ zum 70. Geburstag, edited by Michael Labahn, Klaus Scholtissek, and Angelika Strotmann, 158–83. Paderborn: Ferdinand Schöningh, 2004.

———. *Das Evangelium Nach Johannes: Kapitel 1–12*. Regensburger Neues Testament. Regensburg: Pustet, 2009.

Thettayil, B. *In Spirit and Truth: An Exegetical Study of John 4:19–26 and a Theological Investigation of the Replacement Theme in the Fourth Gospel*. Contributions to Biblical Exegesis and Theology. Dudley, MA: Peeters, 2007.

Thomas, John Christopher. "The Fourth Gospel and Rabbinic Judaism." *Zeitschrift fü r die Neutestamentliche Wissenschaft und die Kunde der Älteren Kirche* 82.3–4 (1991) 159–82.

Thompson, Marianne M. "Reflections on Worship in the Gospel of John." *Princeton Seminary Bulletin* 19.3 (1998) 259–78.

Tolmie, D. F. "The Ioudaioi in the 4th Gospel: A Narratological Perspective." In *Theology and Christology in the Fourth Gospel: Essays by the Members of the SNTS Johannine Writings Seminar*, edited by Gilbert van Belle, J. G. van der Watt, and P. J. Maritz, 377–97. Leuven: Peeters, 2005.

Tomson, P. J. "'Jews' in the Gospel of John as Compared with the Palestinian Talmud, the Synoptics and Some New Testament Apocrypha." In *Anti-Judaism and the Fourth Gospel*, edited by Reimund Bieringer, Didier Pollefeyt, and Frederique Vandecasteele-Vanneuville, 176–212. Louisville, KY: Westminster John Knox, 2001.

———. "The Names Israel and Jew in Ancient Judaism and in the New Testament II." *Bijdragen* 47.3 (1986) 266–89.

Toussaint, Stanely D. "Significance of the First Sign in John's Gospel." *Bibliotheca Sacra* 134.533 (1977) 45–51.

Townsend, John T. "The New Testament, the Early Church, and Anti-Semitism." In *From Ancient Israel to Modern Judaism*, edited by Marvin Fox, 171–86. Atlanta: Scholars, 1989.

Troost-Cramer, Kathleen. "De-centralizing the Temple: A Rereading of Romans 15:16." *Journal of the Jesus Movement in its Jewish Setting* 3 (2016) 72–101.

Trudinger, P. *The Cool Gospel: Essays on St. John's Gospel for Reflection and Resource*. Kingston: R. P. Frye & Co., 1988.

Ullucci, Daniel C. *The Christian Rejection of Animal Sacrifice*. Oxford: Oxford University, 2011.

Um, S. T. *The Theme of Temple Christology in John's Gospel*. Library of New Testament Studies. New York: T. & T. Clark, 2006.

Umoh, Camillus. "The Temple in the Fourth Gospel." In *Israel und seine Heilstraditionen im Johannesevangeluim*, edited by M. Labahn, K. Scholtissek, and A. Strotmann, 314–33. Zürich: Ferdinand Schöningh, 2004.

Van Belle, G. "The Faith of the Galileans: The Parenthesis in Jn 4:44." *Ephemerides Theologicae Lovanienses* 74.1 (1998) 27–44.

vanTilborg, S. "De Zelfpresentatie Van Jezus in Het Johannes-Evangelie: Een Christologie Tussen Letterlijke En FiguurlijkeTaal." *Tijdschriftvoor Theologie* 34.2 (1994) 128–44.

Vasholz, R. I. "Is the New Testament Anti-Semitic?" *Presbyterion* 11.2 (1985) 118–23.

Vawter, Bruce. "The Gospel According to John." In *The Jerome Biblical Commentary*, edited by Raymond E. Brown, Joseph A. Fitzmyer, and Roland E. Murphy, 414–66. Englewood Cliffs, NJ: Prentice-Hall, 1968.

Vermes, G. *Scripture and Tradition in Judaism*. 2nd ed. Leiden: Brill, 1973.

Voelz, James W. "Anti-Semitism in the New Testament: Is It a Problem of Semantics?" *Concordia Journal* 24.2 (1998) 121–29.

vonWahlde, U. C. "Literary Structure and Theological Argument in Three Discourses with the Jews in the Fourth Gospel." *Journal of Biblical Literature* 103.4 (1984) 575–84.

Wengst, K. *Bedrangte Gemeinde Und Verherrlichter Christus: Ein Versuch über Das Johannesevangelium*. Munich: Kaiser, 1990.

Wenham, Gordon J. "Sanctuary Symbolism in the Garden of Eden Story." In *Proceedings of the Ninth World Congress of Jewish Studies, August 4–12, 1985: Division B*. Vol. 1, *The History of the Jewish People (From the Second Temple Period until the Middle Ages)*, 19–25. Jerusalem: World Union of Jewish Studies, 1986.

Wick, P. *Die Urchristlichen Gottesdienste: Entstehung Und Entwicklung Im Rahmen Der Fruhjudischen Tempel- Synagogen- und Hausfrommigkeit*. Beitrage Zur Wissenschaft Vom Alten Und Neuen Testament. Stuttgart: Kohlhammer, 2002.

Williams, Margaret. "Being a Jew in Rome: Sabbath Fasting as an Expression of Romano-Jewish Identity." In *Negotiating Diaspora: Jewish Strategies in the Roman Empire*, edited by John M. G. Barclay, 8–18. New York: T. & T. Clark, 2004.

Willis, Robert E. "A Perennial Outrage: Anti-Semitism in the New Testament." *Christian Century* 87.33 (1970) 990–92.

Yoon, C.-W. "Revisiting Judaism in the Gospel of John." *Korean New Testament Studies* 17.3 (2010) 597–621.

Young, Frances M. *The Use of Sacrificial Ideas in Greek Christian Writers from the New Testament to John Chrysostom*. Philadelphia: Philadelphia Patristic Foundation, 1979.

Zumstein, Jean. "L'Interprétation Johannique de la Mort du Christ." In *The Four Gospels, 1992: Festschrift Frans Neirynck*, 2119–38. Louvain: Peeters, 1992.

Subject Index

Abraham, 7, 12n34, 19, 27–32, 31n30, 34–36, 52, 54n130, 55–57, 71–72, 72n11, 77, 80, 90, 92, 135n89, 141n116

Akedah, 3–4, 6–7, 18–20, 20n69, 23, 27–38, 30n24, 31n30, 34n39, 40, 53, 55–58, 60–61, 60n152, 63–65, 63n161, 67–68, 69, 72–73, 76–79, 78n36, 81n47, 90, 122, 146
    Jesus' arrest, 71–73

Annas, 71, 76

atonement, 3, 5n13, 6–7, 20–21, 23, 26, 28n18, 33–38, 40, 56, 61, 62n160, 65, 81, 84–85, 85n70, 87, 87n83, 94–95, 99, 101, 136,
    Day of, 81

bread, 6–7, 33, 39, 42–43, 45–52, 47n98, 54, 67, 86, 123

Bread of Life Discourse, 3, 6–7, 39, 43, 45, 47, 86, 114

Caiaphas, 14, 71, 72, 76–77

Cana, 39–40, 40n67, 42–44, 42n82, 66, 80, 83–84, 86, 99, 101, 106, 113–14, 124, 131

crucifixion, see sacrifice—Jesus as.

Dead Sea Scrolls, see Qumran.

Dedication, Feast of, 106, 138

Eden, Garden of, 4–5, 69–70, 91–93, 110, 113

Elephantine, 107, 114

Farewell Discourse, 50, 84, 112

Galilee (Galileans), 16, 21, 103–6, 105n36, 108, 114, 116, 116n5, 117, 124, 124n36, 127–28, 130n68, 131–33, 132n77, 136, 140, 142–43, 147

glory (presence/shekhinah), 1–2, 6, 15, 17–18, 22, 25, 29, 40, 42–43, 56, 84, 88, 95, 96n5, 99, 112, 117, 130, 133–34, 136–37, 139–40, 142–43, 145, 147

Good Shepherd Discourse, 57

high priest, see priest.

hyssop, 78, 81, 86–88, 87n81, 87n83

Isaac, 3–4, 6–7, 18–20, 23, 27–38, 28n17, 28n18, 30n24, 31n30, 37n58, 44, 52, 54n130, 55–58, 60–61, 60n152, 63–67, 63n161, 69–73, 72n11, 76–79, 78n136, 79, 85, 90, 94, 146–47
    Binding of, see Akedah.

Jerusalem, 14–16, 18, 25, 40n67, 43, 69, 96, 103–4, 105n38, 107–11, 117, 127–28, 131, 134, 142–43, 147
    authorities, 12, 73, 83, 96n5, 104, 107, 117, 119–23, 121n20, 123n32, 126–30, 132, 134–35, 134n84, 137, 139–41
    Priesthood, see Priest.
    Temple priesthood, see Temple.

SUBJECT INDEX

Jews (Ἰουδαῖοι), see Judeans.
Josephus, Flavius, 18–19, 33, 35–37, 54, 74, 96, 106, 119, 126
Judea, see Judeans.
Judeans (Ἰουδαῖοι), 2, 8–9, 12, 15–17, 22, 36, 39–40, 40n67, 96n5, 103–6, 105n36, 105n37, 108–9, 112, 115–45, 147

lamb, 7, 27, 34–37, 50, 58, 60–64, 67, 72–73, 72n13, 76, 78–79, 78n36, 85, 114
   of God, 6, 33, 37, 58, 58n143, 60–62, 66, 73, 85n70, 88
   Paschal, see Passover.
Leontopolis, 107, 114
logos (λόγος), 1, 29, 43–47, 49, 65, 69–70, 91, 129–30, 129n64
   as high priest, see priest, λόγος as.
   Jesus as, 46–48, 47n98, 51–52, 81, 91, 130
Lowe, Malcolm, 16, 116, 122, 126–29, 140, 143

manna, 45–46, 46n91, 48–49, 51–52, 85–86, 123
   as λόγος, 48–49, 51–52
   Jesus as, 51
Memra, 29

Passion narrative, see Sacrifice—Jesus as.
Passover
   as atonement, 3, 33–35, 37, 61–63, 66, 79
   Isaac as prototype, 3–4, 6,
   Jesus as paschal victim, see Sacrifice—Jesus as.
   lamb, 3, 5–6, 8, 19, 27–28, 28n17, 31, 32–35, 49, 52–54, 56n136, 60–68, 72–73, 78–81, 78n36, 85–88, 85n70, 87n79, 87n81, 87n83, 94, 107, 146
Paul (apostle), 25, 25n8, 57n140, 96, 97n8, 100
Philo of Alexandria, 2, 18, 19, 25n8, 31, 31n26, 34, 34n41, 43–49, 46n91,
49n103, 51–54, 54n130, 63, 65, 69, 70, 74, 77, 78, 81, 93, 108, 119, 130, 148
priest, 5–7, 18–19, 24, 27, 27n12, 39–42, 54, 54n130, 71–74, 72n11, 76–78, 81–85, 91, 91n93, 93, 101–3, 101n28, 108, 113, 118, 119n15, 136n89, 139
   garments of, 44–45, 91, 93
   λόγος as, 43–44, 70, 77, 81–82, 130, 148
   Jesus as, 6–7, 6n15, 23, 27, 27n12, 40–44, 69–71, 77, 81, 83, 85–86, 91, 101, 113, 130–31, 133, 148
   priestly tradition, 23
   robe of (χιτών), 74–77, 91
   turban of, 85n71, 91

Qumran, 2, 5–6, 17, 24–25, 96–97, 100, 102, 107, 119, 126, 137, 144

Reinhartz, Adele, 12n34, 122–27, 125n40, 129, 141n116
resurrection, 1–2, 5, 26, 30, 57, 60, 63–64, 64n166, 69–71, 84–85, 85n70, 86, 89–91, 148
   of Lazarus, 124
ritual theory, 21, 100–102, 114
Rome (Roman), 8, 26, 66, 98–100, 98n14, 106–7, 145

sacred space, 17n59, 18, 21, 97–98, 102–44
sacrifice
   as worship, 2–3, 3n7, 4–9, 16, 18, 24n4, 114, 116–17, 126, 128, 131, 143, 145–46,
   Jesus as, 3–4, 6–7, 3–9, 13, 18, 34, 39–41, 43–44, 50, 60–64, 69, 71–88, 82n55, 90–92, 94, 100, 104, 108, 114, 126, 132–33, 143, 145, 147–48
   of Isaac, see Akedah.
Samaritans, 11, 16, 105
Samaritan Woman (John 4), 4, 11, 49, 87n79, 105, 109–14

SUBJECT INDEX

servant (Suffering Servant), 44, 58–66, 71, 78–79, 78n36, 85, 85n70, 89–90

spatial theory, see sacred space.

Tabernacles, Feast of, 41, 51, 82–84, 106, 110, 137

Tāmîd, 6–8, 18–19, 23–24, 27–40, 51, 53–54, 61, 64–69, 72–73, 78, 85–86, 88, 90, 114, 146
    as atonement, 35–38, 54, 69

temple, 9, 12, 12n35, 13, 15–35, 24n4, 25n8, 26n10, 27n12, 29n19, 33, 33n38, 34n39, 37n58, 39–44, 40n70, 51, 56–57, 66–71, 73, 77–82, 78n36, 83–85, 88–93, 89n87, 95–99, 96n5, 97n8, 98n14, 99n21, 100–103, 105–11, 111n64, 113–14, 116–19, 118n10, 122–23, 126–27–29, 129n60, 130–36, 132n73, 134n84, 136n91, 137–38, 140–41, 140n108, 141n112, 143–48

    as Eden, see Eden, Garden of.
    eternal, 26, 69, 91, 137, 139, 145
    incident, 39–40, 42–43, 66, 84, 89, 113–14, 139, 145
    Jesus as, 1–2, 4–6, 8, 13, 15–18, 21, 51, 56, 63, 77, 83–84, 88–89, 89n88, 91–92, 99, 103–4, 108, 111, 111n64, 111n65, 112–14, 117, 118n10, 126, 130, 133–34, 136–37
    Qumran view of, 6, 96
    relocation of, 7, 13, 16, 18, 86, 96–97, 112n66, 114, 116
    Roman, 66, 95, 99, 100
    vessels, 98, 98n14, 106–7

Tôdāh, see also Bread, 6–8, 18, 23–24, 27, 38–54, 65, 67–69, 72, 84–86, 88, 90, 114, 146

wine, 6–7, 39–44, 49, 51, 54, 67, 80, 83–84, 84n67, 86–89, 101, 113–14, 131

Ancient Document Index

Ant.

1.13.4	35
1.224, 226	33
1.232	36
3.161	74

Congr. 96 — 53

Contempl. 87 — 52

Her. 79 — 46

Jos. Asen. — 42, 110

*J.W. VI.*422 — 54

L.A.B. — 19, 29, 30, 36n50, 37

18.3	28
18.5	19, 34
32.3	19, 28, 28n18, 56
32.12–13	31n30
40.2–4	28, 28n18, 34, 35

Leg.

II.56	74
III.165	53
III.172	53
III.173	46
III.179	47

Mos.

I.180	52
II. 117–26	93

QE

I.3	52n118, 54
I.10	54

*QG IV.*102 — 46

Sacr. 62 — 53

Somn.

I.215	43
II.72–76	53
II.249	44

Spec.

I.84–97	45
I.195–97	53
I.224	53
II.145	52, 54
II.163	54n130

ANCIENT DOCUMENT INDEX

Gen

1:1ff.	70
2:10ff.	93
15:1–20	80
18:9–15; 21:1–2	56
22	27, 28, 32, 55, 57, 63, 71, 72
28:10–22	89, 90
37:3	75n26

Exod

12	72n13, 79, 87
12:10, 46	79
12:13	28
14:24	32
15:9	32
16	48, 49
24:3–8	80, 88
24:16; 33:18; 40:34	43
29:4; 30:17; 40:30ff.	42
28:4–5; 29:5	74
28:5ff.	91
28:31–32	74

Lev

16:4, 24	42
23	15, 83, 131

Num

8:5–22	42, 81
9:12	79
11:4, 13, 18, 21, 33	49
14:4	87
19:6	87
19:9, 13, 18, 20, 21	81
21:6–9	55, 80

Deut

12:5, 11, 13–14, 18, 21, 26	103
14:23–25	103
15:20	103
16:2, 6	103

1 Sam 8:7   140

1 Kgs

8:27	83
8:66	83
12:16–20	139

2 Chr 7:8–10   83

Neh 1:9   103

Ps

22	74, 75, 75n26
22:1	75
22:19	74
33(34):21	78n36, 79
34:21	78n36
45	138
51:9	87
82:6	138

Prv 8   129n64

Isa

4:4	82
6	139
35:6a–7	110
49:10	110
52:13	64, 90
53	44, 58–66
53:4–6	79
53:7, 12	58, 62
53:8a	71
53:10	64
53:12	65

Jer 7:1–7   118

Ezek

3:23	143
9:3; 10:4, 18–19	143
10–11	40n70, 43, 57, 117, 133, 157
11:16	40n70
11:22–23	143

40:38	81	*Abr.*	
43:1–5	70	170	19
44:4	43	177	31
47:1–12	70, 82–83, 93		

Dan 12:3   60

Apoc. Ab.   70, 92

Joel

3:18	93
4:18	110

2 Bar.   26n11, 93

3 Bar.   26n11

Zech

9:9	128
14:8	82, 93

Jub.   32n31, 34n39, 56n136, 72

16:12–13	56
16:15–18	36
18	54n130
18:13	18, 19, 29n19, 30, 32, 35
49	33

Bar 4:1; 3:12, 37   129n64

1 En.   70

14:8–25	93
8:8	70

T. Isaac   42

2 Macc.   36, 58, 65

Matt

16:5–12	47n98
21:9	131n69
27:2	71
27:35	74
27:46	75
27:49	79n41
27:59	91n93

4 Macc.   19, 29, 30, 35, 36, 37, 65

Sib. Or. 4 4:8–11   26n11

Sir.

Mark

8:14–21	47n98
14:51–52; 15:46	91n93
11:10	131n69
15:1	71
15:24	74
15:34	75

Sir. 48:24–25	60
1:1	129n64
15:7	129n64
24:7	129
24:21	47n98

Wis.

2, 4, 5	58
9:2	129n64

ANCIENT DOCUMENT INDEX

Luke

16:19	91n93
22:54	71
23:34b	74
23:53	91n93
24:53	96

John

1	43, 91
1:1	29, 46, 70
1:3	41
1:5	51
1:10	47
1:11	142
1:14	1, 29, 46, 56, 134, 139
1:19–28	129
1:29, 36	6, 58–66, 58n143, 73
1:31	1, 47, 129
1:44	142
1:46	142
1:47	13, 130
1:47–49	130
1:49	15, 130
1:50–51	1, 41, 84, 89, 90, 130, 134
2	44, 83, 118, 145
2:1–11	39–43
2:1–25	1, 4, 56, 80, 84, 89, 92, 95, 99, 109, 113, 129, 131
2:14–25	40
3:1, 10	119
3:1–15	131
3:1–36	113
3:3–8	75, 105
3:6, 8	50
3:10	11
3:14–15	55, 64, 80
3:16	60
3:34	71n9
4	4, 11, 25, 44, 105, 132
4:1–42	16n53
4:5–26	49, 49n106, 104, 109–114, 133
4:10	133
4:12	133
4:22	133
4:27	104
4:34	71n9
4:43–44	142
4:45	142
4:48	142
5	106, 121, 134
5, 7, 8	145
5:1	138
5:22, 27, 30	82
5:23, 24, 30, 36, 37, 38	71n9
6:4	138
6:11–13	142
6:15	142
6:22–59	3, 6, 7, 39, 43, 45–52, 47n98, 49, 49n103, 67, 71n9, 80, 86, 128
6:26	142
6:32–33	47
6:34, 48	48
6:40	48
6:49–51	48
6:54–58	48
6:63–64	49, 51, 72, 110
7	41, 51, 83, 121, 139
7–8	84
7:2–3	128, 138
7:14–18, 23–30, 33–36	135
7:16, 18, 28, 29, 33	71n9
7:17	47
7:18	56
7:38–39	82
7:40–52	142
7:41–42	104
7:42	15, 130
7:52	104
8	135n89, 136
8:12–20	51, 136
8:16, 18, 26, 29, 42	71n9, 82
8:17	11
8:21–24	136
8:22–59	135

8:28	64	15:3	42
8:31–59	12n34, 47, 72n11, 120n17, 133	15:13	57
		15:21	71n9
8:44	137	15:26	112
8:48–49	132	16:2	71n10
8:59—9:1	134	16:5	71n9
9	10, 12, 122, 134	16:8, 11	82
9:4	71n9	16:13	112
9:13, 15, 16, 40	134	17:5, 22, 24	56
9:22	123	17:17	47
9:28	135	17:19	7
9:29	104	17:38, 18, 21, 23, 25	71n9
9:35–37	134	18	69
9:39	82, 83	18:4	72
9:40–41	135, 137	18:12–20, 38	1, 71, 77
10	139	18:15	75
10:1, 16	77	18:24	71
10:11	7, 64	18:31	11
10:14–15	64, 76	18:36	137
10:17–18	7, 55, 57, 64, 73	18:38	140
10:22–33	138	19	75, 85
10:34	11	19:12, 15b	139
10:36	71n9	19:13	82
10:40	139	19:14a, 29, 33, 36	69, 73
11	123	19:15	119, 130, 140, 141
11:4, 40	56	19:17	57, 72
11:7–8	121	19:20–22	130
11:25–26	48n99	19:23–24	44, 45, 74, 75
11:42	71n9	19:29	87
11:49	76	19:30a	88
11:50	71, 76	19:34	6, 7, 79–80
11:54	121	19:36	78n36, 79
12:12	127	19:38	123
12:18	69	19:40, 41	91
12:23, 41, 43	56	20:5–7	85, 91, 91n93
12:31	82	20:15b	91
12:32–34	64, 72	20:19	123
12:41	139	20:21	71n9
12:44, 45, 49	71n9		
13:1	39	*Heb*	
13:1, 3	72	9	81n47
13:1–11	42	11:19	57
13:4	39		
13:20	71n9	*1QH* 4:5—5:4	58
14:6	112		
14:17	112	*1QH* 8:35–36	58
14:24	71n9		

ANCIENT DOCUMENT INDEX

1QH 16:16	110
4Q225	18
4Q255	35, 36
4Q161–165	60
4QpsJub^a	18, 35, 36
Exod. Rab. 15.11	56
Frg. Tg.	34, 36

Gen. Rab.

22	3, 28, 29n19, 35
56.4	34, 35
56.8	36
Lev. Rab. 2	34, 36
m. Tamid 4.2	86
Mek. R. Ishmael	28
Mek. R. Simon	30, 31–32
Midr. Rab. Gen. 56.9	31
Pirque R. El.	29–30, 90
Tg. 1 Chr 21:15	30, 90
Tg. Gen 22	34, 35, 37, 63, 79
Tg. Gen. 35:9ff.	41, 83
Tg. Job 3	63
Tg. Lev 22:27	3
Tg. Neof. I	36
Tg. Neof. Gen. 22	29, 33n37
Tg. Ps.-J.	36
Tosefta (Sukkah III.3)	82
1 Clem.	30
1 Clem. 10:7	29
Barn. 7:2	73
Peri Pashas #25: 59, 69	72

www.ingramcontent.com/pod-product-compliance
Lightning Source LLC
Chambersburg PA
CBHW062047220426
43662CB00010B/1683